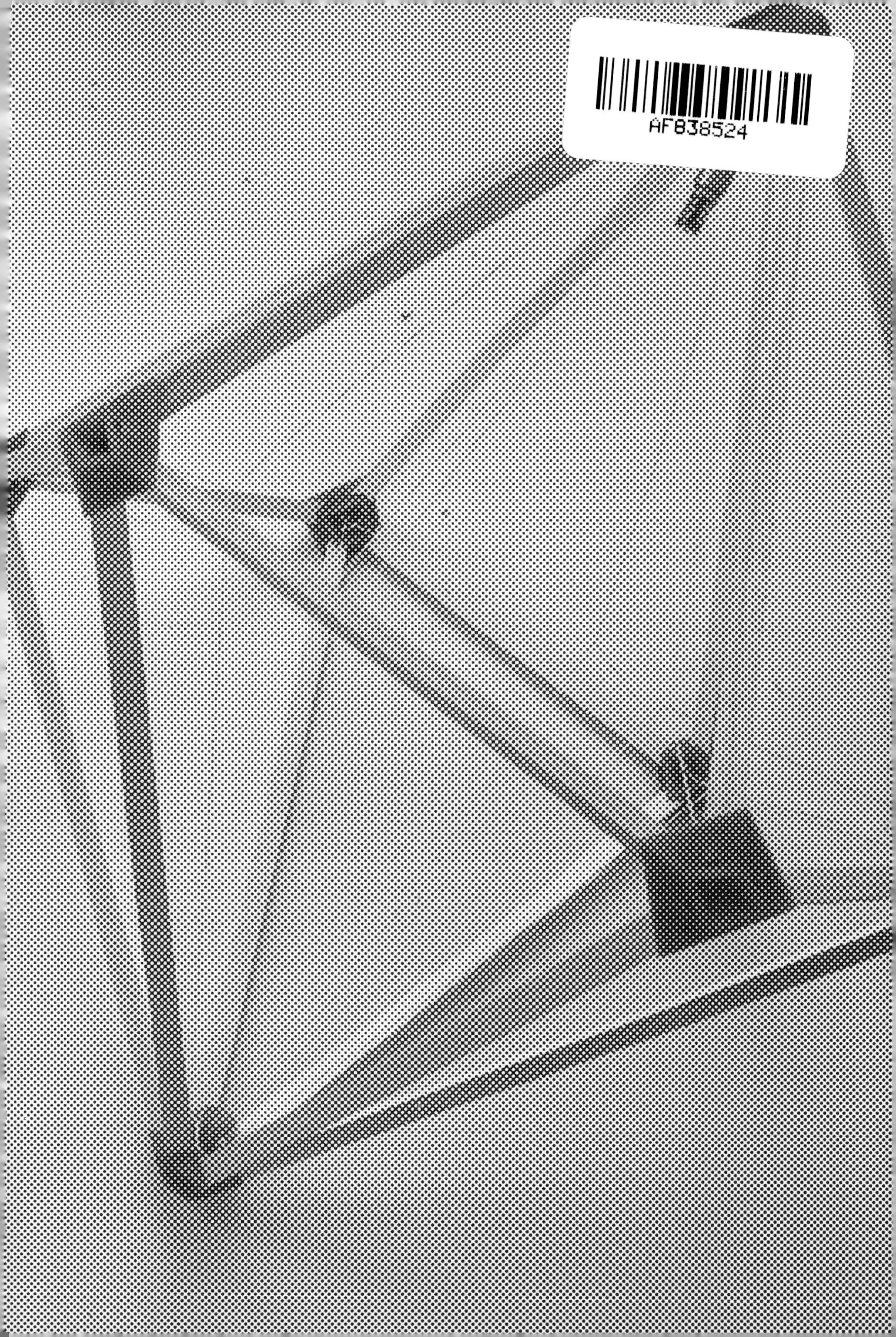

Olafur Eliasson
Green light—
An artistic workshop

Edited by
Daniela Zyman
Eva Ebersberger

Thyssen-Bornemisza Art Contemporary

Sternberg Press

Table of Contents

The Will to Act Is a Renewable Resource

Francesca von Habsburg

Green light—An artistic workshop is an experiment that Olafur Eliasson and the TBA21 team have been developing for several years. The first *Green light* workshop, which began in Vienna in February 2016, started transforming lives upon inception, our lives and the way immigrants' lives are perceived by the general public. Now, as it gains traction, it is becoming a true agent of change. Olafur and I are always asking ourselves what we can do to address the most challenging and urgent issues of our time and bring about social transformation. We are both dedicated to the environment, climate change, and the oceans, but somehow the refugee crisis is a human crisis that touches us deeply and at the same time touches on all of the above.

The most recent wave of immigrants to Vienna started in the summer of 2015 with countless people struggling through the long walk and terrible abuse along the way. Some arrived by train but most on foot. We rushed to the hubs, where we could distribute clothing and food, and NGOs were overwhelmed by the generosity of the Austrians. This tone held up for a long while. Austria has accepted many waves of refugees over the centuries. It is part of the country's rich heritage. At TBA21 we held meetings where emotions ran high. We wanted to offer the exhibition space at Augarten as a refuge. That is when we first came across regulations that make everything incredibly complicated. It was inconceivable how difficult the government made it to offer basic shelter. And although we have a residency building, several kitchens, and bathrooms, you would be amazed to know that that simply was not good enough.

Working through these technicalities and all the legal aspects of this project as we moved forward was about 50 percent of the effort overall. While we were battling the impossible, Olafur had been working with TBA21 on a workshop idea. We had long wanted to create a participatory project, a production line of sorts. We sat down together to talk about ways to respond to the situation, and out of that conversation *Green light* evolved. Now, instead of simply housing the refugees, we would be able to perform a much more valuable function that would engage them, help them integrate, teach them European languages and about our culture, and do even more as the project evolved.

Green light offers practical and humanistic solutions to the refugee problem in an open and generous way. This makes change possible. It is not only we who have to change; it is the system we live in and by. It is simply no longer relevant. It was built over three generations of relative peace and prosperity for Europe, but now we are somehow not living in a time of peace and independence. And as we are already experiencing, walls are going up, and there has been a huge swing to the right. A populist backlash is on the rise, and we are even seeing nuclear tensions reminiscent of the 1980s. Depending on where you live, this can be outright terrifying, way more terrifying than the faces of the families trying to make their way to a better life.

As Al Gore has said, the will to act is a renewable resource. It is not an act of charity; it is participatory and mandatory in these times of conflict and fear. We need to let these projects grow and grow with them. We need to understand that art can be that transformational agent binding us to a new world that is rooted in ethics. We have created a locus where politics are not left at the door but are invited in to be challenged by the creative energy of hope and transformation.

Olafur and I feel aligned in our desire not only to raise awareness but also to influence policy making on a larger scale. How do we work toward that goal and find the opportunities that help shift public opinion and develop a new language that describes action and shifts in political thinking? From my side, I have committed the work of TBA21 to the most pressing topics of today, not only in a descriptive fashion but also by applying the language of art to concrete actions and solution finding. It's a turning point for the foundation as it increasingly looks at becoming an agent of change. I find that bringing ourselves to reevaluate just about everything regarding the way we engage in the world is a good and very necessary thing to do, as apathy begins to feel increasingly dangerous. *Green light* is part of this process, and so is everyone who participates in its workshop in any way. *Green light* is not to be gazed at; it is to be engaged with!

As Timothy Morton says in his wonderfully crafted text: "... the things [Olafur Eliasson] makes are wholes that are less than their parts, because you can use them in all kinds of ways!" He has given me food for thought because I have always believed that the sum of the parts is bigger than the whole, but again, what makes that true? By reversing that age-old concept, we may begin to understand how making a difference is possible.

I would like to thank all those who have made this project possible, and the list is long. I want to mention everyone by name as this project is mostly about the people who made it happen:

First and foremost Olafur Eliasson and Studio Olafur Eliasson, in particular Caroline Eggel, Kerstin Palermo, Brita Jaichner, Kajana Wagner, Anna Engberg-Pedersen, Camilla Kragelund, Kristina Köper, and Geoffrey Garrison;

the entire team at TBA21 – Daniela Zyman, Boris Ondreička, Franziska Sophie Wildförster, Philipp Bauer, Sophie Bayerlein, Karin Berger, Rocio Burchard, Isabella Cavaletti, Azra Demir-Ramovic, Ziva Drvaric, Eva Ebersberger, Georg Eder, Beatrice Forchini, Elodie Grethen, Christina Gruber, Fanny Hauser, Andrea Hofinger, Tereza Horakova, Barbara Hörhan, Susanne Janetzki, Ulrike Janetzki, Philipp Kolla, Philipp Krummel, Claudia Naue, Rhiannon Pickles, Daniele Perra, Gérard Rabara, Clemens Rettenbacher, Markus Reymann, Mariana Rodriguez-Yanez, Yusuf Haibeh Said, Markus Schlüter, Anna Schmoll, Heidi Scholdra, Cory Scozzari, Simone Sentall, Lisa Slawitz, Paulina Sosna, Frederike Sperling, Elizabeth Stevens, Katharina Stöhr, Anahita Tabrizi, Markus Taxacher, Nataša Venturi, Florence Wehinger, David Weidinger, Sandro E.E. Zanzinger;

the *Green light* participants in Vienna – Aliakbar Ahmadi, Shamahmood Ahmadi, Tahajud Alghrabi, Raafat Alhashimy, Naima Ali, Anas Aljajeh, Dunia Aljasararee, Milad Amiri, Mohammad Amiry, Majid Ayubi, Ali Ayzouki, Murtaza Azimi, Tawab Baran, Ibrahim Al Bayati, Fatima Chuchari, Ghifar Al Darkazanly, Beiroza Daud, Ayman Al Dawahra, Ebrahim Ebrahimi, Farhad Farhamand, Husseyin Haj Hassan, Nedwa Hasan, Hussein Hosseini, Liya Kasa, Homa Khosrawi, Ibrahim Mawazini, Fayaz Mir-Amiry, Akbar Muratov, Mayhoub Neesrin, Sahed Niazi, Nesar Ahmad Nourzai, Zia ul Haq Oryakhel, Kelvin Osazuwa, Alarabi Raberi, Emran Ali Rahimi, Hossein Rezaie, Kalaji Samar, Saber Sawari, Issa Shafaei, Qasim Tahmasebi, Milad Wasil;

Peter Wiesinger and Marianna Amon from mytraining.at; all the artists, individuals and organizations who contributed to *Green light—Shared learning* – Atıf Akın, Daniel Aschwanden, Tarek Atoui, Mary Broadcast, Matti Bunzl, Damian Christinger, Benjamin Daud, Displaced, Alexander Ehrmann, Sina Farahmandnia, Paul Feigelfeld, Brigitte Felderer, Raimund Haindorfer, HANDS ON, Karin Harather, History(ies) of Migration, Mária Hlavajová, Barbara Holub, Mary Kreutzer & Leila Hadj Abdou, Janet Kutschert, Rasmus Nielsen, Sandra Noeth, Ahmet Öğüt, Ben Paine, Johannes Porsch, PROSA, Andreas Roepstorff, Renate Rummerstorfer, David Rych, Stefanie Schlögl, Georg Schöllhammer, Shuddhabrata Sengupta, Renate Stuefer, Herwig Turk, Heidemarie Uhl, Therese Zahud, Zavoloka; the project partners Vienna – Georg Danzer Haus/Verein Fluchtweg, Vienna (Marianne Engelmann, Kemal Köse); Caritas Vienna (Ingrid Rachbauer, Andreas Pawlowsky, Irene Fähndrich-Martin); Red Cross Vienna (Thomas Prinz, Elisabeth Palugyay, Alexander Tröbinger).

For their interest and support I would like to thank the Federal President of Austria Alexander van der Bellen, Federal Chancellor Christian Kern, and Federal Minister Thomas Drozda.

In Houston, Texas, special thanks to Alison Weaver at the Moody Center for the Arts and the Interfaith Ministries for Greater Houston, and the *Green light* participants – Hayfaa Al Gburi, Zinab AlAjil, Raghad AlAjil, Hanaa Suwaed, Azad Ismail, Mohammad Sheikh Horo, Najah Al Sholi, Samir Al Khateeb, Elham Hasan, Nawfal Almohy, Dayami Rodriguez-Lopez, Abdulhannan Sheikho, Samira Houshmand, Omid Jahanshahi, Marianela Medina-Cuellar, Fatemah Jahanshahi; also to Jiří Fajt and Adam Budak at the National Gallery in Prague.

In Venice, our thanks go to the Biennale team – Christine Macel, Andrea Del Mercato, Manuela Lucà Dazio, Debora Rossi, Maria Cristiana Costanzo, Cristiano Frizzele, Jörn Brandmeyer; to the *Green light* project partners Emergency, and Georg Danzer Haus; the participating NGOs – Il Villaggio Globale; Giuseppe Olivotti; Il Lievito; Gea; Co.Ge.S Don Lorenzo Milani; Diocesi Patriarcato di Venezia; Fondazione Groggia; Curia Patriarcale e Fondazione Santa Maria del Porto; Cooperativa Coges; Opere Riunite Buon; Caritas; the *Green light* participants – Sangare Adama, Naima Adan Mohamed, Seedorf Aigbah, Frank Agbonteam, Miso Ajayi, Marwan Alfrij, Naeel Alfrij, Promise Awose Iyekeretin, Lamin Camara, Enerhu Diamond, Ubaka Dumbiri, Andrew Eboigbe, Marcel Esene, Abdoulie Faye,

Yankuba Gassama, Monday Hitila, Denis Igbinedion, Jerry Angel Imariabe Edosomwan, Bakary Jawla, Yousaf Khan Undarh, Shen Limei, Philip Lucky, Asho Mohamed Saaiid, Qadeer Muhammad, Ahmed Muhammed, Akissi Odile N'Guessan, Mahamadou Niakate', Wahidullah Niazi, Akam Noordien Aulla, Iyore Odeh, Dickson Ogwezy, Kelvin Omon, Kelvin Omorogbe Nosakmare, Mo QiuChiang, Lamin Sallah, Azhin Taha, Hawrin Taha, Zubaida Tahiri, Mohammad Usman, Nasrin Hossein Zarandi;
the *Green light* team – Elisa Danese, Laura Schiattone, Rita Fabbri, Mohammed Salhi, Diana Leone, Marta Ruffato, Pietro Consolandi, Giulia Angeloni, Lucia Brergamaschi, Clara Machado Alves, Julian Nativo Matias, Enrica Zaccone, Alessia Prati; Marco Franco, Adriana Navarro, Troels Brun; Kvadrat and Moroso for their support.

And as always thanks to TBA21's main program sponsors Vienna Insurance Group and Wiener Städtische Versicherungsverein.

Assembling a Light, Assembling Communities

Olafur Eliasson

Making art is making a model of the world. It proposes what the world might look like or what the world does, in fact, look like if we only look at it differently. I am especially interested in models exploring our notions of self and other in relation to how we live in our societies and in the globalized world of today.

Art can activate our imagination, listen to us, create beauty, exercise critique; it insists on complexity – rather than easy-to-consume one-liners – and in that, forcefully pushes in the opposite direction of populism. Art challenges notions of identity, of belonging, and estrangement, and questions borders and the distribution of privilege, to mention only some of the things it is capable of doing. To me, *Green light—An artistic workshop* is about all of the above. It is a model of the world that is a part of the world. The *Green light* project began at a specific moment in time, in 2015, when refugees were arriving in Europe by the hundreds of thousands, fleeing hardship, political and economic instability, and war in their home countries. Although these problems had begun years before, many – myself included – often felt emotionally disconnected from the reality of what we read or saw on the news. Art and culture, I believe, can have a pertinent role to play in responding to such events: as a start, it can reverse our emotional disconnect and, whether directly or indirectly, inspire us to take action. This conviction was also shared by Francesca von Habsburg, founder of Thyssen-Bornemisza Art Contemporary (TBA21), and by TBA21's chief curator Daniela Zyman, with whom I had extensive conversations throughout the late summer of that year. We believe that culture is able to shine a light on and shape discussions about contemporary global challenges such as climate change and forced migration, and is able to develop new models of interaction and catalyze positive change.

But how does one proceed from the assembly of a light module to social change? The journey might seem long and convoluted, yet a simple but crucial first step is to trust the potential in the non-spectacular situation of sitting down together and doing something basic with our hands – in this case, working on a lamp that is more easily assembled by two pairs of hands than one. Add to that a multifaceted program of shared learning, with practical workshops, counseling, language classes, cooking, sports and cultural events, and knowledge exchange. What emerges during these activities is a shared social space. And once the initial nervousness has evaporated, moments of relaxed enjoyment unfold, pieces of personal history are exchanged. This elicits a feeling of interconnectedness that is incredibly strong. I believe that allowing ourselves to be open to this feeling is key to intensifying our engagement in society and to participating actively in coming up with solutions in times where forced migration affects us all.

The *Green light* lamp module is a stackable polyhedral unit, initially developed by the late Einar Thorsteinn, a mathematician and architect who was a close friend of mine. Einar called it the "super cube," and it is one of numerous geometric studies that he and I began together and that my studio team and I have continued working on over the years. The *Green light* units themselves are made mostly of recycled and natural materials and fitted with small green LEDs. They can be hung alone or assembled into larger light sculptures. I love the fact that you can make unruly, wild growths of lamps from them as well as ordered structures like a luminous wall or a sphere. The question for me is not so much what the lamp is, but what it does, both in the social spaces out of which it emerges and in the physical spaces in which it is installed. Every *Green light* has agency.

I undertook the *Green light* project with TBA21 with the hope of developing a scalable model that would work in an art context, but could reach beyond it and also be implemented in a school, a public library, or a political institute. So far, we have been able to bring different versions of the project to Salzburg, Basel, Houston, and Prague, in addition to Vienna. And, now, we are presenting the *Green light* model at the Venice Biennale in an attempt to bring one of the most urgent issues today to the heart of the art world. Next up is Yokohama, and further stations are under consideration. While the *Green light* community expands, I hope that cities, national governments, and policy-makers also begin to see the potential of creative approaches to welcoming refugees, addressing concerns among their populations, and devising collective solutions. Populations around the world will become increasingly multi-ethnic and multicultural and it is clear that the near and distant future will continue to be shaped by migration. We therefore need solutions, now and into the future, at all levels of society.

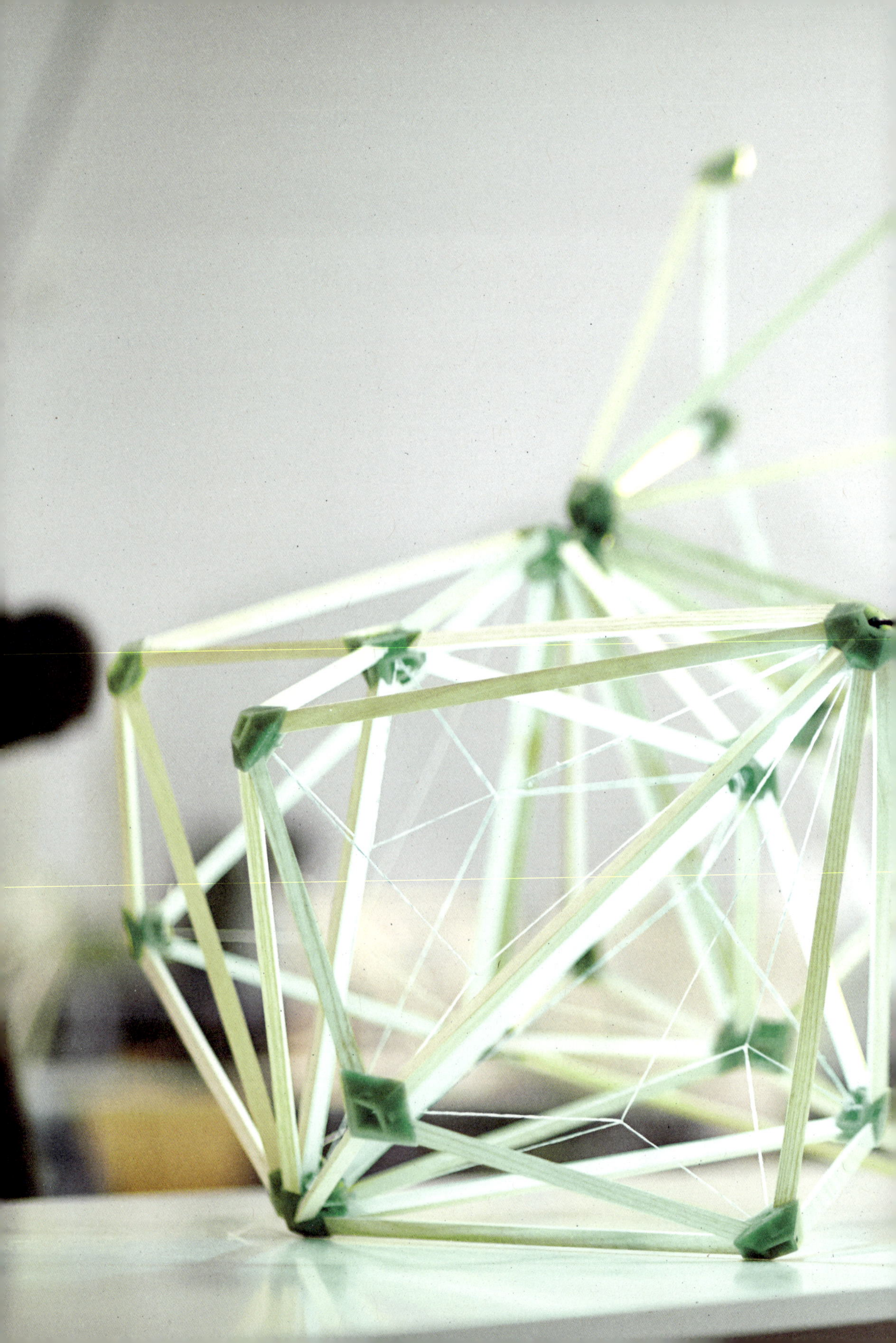

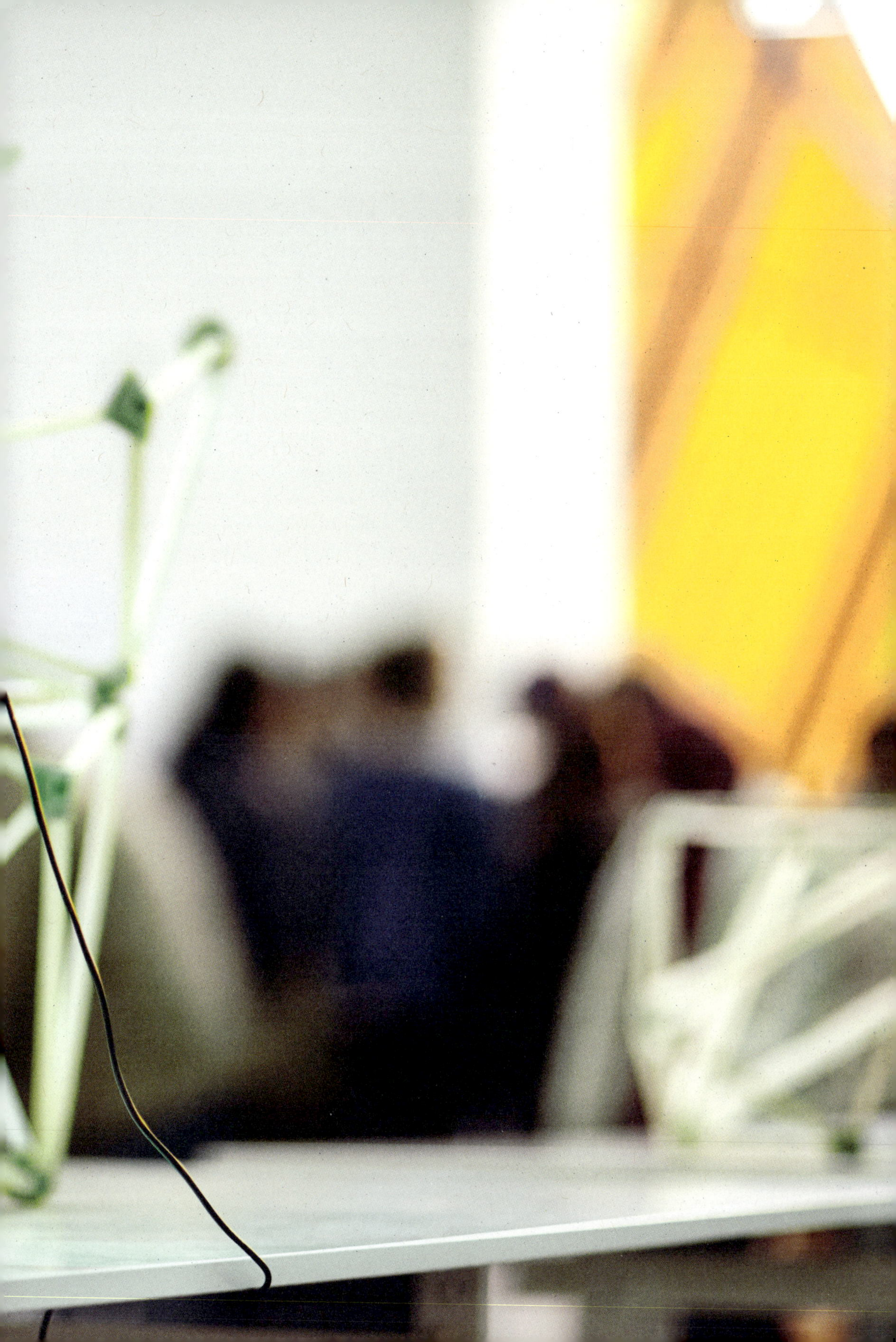

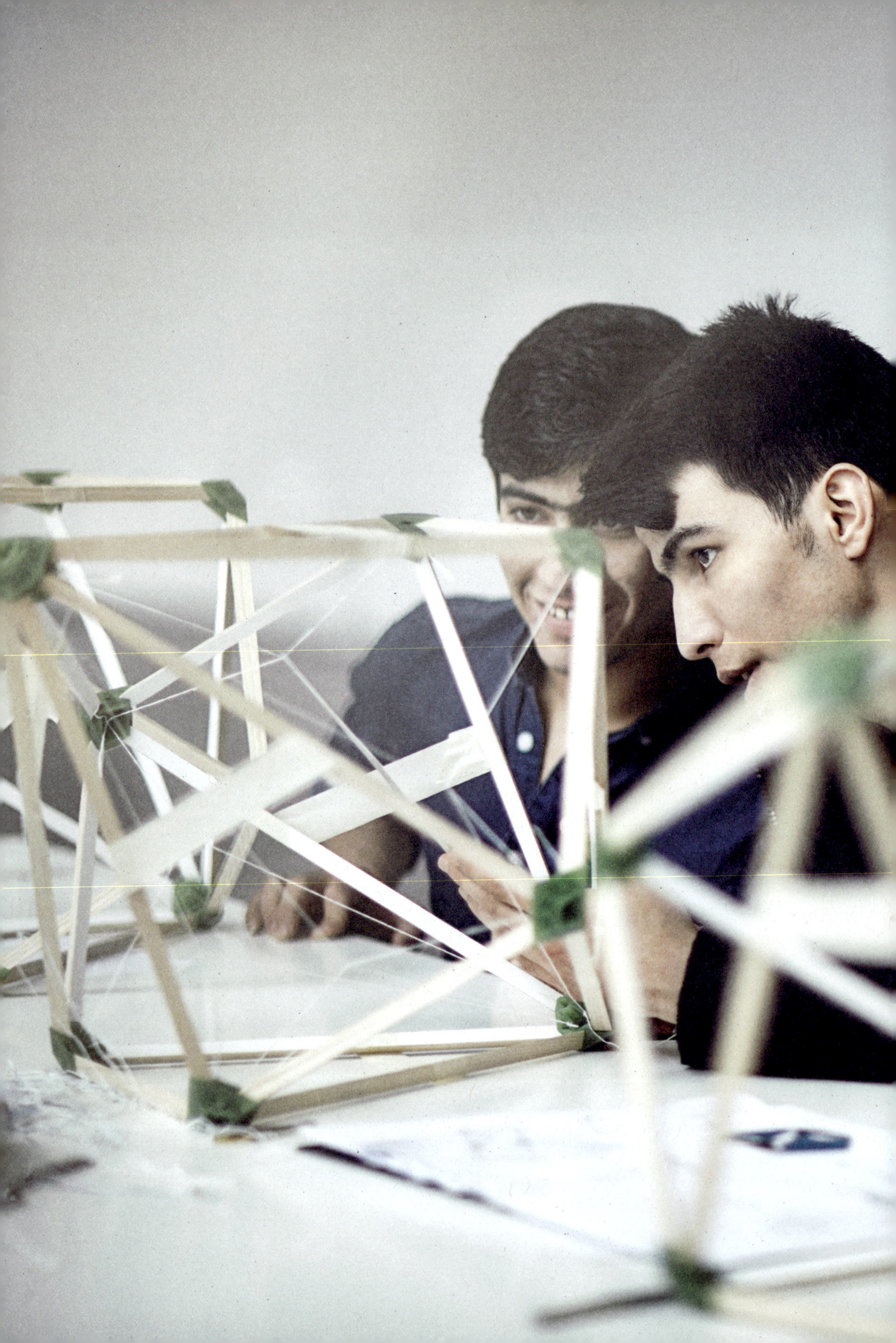

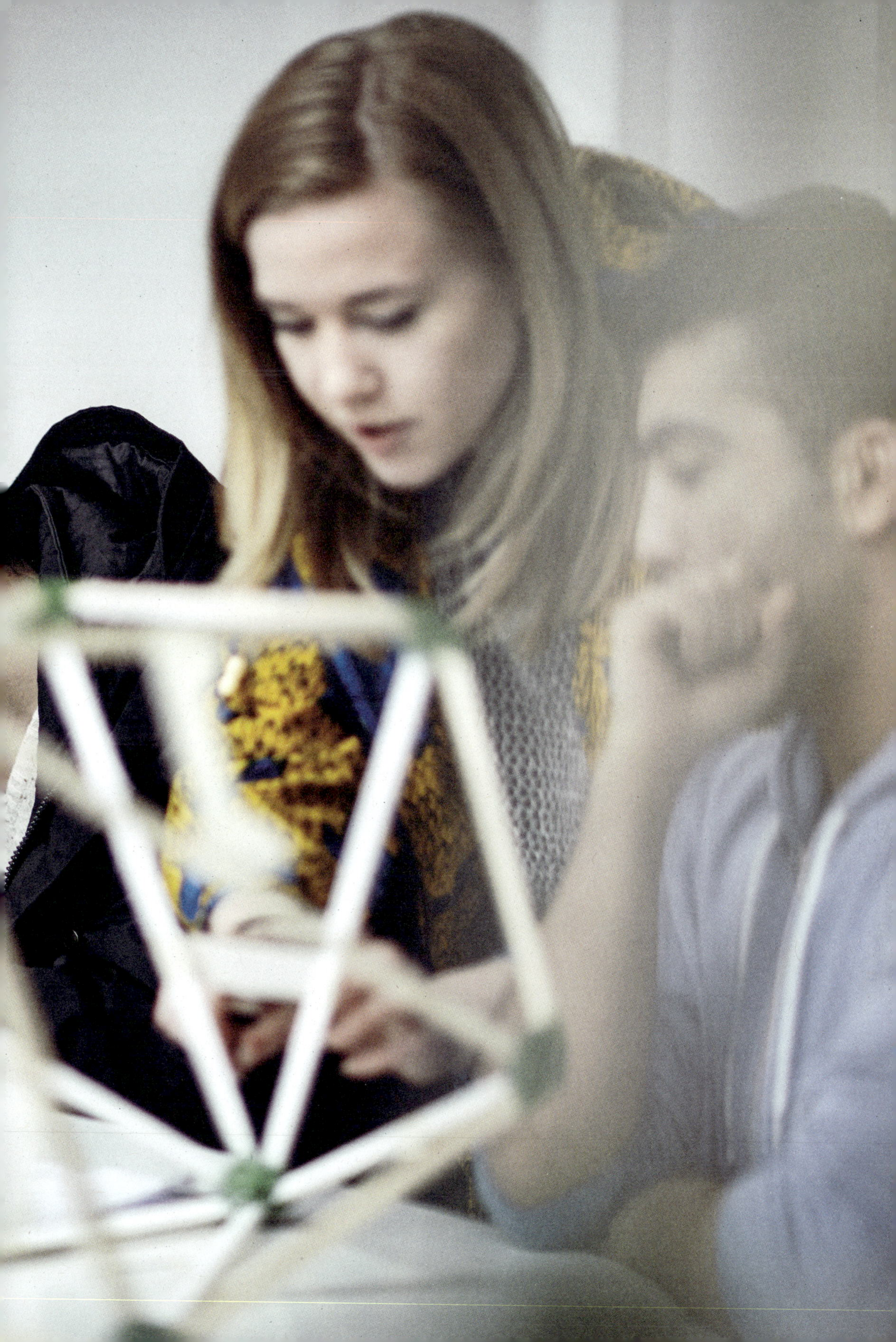

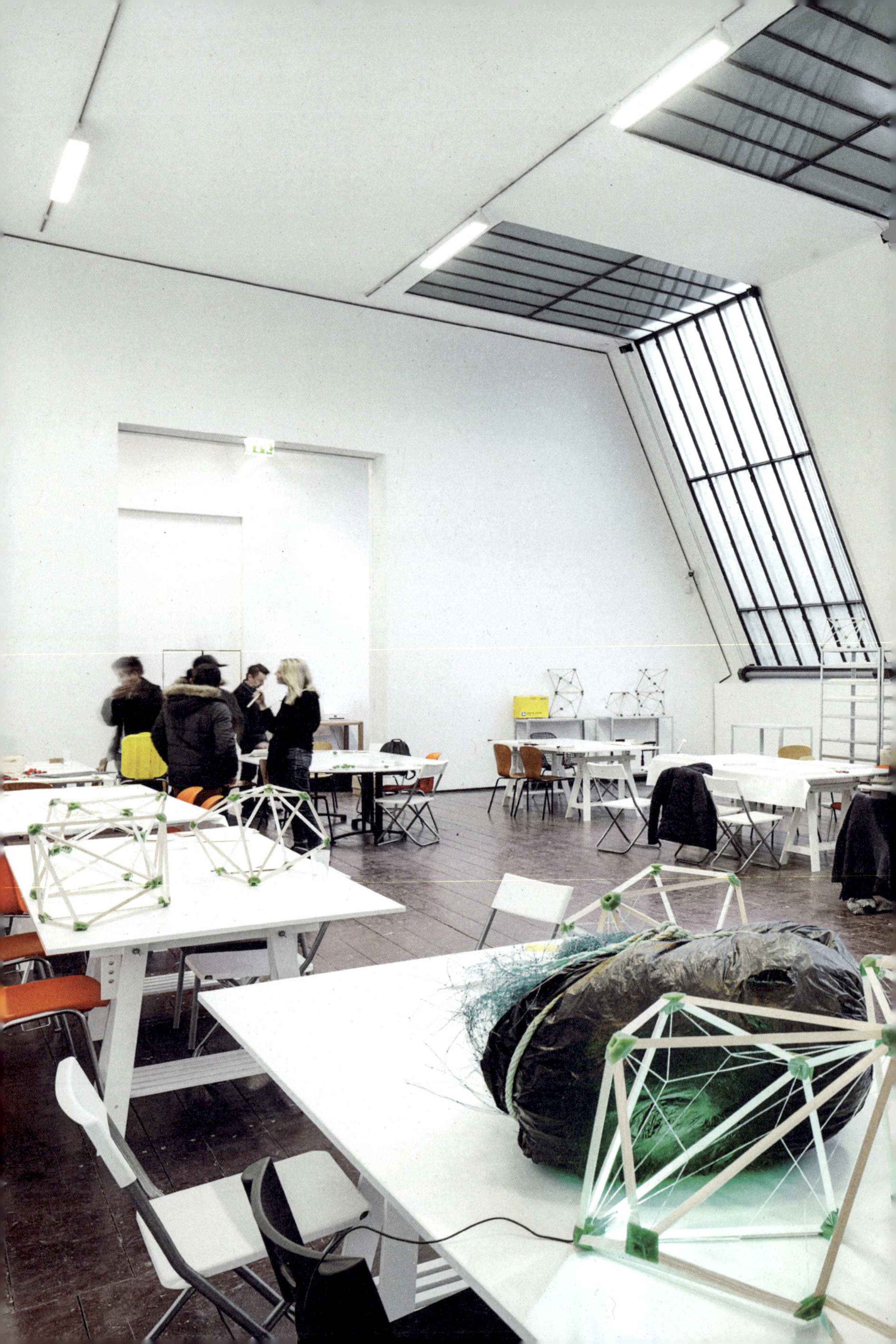

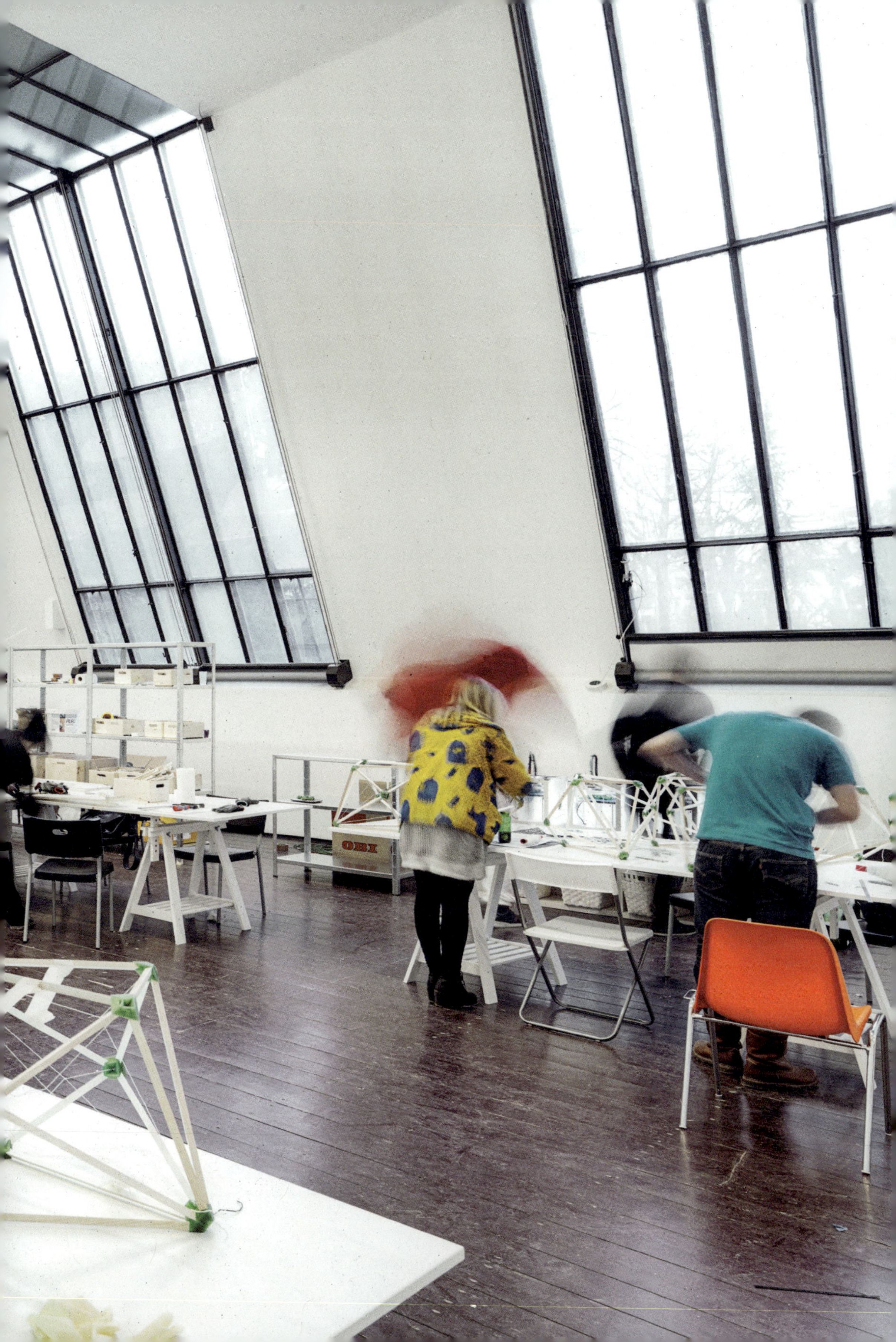
OBI

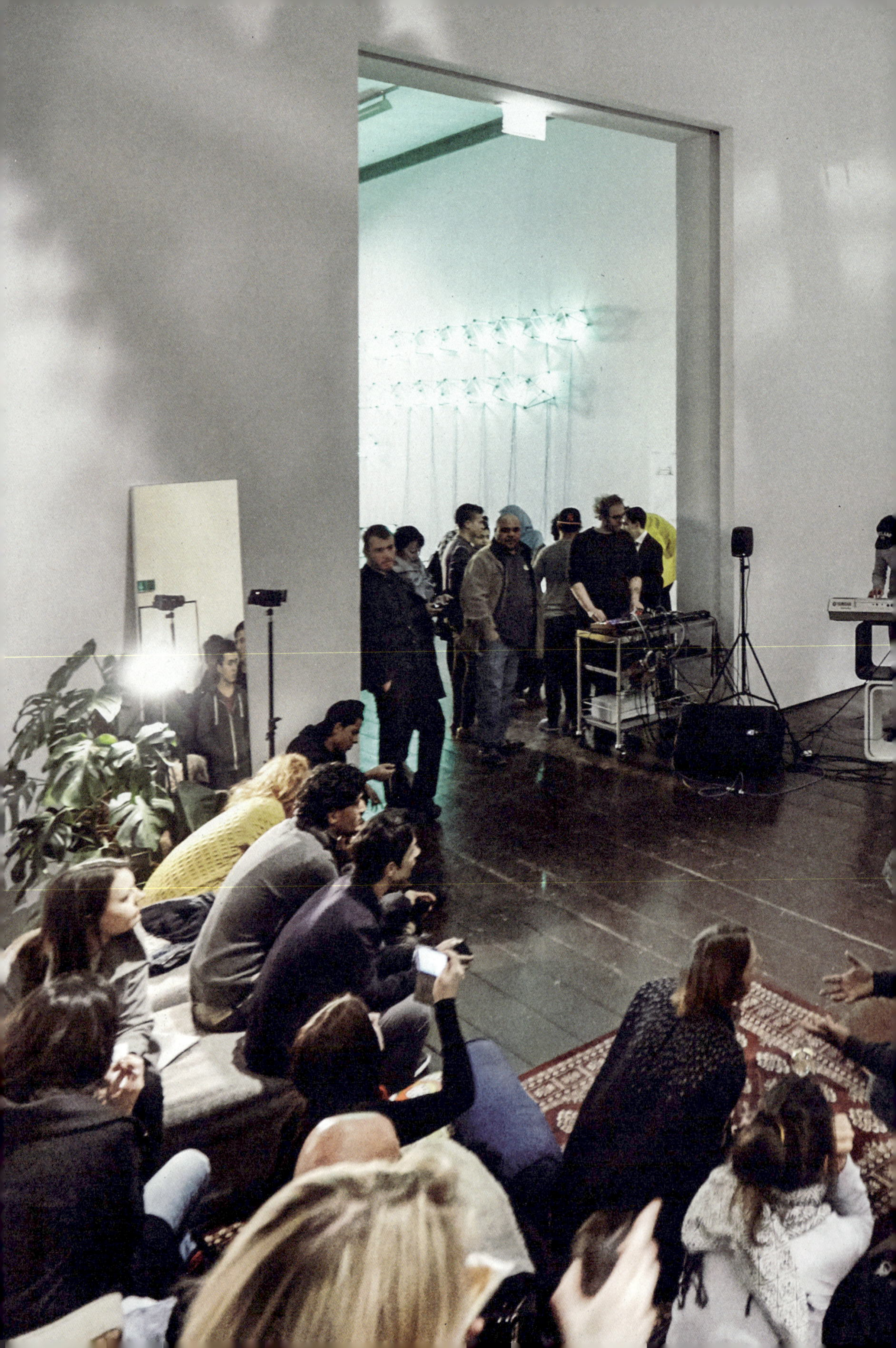

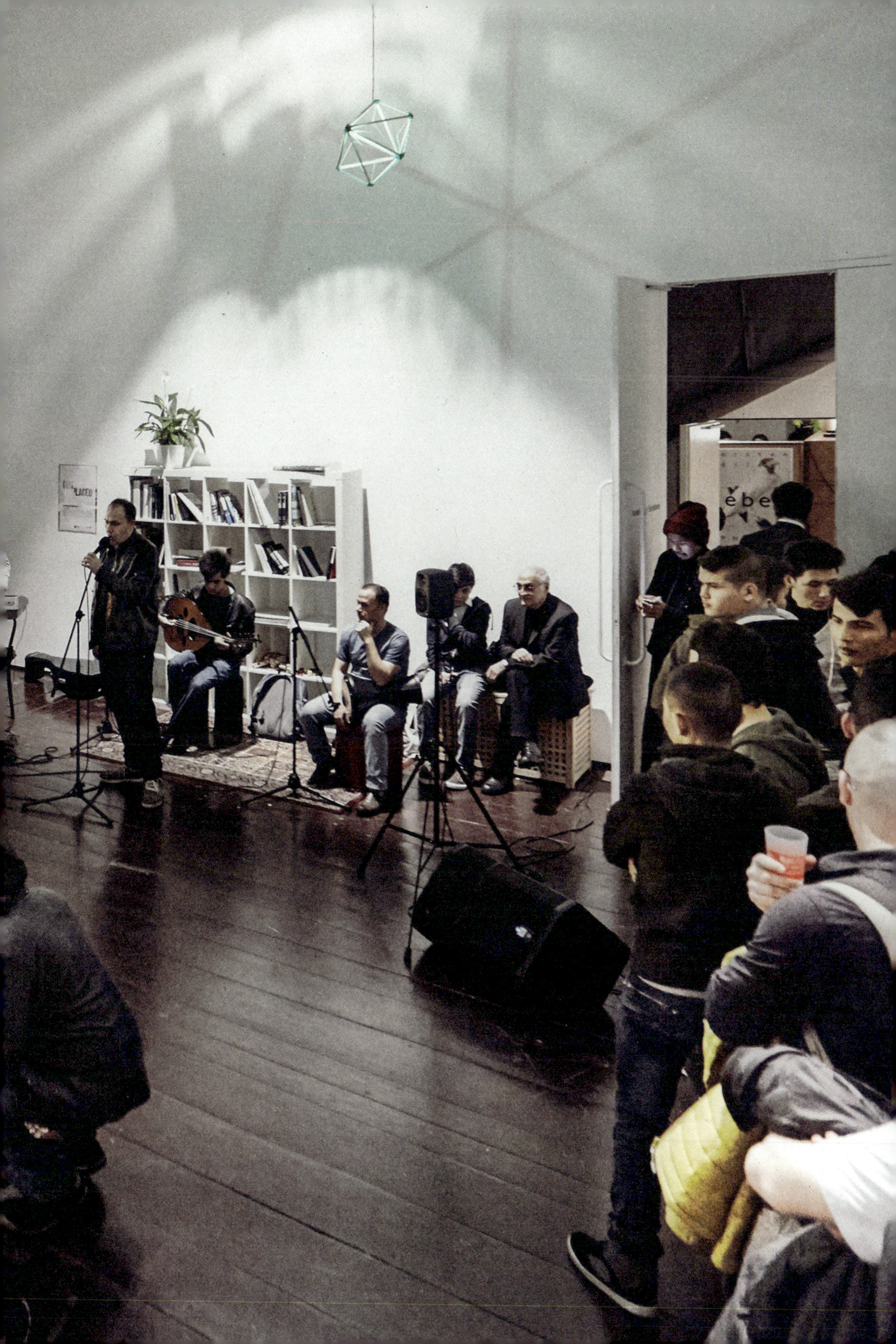

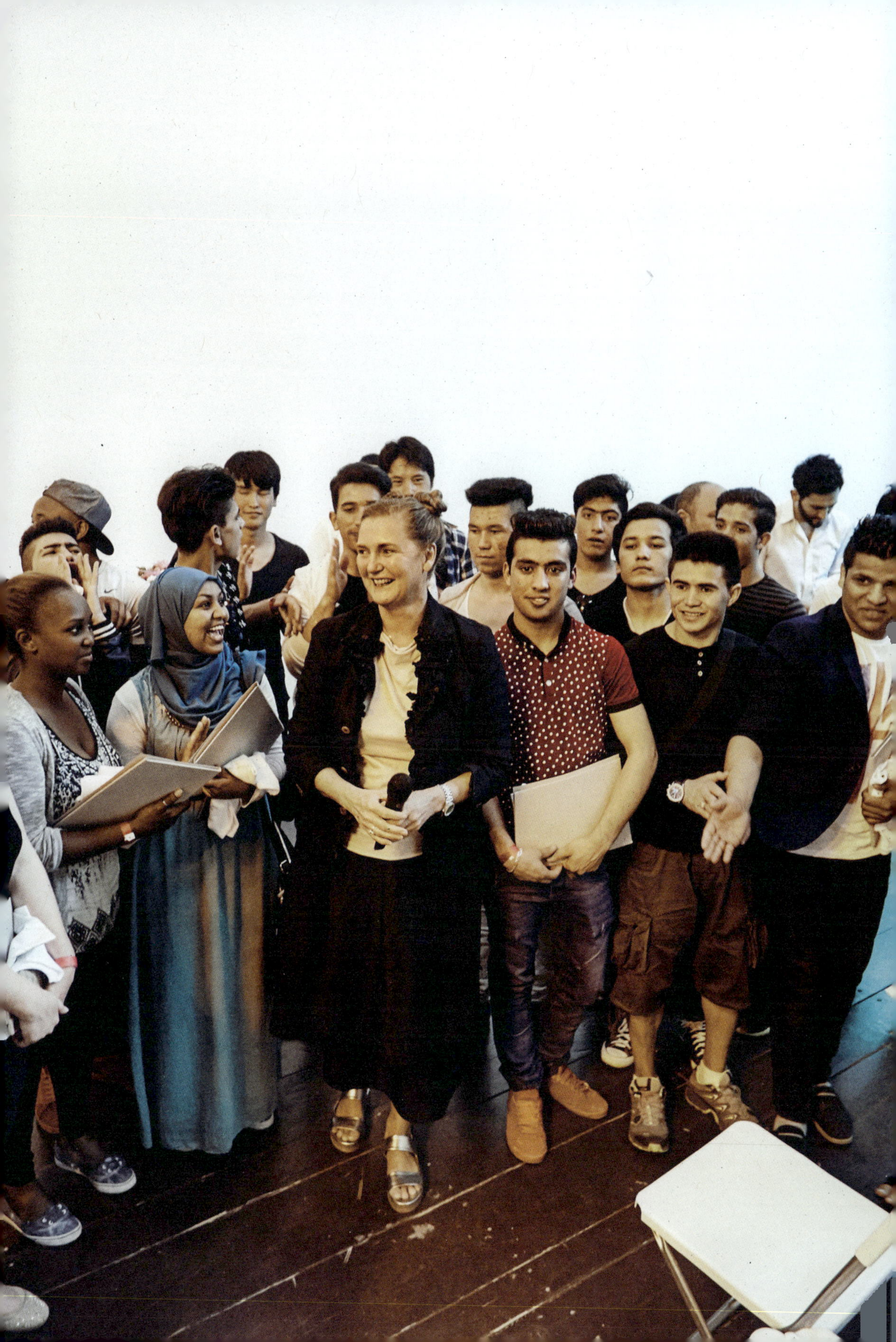

Hosting the Spirit of *Green light*

Olafur Eliasson in conversation with Andreas Roepstorff

OLAFUR ELIASSON I want to thank you all for cohosting us and one another because I think there is something very important going on here—the decentralization of hospitality, which means there is no center, but rather only periphery. Obviously, this is not completely true, because there is an organization, TBA21, behind this, but I would still argue that *Green light* aims to decentralize hospitality.

The reason I invited Andreas to come here today is that his work shows that systems can change. Systems are normally defined as hierarchical, top-down, institutional, and exclusive—also systems that claim to be inclusive are in fact exclusive, systems that claim that we can identify with them but that we actually struggle to identify with. Let me give one example: one system that we like is the EU, but we have no emotional understanding of what on earth the EU is. Another system is the UN: we have come to love the UN, but we have no emotional narrative to understand what the UN is. We all think that these systems are important, but we feel disconnected. So I am very interested in when we feel connected and when we feel disconnected.

For me the refugee crisis introduces a similar challenge. We know a lot about the refugee crisis from the media and from one another because we talk about it, but the emotional narrative is very difficult. It is so abstract! I know what I think about the crisis, refugees, EU, the climate—you name it. I know what I think about it, but it is so difficult for me as a civic participant to engage with. If I cannot feel the "we," I am also a populist, because populism means anti-we. So I suffer because I have become numb and I don't have a sense of we. That is why I called Andreas and asked him to help me!

ANDREAS ROEPSTORFF Thank you, Olafur. This has been a really, really interesting afternoon. It is wonderful being in this room, seeing how it is getting a little bit darker, and in this darkness the green light moves from being a metaphor to creating an environment that encloses us. There is something very interesting about the color green—does it make sense to speak of an evil green? Or green might be seen as naive or envious, and there is also something about growth that seems to go with the green.

Atıf Akın said something interesting earlier; he said that Western history has largely been built in exile, by refugees. And the argument is, more or less, that different modules are being brought together, are being reconfigured—and out of that reconfiguration what we know as Western culture has arisen. I was wondering whether this might be one of the metaphors of *Green light*, as a construction. Is it exploring not so much the feeling of we-ness, of becoming one, but that feeling of modular assembly? Individual modules are being combined with one another to create something that transcends the individual. This motif of greenness, of modules that all look the same but somehow get recombined into something else, is what this afternoon has been about for me. And maybe that is better than being sucked into a we that dissolves each of us.

Constructing "We-ness"

AR Going back to the question of these larger institutions that we do not feel that we are part of. It is a really difficult notion to open up to! How do you get across the idea that you belong to some entity that other people belong to as well? In the fields of cognitive science and anthropology, researchers are very interested in exploring the "we-mode." Is there some kind of a feeling of belonging together as a species or as a group? The way to construct a we-mode might be through an invitation to sharing. The we-mode is characterized by instances of sharing. It might be instances of sharing acts, of sharing language or food, because these transform the "I" and the "you" into some kind of we-ness.

OE I like that—the we-mode. That is a good word to remember, we-mode. Also the other word, we-ness. It is nice to be in the cultural sector and claim to occupy the word we-ness before some commercial company exploits it. Let's just sit for a second in the we-ness together. I am so excited about this idea that interdependence is something that you cocreate. Obviously you take for granted that if you pay taxes the government will make the we-ness for you, the civic interdependence—*gesellschaftlicher Zusammenhalt*. Actually, despite paying taxes, we are left in a situation in which we also have to cocreate our realities, our we-mode.

You talked about sharing—so what type of spaces would you, Andreas, see as representing a kind of sharing in which I don't demand that you think the same thoughts that I think. Is it in parliament? We tend to think of democracy as a great host for disagreement. But the truth is that this system is also being influenced by populism, which has made it into parliament. So essentially, what other spaces, if not democracy, allow us to celebrate our shared base? I think culture to some extent is such a space, but if it is not, where do we find the type of sharing that welcomes the fact that we cannot agree on everything. What spaces are left?

AR Maybe the best space to start with is a concrete space. What is critical is that once spaces get concrete people can get together, even very transiently. A place where you can relate to one another without dissolving into one another. It seems that what we are doing when we are together, even very temporarily, is that we become hyperfollowers of one another.

We did a very simple experiment with tapping, in which basically what I was producing became everything that you heard and what you produced became everything that I heard. Out of that emerged a very interesting pattern. People would start to fall into rhythms, but since you could only know what I was doing based on what I did previously, you tried to align with me. If I was slow, you would also become slower, but I would try to be faster to align with you. And as a result of that, we were never in sync with each other but were kind of dancing a beautiful dance of hyperfollowing each other. Because we each try to anticipate what the other is doing, we create this dance of having something that emerges stably between the two of us without one of us falling into the pattern of mimicking the other or becoming the other. So a good place to begin is with hyperfollowers in concrete spaces.

The Hyperfollowers

OE Do you think that public space is a platform where this can happen? Public space is such a broad term, but let's just say it is a space that is not privatized. That is a better way to put it.

AR This space that you create today here is a public space, a sort of temporary space and yet a public space. I think there is something about this concreteness of being together that allows these processes to happen.

OE So hyperfollowers create a kind of hospitality. And I like that you point to this space here because I always feel proud when cultural spaces support a feeling of we. I could not agree with you more. But we should not forget our own limitations. I had the good fortune to speak with a lot of talented journalists earlier today, and there was this interesting assumption that this space, our common space, is a neutral host containing the newly arrived refugees. There was this assumption that Vienna is standing still, and that the people are on the move coming here. Whereas I would suggest in terms of your hyperfollowing concept that we are also on the move. Our movement is a movement toward populism; it is a movement of nationalism; it is a movement of a certain type of arrogance, but it is also a movement of compassion. So we are not not-moving, do you understand? And this is interesting, and I say this also a little bit to celebrate the great Doreen Massey, who passed away two weeks ago, who would say that it is a meeting up of trajectories. Hyperfollowing becomes a sort of exchange.

As one press person said on the phone, clearly the refugees have been traumatized to various degrees and are struggling with post-traumatic stress. Yes, for sure they are, and if we are lucky, we can host their trauma with such generosity that there is an element of detraumatization. But let's not make the wrong assumption, that the Viennese are not traumatized by populism. Vienna and Europe have been traumatized by a sort of arrogance, by non-compassion-based activity, and exclusion.

Embodied Spaces

AR The idea about a neutral space is an interesting one. In my experience it takes an enormous amount of energy, effort, and power to maintain something that looks like a neutral space. Spaces are always politicized. Spaces are also changing; spaces are always reflecting the type of processes that go on within them. The experience of walking around in this part of Vienna, as I was just flying into town today, has been really opening and welcoming. My first experience in Vienna was about twenty-five years ago, when I was here as a student at a conference. Somehow no matter what I did in the city, someone told me off when I walked the street or sat in the tramway. I am usually not told off in a public space, so the experience was that it was a neutral space, but a space that could be kept neutral only by constantly enforcing norms for what was wrong and what was right, for how to behave. It was not in a kind of disdainful way but simply stating to the wild person coming from the north that there are certain ways to behave or not to behave. And of course these norms, as well as that enforcement of particular norms and rules for engaging with one another, are also part of social space. It might even be a necessary part of the social space.

Thus the notion of space as simply being there, as an empty area where billiard balls roll around bumping into each other, is just not a good characterization of human lives. Rather, the history of the space and the patterns of interaction that were already there also shape what can happen in the here and now. This is why it is so important to think about spaces, to think about creating spaces that allow particular modes of being together, because in setting up spaces, you also set up rules of interaction, ways of engaging with one another. You create hierarchies, suggestions for what can be done and what cannot be done. In that sense to explore spaces is really a political, an artistic, a creative way to enable rules of engagement for human interaction.

OE I agree. Can you say something about how we physically embody something, how we actually become a spatial agent? How do we make sure that we at least don't become disembodied?

AR The notion of what it means to embody is a critical one. Let's just shift frame for a moment and look at artificial intelligence. Some twenty years ago we held the notion that chess was the ultimate test of intelligence. So when Kasparov played and lost against Deep Blue, that was a paradigm shift. A couple of months ago we saw a similar thing repeating itself with the game of Go. Previously it was thought that it was such a complicated game that no computer would ever master it. But we can see that when it comes to those kind of processes, in particular rule-bound games, there is no doubt that we will increasingly come up with algorithms that can do a lot better than we can. What humans seem to be really good at, probably better than any other system that we know of, is being embodied, acting in the world and realizing that it is through being in the world with others that we have access both to the other and to ourselves. So the critical starting point here is to say, "Yes, we are embodied!" We can be outcompeted in formal games, by computational processes, etc., but what people are really good at is being in the world as bodies with others. And the moment when you are that, when you are here as a body—also a body with a mind—it is almost impossible not to be affected by others. The experience of being affected, of being touched by others, of being bodies interacting with one another, that realization is a critical instance of what it is like to be human.

OE The reason I am so excited about this is that exactly these types of considerations—if not so beautifully articulated—are what I toss around in my studio throughout the day. And of course the worst fear I have is of becoming disembodied like a chess-playing computer. You can be really smart but create no consequences.

Intersubjective Objects / Interobjective Subjects

OE Do you know the experience of standing in front of a work of art—and certainly this does not happen often, for me at least—and you say, "Oh, I know that feeling! I identify with it; it is something that I had not yet verbalized!" This green sphere is a form in a way, a language—it gives language to an idea. It speaks, verbalizing on my behalf something that I was working on emotionally but had not yet come to the point of articulating. It was not given a shape, a form, a sculptural language, a space in architecture, an urban plan, a landscape.

So one could go on with this conversation, heading into some psychological conundrum, but the point is that a work of art reflected me. It actually hosted my experience—I felt seen by the work of art. It is looking at me, and I am the one being watched. I am the object; the work of art is the subject. We are both subjects and objects. Subject and object do not matter, as in the triple-O theory formulated by Timothy Morton, object-oriented ontology. But you see, slowly you are hosted—and now that is the question. Where does embodiment actually take or claim space? Because it does take space.

AR Bruno Latour wrote a beautiful article years ago called "On Interobjectivity," in which he pursued the idea that humans are characterized by interobjectivity rather than by the more traditional idea of intersubjectivity. If you want intersubjectivity, pure, Latour suggested, you should go see a baboon tribe. That is all about hierarchy, social emotions that are being played out aggressively and unaggressively. Instead, Latour suggested, what really seems to characterize us as humans is the ability to set objects out in the world in such a way that they become, on the one hand, extensions of ourselves and, on the other, a configuration of the space within which our lives unfold and reconfigure.

We are involved in some interesting work with archaeologists who study the very early record of object production. Researchers used to think the "early Europeans" invented complex objects and decorations, for example, in Lascaux, France, some thirty thousand years ago. However, it seems now that a lot of those "inventions" that were ascribed to Western Europe really originated in Southern Africa, probably sixty or seventy thousand years earlier. This is a very interesting and in a sense beautiful development. One of the questions we explore with the archaeologists is the tangible way in which patterns and marks on things have been put out in the world, at first maybe just by coincidence but later as markers of something. One idea is that when the marked object appears, then what you also put out there is a form of agency, that is, a sense of a person comes out with the object. Thus, by living in a world with made objects, you come to live in a world with other people's agencies as well. Via the object the world becomes in a sense, animistic, because behind every object there is agency, and thereby you may get intentionality, the presence of other people. At least this is one hypothesis, one idea that we are exploring, the evolution over time of environments of intentionality. That may have created quite unique ways in which people can deal with one another. Objects become "technologies of the mind"; they are a kind of externalization that creates ways to be with ourselves and others, that create ways to transform the world.

The Sharing Game

OE And if you think about it, isn't that just what the object called *Green light* does? It hosts exactly in a funneling way—funneling, just like a vortex that drives you down a black hole, but like a green hole, it hosts the effort.

This is so interesting because we work within what is called the cultural sector, and that to a great extent, is a supplement to the rational sector. But why is the cultural sector marginalized instead of being seen as the vehicle or the identity machine, the we-machine, the we-mode, the we-ness creator? I generally have great confidence that the book of cultural strategies actually has more solutions to conflicts—let's call them counternationalistic or anationalistic agencies—than the political sector. Why do you think that the cultural sector is not seen as the guiding light in Europe?

AR That is a good question!

OE The guiding green light in Europe.

AR The guiding green light! Well, I think what it might take for the cultural sector, or any sector, to achieve what you are asking is the return of agency to the people who are consuming it, who are taking part in it. The interesting shift from being consumers of objects to being somehow coproducers of objects or situations, etc. It seems to me that this is really the critical challenge that we are all facing now. At the moment materiality is almost produced automatically, so the knowledge of how particular items are produced, either as symbolic ideas circulating around us or in the objects that we are surrounded by, is disassociated from you. I think if there is a change needed, then it is to regain that feeling of agency, of being part of the objects we are surrounded by. If the we-ness is also an experience of taking responsibility to form certain things, then the critical element is that when you are confronted with them, you should hopefully realize that you should see yourself in these particular projects or in these particular objects.

We constructed a simple experiment, in which people first had to build something together and then they had to play a sharing game with each other. This is an investment game; it is called a public goods game among economists. The idea is that I put something into a pool and you put something into a pool. We don't know what the other person puts into the pool, but this pool magically grows and we share whatever is in it. Now the best for me would be if you put everything into the pool, I get half of your things and then I keep everything for myself. Of course for you this would be a very bad strategy, and the crucial question is if we could come up with a situation in which we both trust each other to invest the maximum. What we found in this experiment is quite surprising, namely that when people built something together, which they knew the purpose of, then they were basically investing everything in the communal pool afterward. Whereas when people didn't know the purpose of what they were doing, then they were much more reluctant to engage in the simple collective play of investing in a sharing kind of way. And very interestingly, when they knew what the result of the work was all about, they were also much more willing to trust or invest in another person whom they hadn't met previously.

OE So that means that when they knew the narrative, their we-ness was experienced more deeply.

AR It was almost as if when you don't know the outcome of the labor that you are involved in, you become, so to speak, disembodied. If you become disenfranchised from what you are going to make, this also translates into the relations of how we can do things with each other. This of course is something that Marx had some early thoughts on. This is perhaps another version of embodiment, somehow what we are doing with our objects translates into what we do with each other—and vice versa, what we do with each other translates into what we do with objects. From that perspective I find the kind of thing that you are doing here both a really interesting experience and an interesting experiment. Potentially it is exploring the idea that by doing things together, by constructing things together, by taking shared responsibility, that sense of shared responsibility both gets inherited into the objects and defines what we have between ourselves. And that is a version of the type of concrete spaces that we talked about earlier.

The Unpredictable Talent

OE Maybe you could say something about stability and the scale of events, because clearly we are on the nano scale of the refugee crisis with *Green light*. We are barely touching it with a needle, but still we are doing something! I was very curious about your research on the stability of systems, because it is also about democracy, right?

But what do you do with a person who is in fact not predictable? How do we still say to that person: "You are welcome! I don't understand you exactly, but you are still welcome?" Now that takes a little bit of talent, what I call "unpredictable talent." This is a very significant part of the success here, when Franziska [Wildförster] approaches someone and says: "Maybe if you just write a poem which expresses your dissatisfaction, maybe this is stronger than when you say that you are so happy being in Vienna!" The unpredictable curatorial muscle is very much part of the success, which makes it so difficult to scale up. It is easy to do the *Green light*, but to actually say: "I know you are not happy," that is much more difficult on a larger scale. Getting back to you, Andreas—the stability of systems, of course bigger systems are more stable, that is nothing new, but how can we scale up what Boris [Ondreička] and Franziska do, and eventually also Francesca [von Habsburg]? The unpredictable component!

AR I mentioned earlier the idea of the hyperfollowers. We had a situation in which basically I would be tapping, you would be tapping, and I would hear your tapping while you would be hearing my tapping, and we would constantly adjust to each other. What we saw was that people are somewhat unpredictable; they don't act like a static metronome. But if they are responsive at the same time, if you can adapt to me and I to you, then the emergent system can be very stable. We also saw in these experiments that if there is a situation in which the other person is both unpredictable and not responsive, then it is really difficult to coordinate. So a way to get around unpredictability is to set up ways to introduce responsiveness into a system, because that allows us to become hyperfollowers, to fall into these patterns of mutually coordinating with each other. Now the question of scale is a very interesting one. There is a famous British anthropologist, Robin Dunbar, who has an interesting idea about language. What language allowed us to do is to expand into larger groups. Again, if you look at baboons, they can host a group of about thirty to forty individuals, and the idea seems to be that the way that they solve conflicts is that they spend a lot of time grooming one another. You can only groom so many others if you have to do it body to body. Dunbar's idea is that with language you can extend that to a group of say three to four hundred people, this is the group that you can keep track of and that you can groom through words, for example, through gossip and flattery. But Dunbar has some difficulties explaining how we can move into even larger groupings. There is a Dunbar's number, which says that one to three hundred might be what people can contain. This is both a very interesting and a somewhat dissatisfying idea, because we know that we organize ourselves into much larger groupings. If you look at something like a nation-state, we know a few things about what it takes to create the idea of being able to coordinate within the borders. Denmark is in many ways an interesting case here. It seems that an idea of homogeneity within the borders and differences from others is a very effective way to set up this feeling of we-ness within such a situation.

There is a need for explorative work about how we enact social organization that takes us beyond the three or four hundred people, into larger collectives, but without falling into the trap of the nationalisms of the nineteenth and twentieth centuries. Here the main way to create these kind of stable communities was to assume and produce homogeneity on the inside as opposed to differences on the outside.

An interesting case, one fitting to Vienna, may be to look at empires rather than nation-states. They may provide another solution to this problem, because an empire is more concerned about the center than the periphery. The difference at the border may be less important; it's more of a gradient. What may be needed is another way to think about how to get out of the notion of borders and how to create systems that are sufficiently responsive for us to feel part of it and to contribute to it, in order to allow us to scale up. It may not just be homogeneity but also differences and responsiveness vis-à-vis larger systems. That might be a challenge, not just of contemporary states but also of entities such as the EU or the UN.

OE Thank you for bringing up the issue of borders, nation-states, empires, and the new models that are needed. For this to work, the need is obviously to scale it up. I was just calculating that if Germany has one million refugees, and we had fifty people here last month, that means we would need twenty thousand *Green light* workshops in Germany alone! So do you see the importance of this type of thinking, the scalability of the system? Because clearly it is easy for me to say that the sustainability of cultural strategies is a more socially inclusive model on this scale. But I think we should leave it here; it is a lovely place to stop.

This conversation was conducted on April 7, 2016 at TBA21 in Vienna, as part of *15 Acts of Participation*, a full day event with lectures, events and performances, in the context of *Green light—Shared learning*.

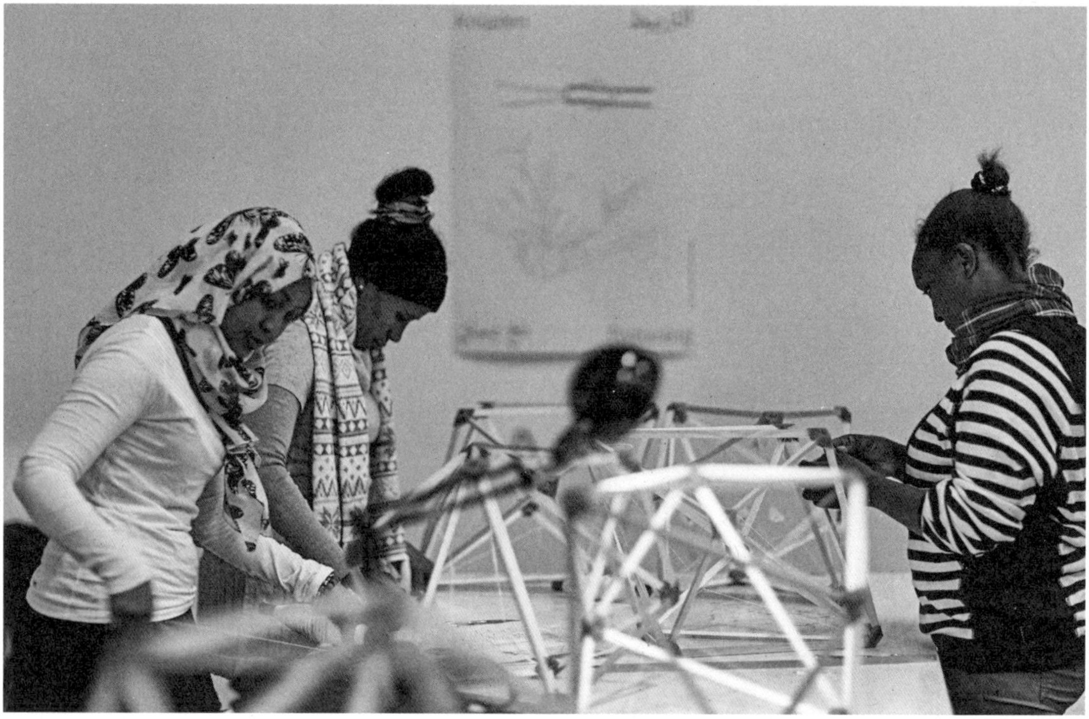

Assembly of *Green lights* by Naima Ali, Armen Muse, and Liya Kasa

We became one family

Naima Ali (22) is from Somalia. Back in Somalia she worked in the family household. Together with fellow *Green light* participants Liya Kasa and Armen Muse, she arrived in Austria in autumn 2015. Her cooking skills were greatly appreciated by the *Green light* team. She is still going through the asylum seeking process and is living in a refugee accommodations run by the Diakonie in Vienna.

Naima, how did you get to *Green light*, why did you join the project?
I joined because when we were there, we weren't in the camp feeling bored. To come here was nice, really nice.

How did you end up in Vienna?
[laughs] Vienna is nice, I didn't know Vienna before, not even Austria. Here, we found happiness, but not only happiness: we are safe here. So, that's the main point I think. Our country isn't safe, which is why I came here.

When you started to work on *Green light*, was there anything that made you feel like "maybe this is not so good for me"?
No, not at all. I just didn't understand how we could make the lamp, if it was going to be too difficult. Even when they were explaining it, I didn't know if I needed to have specific knowledge or something like that. But it turned out to be easy and we all helped each other, managed to understand each other. Even if some people were from Afghanistan, some people from Somalia, and so on, we became one family, you know?

The idea of *Green light* was to use the specific qualities of art to bring people together. What do you think about that?
It happened naturally. There were so many people involved who didn't know each other and didn't even share a language, but we understood each other. We worked together in the same room, laughing and so on. It was nice.

There is the idea that you don't have to speak the same language if you work together.
Yeah, we were people from five different countries working at the same table and we understood each other. For party conversations, we would use German or English, but my English is not that good. While working we used body language and we understood each other enough to work together, it was great.

Armen, Liya, and you came together. Did you also meet other people in the project?
Yes, for instance Fatima, the two Ibrahims, Ghifar, we got to know all of them here. Now we are a family here. We know each other now, and we see each other.

Working, and working together, but what about the learning process? *Green light* was always about working together and learning together. What do you think you learned here?
German! As I told you, I didn't know

anything. Now I can understand it at least, and I know some words.

Living in a group, working together: What about social skills?
When we made the *Green light*, a lot of people came here to see it. And we explained it—that was a first time for me. I never explained something to a lot of people before. It was difficult, but it was also nice. And I helped people, telling them that they could do something like this too. [laughs]

We want to do *Green light* workshops in other places. What do you think about it?
I think it's good to continue. Not for us, but for a lot of refugees who need what we needed then. Maybe now we'll stay here, because now we know something. Before we didn't know anything. We were staying at the camp. We didn't know anywhere to go. Some people need a project like that, actually, many people do. So if they get this chance, it would be very nice because then they'll get what we got before: we got happiness, we got each other. Time at the camp passes slowly. It's not good to stay around there and be bored. Here people can come, get knowledge, meet people, even learn the language, especially because the TBA21 staff helped us to communicate in German. So they would get all these things. And it's nice because if you know how to explain, how to communicate with people, maybe you'll feel happy.

It creates a different place.
Yeah. There are a lot of people in the camp, but no one is sitting together and talking. You might know some people, but that's not the main point. Here, you work together. You are busy, you are working on something, you are doing something, and you are interacting, even if it's only through motions. It's still fun.

That was always the hope—that this would work out. As a refugee, what do you feel that you brought to *Green light*?
Patience. Refugees are not all the same. There are so many different languages, different countries, different cultures. So when you teach each other, it requires patience. If someone needs something—if you don't like a person, or if one person understands something one way and another person understands it another way it requires more explanations I think. And time. Because if we take *Green light* as an example, it lasted a long time. Not that much, but still it was quite a long time. When we work, we understand each other, we teach each other, so it requires patience, time, and, I think, a lot of explaining.

Thank you. Is there anything else that you would like to add?
Yes, sure. First of all, I want to thank the group. And whoever had this nice idea. Second, there are many people just like me who need this project, so I think would be nice if it continues. Because we forget so many things when we are happy. Because when you come to another country, you see so many new things, but maybe you don't know anyone, or you don't speak the language. I, for example, don't have family here, I don't have anyone. But I have a family here now. We were together, we felt good, and it helped me forget so many things that maybe if I were alone I would have remembered. But now I forgot them, so I sit here and thank you

This interview was conducted by Clemens Rettenbacher on October 6, 2016

Teaching each other

Liya Kasa (25) is from Asmara, Eritrea. After finishing primary education, she worked in the family household. She enjoys reading novels and listening to music. Together with fellow *Green light* participants Naima Ali and Armen Muse, she arrived in Austria in autumn 2015. Today, she is living in refugee accommodations run by the Diakonie in Vienna. She has not been granted asylum yet.

I am from Eritrea, I came here last October. I arrived by sea from Turkey. Then through Greece and following some other people on the way we came to Austria. We were with a big group of Syrians and Afghans.

Why did you come to Vienna? Did you want to come to Vienna?
No, before coming here I didn't even know anything about Austria. The way here was very difficult, we got really tired, and then when we got to the border, there were Austrian soldiers there who welcomed us, and so we decided to stay here. We were tired and they were friendly, so we said: "Ok, it's fine here."

How did you get to *Green light*? What brought you here?
When I was with the Red Cross, a person was registering for it, so we just gave our names and they brought us here.

What did you think the first time you heard about the project? What did you expect? Do you remember?
A lady called Milena told us that we would make something together out of things that aren't used. I didn't expect this sort of thing. I said to myself, "Let's just try." But when I got here I realized this was a good thing. And there's the German course. But I didn't expect this.

Let's talk about the workshop. The idea of *Green light* was always to use art and art institutions to bring people together. And to teach each other.

Yes, what do you think about that?
I think it was good because for one, I now know how to create this lamp and I took a German course and I got to meet many new people. It was nice.

Were you interested in art before?
Only in music.

There was some music in *Green light*.
There was this guy from Lebanon, Tarek Atoui.

How was it to work together? Many people were in need of your talents in the project. Whenever I wanted to cook with you, Yusuf would say I couldn't take you away because you are the best at making the lamps. What was the work like?
When you make the lamp, in the end you

have to put in the thread. I was good at that. We were the best at putting in the threads, that's why Yusuf would say that.

What made you so good at it, what do you think?
Maybe because I liked it, that's why. It's complicated, but if you learn it once, it's very easy. That's why I like it.

Working in a group, working with your hands, it changes something in the way you think. Would you agree?
For me, when I put in the thread it was always very hard to fit it into the hole. The hole is very small. So when I get it in and I get to fit it exactly I get a feeling of satisfaction.

There are many challenges in *Green light*. And that also means there are many chances to overcome obstacles and then feel good about yourself. Was it sometimes hard to work with so many different people?
Not for me, because the people here were nice. Some people could get loud at times, but in the end we always worked it out.

If you work together, you have a different way of overcoming problems—like you just said—sometimes there is tension, but you work together and this creates a different kind of group. What do you think about that process?
It's nice when to work with people, because sometimes things are easier when you do them in a group. Something you don't know you can learn from another person. When I first came here I didn't know how to build the lamp. Kelvin taught me then, he showed me and afterward I would show other people, both visitors and participants.

So it's about giving and taking knowledge.
Yeah.

If you think about the special knowledge or role everybody had within the group, something that they could do better than anybody else and that they to the group, what do you feel was your thing that you could use best for the project?
I am an open person. When I was with my friends, they would laugh more. I talked to them so they wouldn't be bored. I also made them finish the lamps, not make half the lamp and finish the next day. I would say, "Let's finish and have some fun after." I think that was good for the project because we didn't leave things half done, we finished them so the next day we would begin anew. When I focus and finish things with a good result it makes me feel happy [laughs]. So it was nice, I like to finish things.

What do you think about the lamp itself? Do you like the design or is there something you would do differently?
If I were the one creating it I would put in different colored threads. I think that would make more sense for the lamp. But it's nice, the design is nice. Putting in different colored threads would be nice though.

How would you describe the workshop to participants who start it?
The *Green light* workshop is about teaching each other. I don't know something and you do, so I will take that thing from you and give it to others. You meet new people and share experiences. This is what *Green light* is about.

This interview was conducted by Clemens Rettenbacher on October 6, 2016

Learning from and about each other

Armen Muse (29) is from Asmara, Eritrea. She left her native country ten years ago and arrived in Austria in autumn 2015, together with fellow *Green light* participants Naima Ali and Liya Kasa. She is currently living in refugee accommodations run by the Diakonie in Vienna. She has not been granted asylum yet.

Where are you from, Armen?
I'm from Eritrea, from a city called Asmara. I haven't been there in ten years. I spent three years in Sudan, then seven years in Syria. On the way here I spent fifteen days in Turkey then came over by sea.

Why did you come to Austria?
Because I can be happy here, I can live a happy life in Austria.

Did you know Austria or Vienna?
No.

How did you learn about the *Green light* project?
My name was added to the list after Naima Ali. She told me about the project and asked if I could come. *Green light* made me very happy, the German classes made me happy. Too much happiness.

Too much?
We came here for work, German classes, and food, and we were very happy. In the camp we were not happy. All you can do there is eat and sleep.

What is the best part about *Green light*? What do you think?
All of it. Work, eating together, meeting people who become like family.

Did the project help you somehow?
After I started to work here, little by little, I started to feel better. Every day I would have a chance to be happy and to see people who are like my family now. That was all very good for me.

What is important about *Green light*?
It was important to meet the people there. And when you do things, you learn more. It was important to learn from and about each other.

What can you learn here?
You can take a German course, meet other people, and you learn to build the lamp.

So, how can you connect people, what do you think?
Since I only speak Arabic, I try to use German more often. This is about making an effort to connect.

Do you like the lamp?
It's nice for the house.

What do you think we could do better when *Green light* is taken to other countries?
You should make it bigger.

This interview was conducted by Clemens Rettenbacher on October 6, 2016

A New Holism

Timothy Morton

The Buddhist concept of no-self is often taken to mean that you don't exist at all. Which would be fine, but then you have to explain why things happen at all, and you have to wonder who it is who, according to that system, becomes enlightened.

The trouble comes from a certain interpretation of Buddhism by Buddhists themselves. Some Buddhists think that emptiness, the idea that things don't really exist, means that the ultimate reality of a thing is some kind of total void. What if we flipped this model upside down and concurred with the other Buddhists, who think that emptiness is sort of the basis of how things can exist, how things can happen, rather than their ultimate nature? I mean, if she exists, Buddha can still use the toilet. She can get money out of a cash machine. Buddha can rescue people at the border. This seems to suggest that Buddha exists in some way.

It's just that Buddha, like you and me, like refugees and every other human on this planet, along with everything else, exists *less* than we might suppose. Things are holey. A more elegant way of saying the same thing is to say that things are *open*. Tim Morton is open. What does it mean?

On a physical level, for starters, there's so much of supposed Tim that isn't strictly Tim. Tim doesn't have some kind of "Intel Inside" sticker on everything about him: *This is a Tim Morton cell, This is a Tim Morton DNA strand, This is a Tim Morton lung*. Tim is made of all kinds of things (I just named three) that aren't Tim. Even if you don't think of evolution, this is true. But if you do, it's especially true.

Furthermore, Tim's ideas aren't strictly his either. Ideas don't have a Tim stamp. If they did then we'd have to know what Tim is first before we could make sure that logical things Tim says (very rarely) are true. And we'd need logic to describe Tim. But logic is what we're trying to prove. So we have a bad circularity. So this idea, that thoughts are symptoms of Tim and Tim alone, can't be right. In the age of Twitter it's obvious that ideas are more like tweets than they are like essential bits of me. If they were, they couldn't be retweeted, detached from me and sent around the world. Because they're not exactly mine in the first place, I can do all kinds of things with them.

It's the same with where Tim lives. Having a baby is a great teacher. You begin to realize that your world is shrinking. What you took to be your very own house, if you're lucky enough to live in one, is less and less yours. You feel like you're inhabiting an ever-shrinking island of you-space as the baby begins to crawl, use objects, knock things over, yell for attention when you were just trying to fix this plug ...

You relax, eventually, when even the one-meter radius island left, the one around your body, disappears, and you realize the truth: *you never had the house in the first place*. You were always kind of squatting in it, like living in a hotel or a temporary camp.

But this is great. You enjoy it more that way. You don't need to keep maintaining it. You don't need to keep maintaining yourself. You don't need to try to be authentic. Whatever you are is holey, open—there is less of you than you thought. When you get married in the USA the tax code treats you as one and a half people. That's psychologically and ontologically true. You are three-quarters of a person. But that means there's so much more wiggle room to do stuff, and to let stuff happen.

That's the way to think of emptiness. It's a feeling. The esoteric schools of Buddhism concur: it's spaciousness, that moment when you go "Ahhhh!" and flop down exhausted on the sofa or the park bench or when you've made it into the country unscathed after a very long journey. The Sanskrit syllable for emptiness is *AH* for this very reason—it's a relieved outbreath, the lovely luxury of always-available wiggle room. Always available, no matter who you are: this was Buddha's radical message. It doesn't matter what class you are, because remember, you're not totally solidly you, so you're not defined by your class. So no matter who you are, or where you are, you can practice finding the wiggle room in any situation. There is something very empowering, in a slightly anarchist way, about that. You have the controls. You don't have to wait for some authority to tell you when to wiggle, because fundamentally, there's plenty of wiggle going on. You just have to tune into it.

Now you might think that this is because you are "bigger" than your life situation, that you go beyond it in some way. But that's not quite the right way to look at it, because of what we've just found out: we are three-quarters people, metaphorically speaking. There's ontologically *less* of us—ontologically meaning "having to do with how things exist." Things—a five-pound note, a computer cable, a razor blade—are less heavy, less of a big deal, than we like to think. They are what they are—they aren't absolute nothing, you can handle a fork and you know that a razor blade isn't a five-pound note.

What is in fact the case is that there's so much more of the not-you things than there is of you. There's so much more non-Tim DNA in Tim in order for Tim to remain alive. Think of the bacterial microbiome. Think of your mitochondria, the energy packets in your cells—they are really bacterial symbionts with their own DNA. If you only had one thought you'd never be able to do anything at all—think of how many billions of those you have, and how open and various they are too, because they're also not totally themselves, they also contain all kinds of wiggle room.

There's so much more of your house than there is of you. Not physically, although that may also be true. But ontologically, having to do with how things are. And if we take "house" to mean "all the stuff in my world that I use to be getting along with stuff"—which is actually a pretty good definition!—then obviously "all the stuff" is a pretty open, which is to say infinite, list. Did I say never-ending? No. I said infinite, which strictly doesn't mean "going on and on for ever and ever," because numbers aren't really solid either. Infinite strictly means *you can't count it.*

What does it mean? Well, I hold the idea that if a thing such as Tim exists, this thing exists in the same way as other things. Doesn't sound like a big deal when you put it like that, "it" being object-oriented ontology. But it's a huge deal. Notice that this doesn't mean things have the same *right* to exist. That would be horrible, and it would also be illogical according to the very idea I'm mentioning here, which is that groups of things exist in the same way as their members or parts. We'll get to that in a moment.

It's a huge deal, because, well, just think about it. A football team, if it exists—I'm not the object police so I'm not going to prove it to you—is one thing. It's a whole. This whole is comprised of eleven parts, the players. Eleven to say the least: we're leaving out the manager and the pitches and the games and the stuff football players get on with (see above).

Therefore—brace for impact—*the whole is always less than the sum of its parts.*

I get such a kick out of writing such a counterintuitive thing, which I've just proved ever so simply that a small child could understand it, understand it probably better than you and me, because she hasn't been indoctrinated into the opposite idea. The opposite idea is what we keep saying to each other, nodding our heads wisely as we show off our superior intelligence: "The whole is always greater than the sum of its parts." What's amazing is, when you read the opposite, you are probably hitting delete on the idea. You are probably thinking you don't need to read any more Tim Morton because there's obviously something wrong with him.

I think that this idea that the whole is greater than the sum of its parts is a tweet, if you like, from agricultural-age monotheism, filtered through Neoplatonic forms of it (whether they are Islam, Christianity, Judaism). God is omnipresent, which means God goes on and on forever, in space and time. And God is omniscient, which means that God, like Santa Claus making that list and checking it twice, can see everything all at once. And God is omnipotent, which means God can do everything and anything. So God is ontologically greater than the entire universe, which you might say are the parts contained within the whole that is God—I'm not going to get into all the wonderful ways of slicing and dicing this concept right now. I'm just trying to sketch out the big picture so you have a sense of where I'm coming from in this argument.

God stands for the King of the agricultural civilization, the being who assures everyone that they belong to a whole, in such a way that this whole is "something bigger" than them. Isn't that what people often say? "I wanted to believe in something bigger, I wanted to be part of something bigger." You are a part of a whole in such a way that the whole is greater. If you die, it doesn't matter to the whole, in the sense that someone else will come along to do your job. That's the kind of thinking that gave us the caste system, against which Buddha was rebelling.

A nation is in fact not a great big whole, but a small whole. You see I think it's very important to be a holist. There aren't *only* parts. If that's true then reducing things to their parts must be the right thing to do. But as Gandalf says in *Lord of the Rings*, "he who breaks a thing to find out what it is has left the path of wisdom." And the path of ontology: If you break open a piece of chalk to find out what it is, you have two problems where just before there was only one—because you now have two pieces of chalk to explain. It's the same with particle accelerators. Or you can be like Mrs. Thatcher and say, "There is no such thing as society." Then you can justify all kinds of cuts because the thing you're cutting doesn't exist as much as so-called individuals do.

But the other way around isn't great either. It's what I call *explosive holism*, this belief that the whole is always greater than the sum of its parts. For example, if you believe this you can be some kind of uncaring utilitarian and say, "Well, it doesn't matter if this polar bear dies, because it's the population of polar bears in general that's more real and therefore more important. The polar bear wouldn't exist without that, so we shouldn't care very much about this particular one." When you're down to just a few, because of global warming, you can see where this idea is going to lead. It's called extinction.

And you can believe that nature is a whole in that explosive, greater-than-the-sum-of-its-parts way. Sounds nice doesn't it? The Gaia hypothesis appears to be like that. But it's not nice at all. If the polar bear goes extinct it doesn't matter because Gaia or nature will replace the bear with something else. The bear, a human, this tree are all parts of a machine, because machines are like that, they are wholes with replaceable (aka less important than the whole) components.

While it's true that without wholes you wouldn't exist—you came out of one called *mother* for example—that doesn't mean they're more real than you. And this in turn means that there's so much more wiggle room down there, within things. Wholes are holey.

Why do we have passports? Because nations are ontologically *small*. They need to be maintained with all kinds of rituals and documents. They may be very big and very powerful, and represented right now by some guy in riot gear with a water cannon. But ontologically, they are tiny. They contain multitudes. They have wiggle room. Stuff can happen. There can be change. You can do stuff, like changing the world.

The intellectual game for the last few decades has been characterized by what some people call cynical reason, which means that sentences like the ones I just wrote are seen as really, really pathetic. I'm supposed to be telling you how paralyzed we are, how much more paralyzed we are than you can possibly imagine, how bad this world is, how difficult to change, and that is supposed to make me seem more intelligent than you. How on earth did we argue ourselves into this corner? Well, again, it has to do with explosive holism. If society, history, capitalism, whatever, really is ontologically greater than us, then we have every reason to be cynical. But it's only greater than us if you let it, in other words if you keep on cleaving to a Neoplatonic theist way of justifying the existence of a certain kind of god. It's just that you've turned society or capitalism into that god. It's funny how this is supposed to make you seem more intelligent, if you are left wing. It's weirdly like some kinds of fundamentalism, which seem functionally to be forms of Satanism, because they believe in many cases that Satan can be more powerful than God, and they obsess about how everything you do and think could lead you away from God into Satan at the slightest notice.

I like Olafur Eliasson very much because he makes things in social space that allow us to feel all kinds of wiggle room. And he does it in a very nonconceptual way, which is to say, the things he makes are wholes that are less than their parts, because you can use them in all kinds of ways, and remember that's one aspect of what we are calling "parts." My world is more than me (remember the argument about having a baby). The world of a bridge or of the *Green light* project is more than the work itself. It's very obvious with the latter, because the whole thing is about building and putting together things, and in turn the assembled thing is never final or complete, always less than its possible futures.

Because there's less of me than I thought, there's also less of my world, which is also a whole. It's real, but it's breezy, perforated, like a sponge. Which means I can share someone else's world, and vice versa. I can't do it totally, because that would mean that when I do so, the whole that results swallows all its parts. Truth can be like that too. "True" can be modal, in other words, things can be partially true, not 100 percent true. You can be half right, 70 percent accurate ... you can share your world 30 percent with a lion. But it's not zero percent, like Wittgenstein thought. Your world and the lion's world can overlap, and this is why you can care for each other. Your world can overlap with a refugee's world, not because you are the same underneath and your differences are superficial. It's not because you belong to the thing called humanity, an explosive whole if ever there was one, usually modeled on some kind of straight white male. You can share worlds because there's ontologically less of you than you supposed.

We are humans. We are not jellyfish. Humans caused global warming, which is already responsible for mass migration and conflict. Dolphins didn't. Humans are different from dolphins. I'm very firm on this point. If we're all made of atoms or entirely reducible to discourses that constitute what it means to be human or Tim or a citizen or whatever, then you can argue yourself to a point where you think that things can be the same—underneath they are all made of the same kind of thing. The way of saying "human" has usually tended to be a violent form of explosive holism that says your specific social and economic (and so on) differences don't matter, or don't matter as much as being part of something bigger. But if there's no "human" at all, how do we care for one another on an international scale, let alone care for other lifeforms, which is what we're now enjoined to do, not because we'll get a prize, but *because we can understand that there are problems*. You don't even need to prove global warming was caused by humans to take responsibility for it. You just have to know it's real. You don't have to know why a cigarette burning in a very dry forest was smoked and chucked away right there. You just have to put it out, because since you can see it and understand what it does, you are just responsible.

But we lack the philosophical and spiritual resources to give us the courage and motivation to do such things. Rightly, anyone with a clue would hate to be reduced to some omnipresent, everywhere-the-same humanity. Try imagining it. You will inevitably imagine something very specific. I think that's interesting actually. When you try to imagine a substance that underlies appearances, you imagine another lot of appearances: maybe it's a dull transparent lump of jelly. The very fact that the thing can be imagined, as in made to appear, means that this will always be the case. I think that there's something in the structure of thought that's telling us something very deep about the world, namely that you can't peel appearances away from being.

The appearances are the parts. The being is the whole. There's always more appearances than being. Being is ontologically small. That's why things can happen. Appearances, which include how things work, what you do with them, what happens when they get irradiated or arrested, pour out of things as if everything were some kind of Pandora's Box. Actually originally it was Pandora's Jar, which is great, because a jar is ... open.

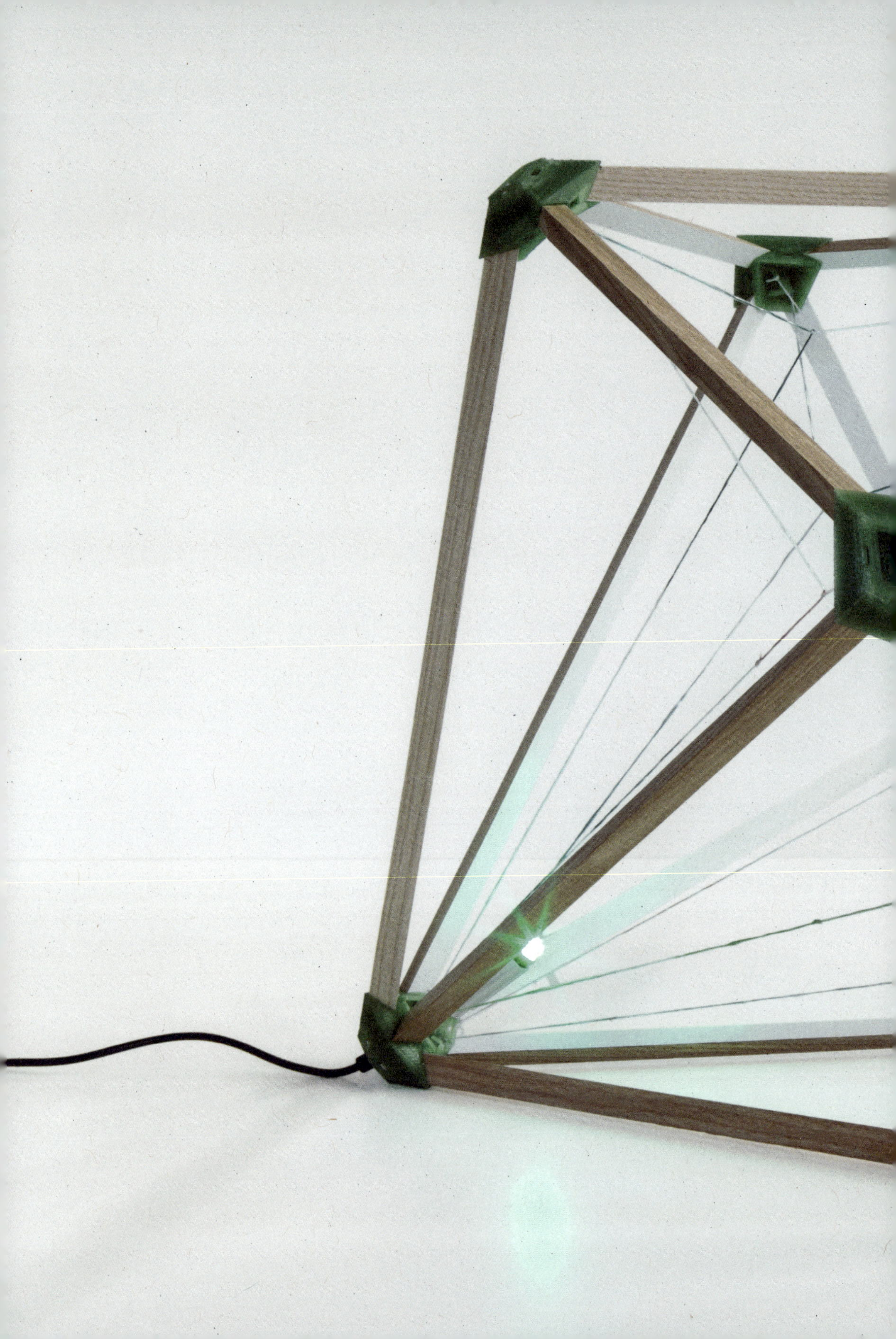

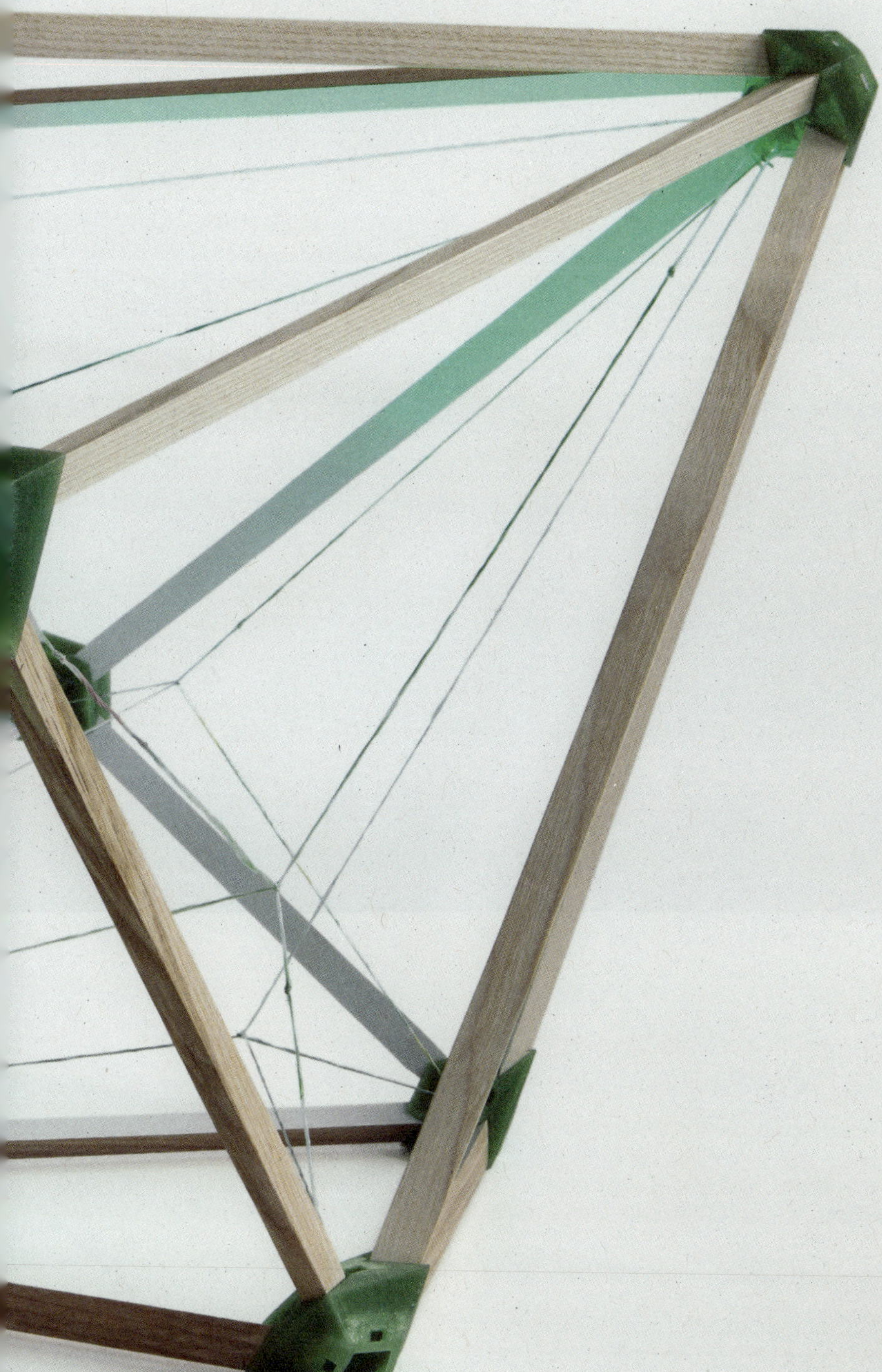

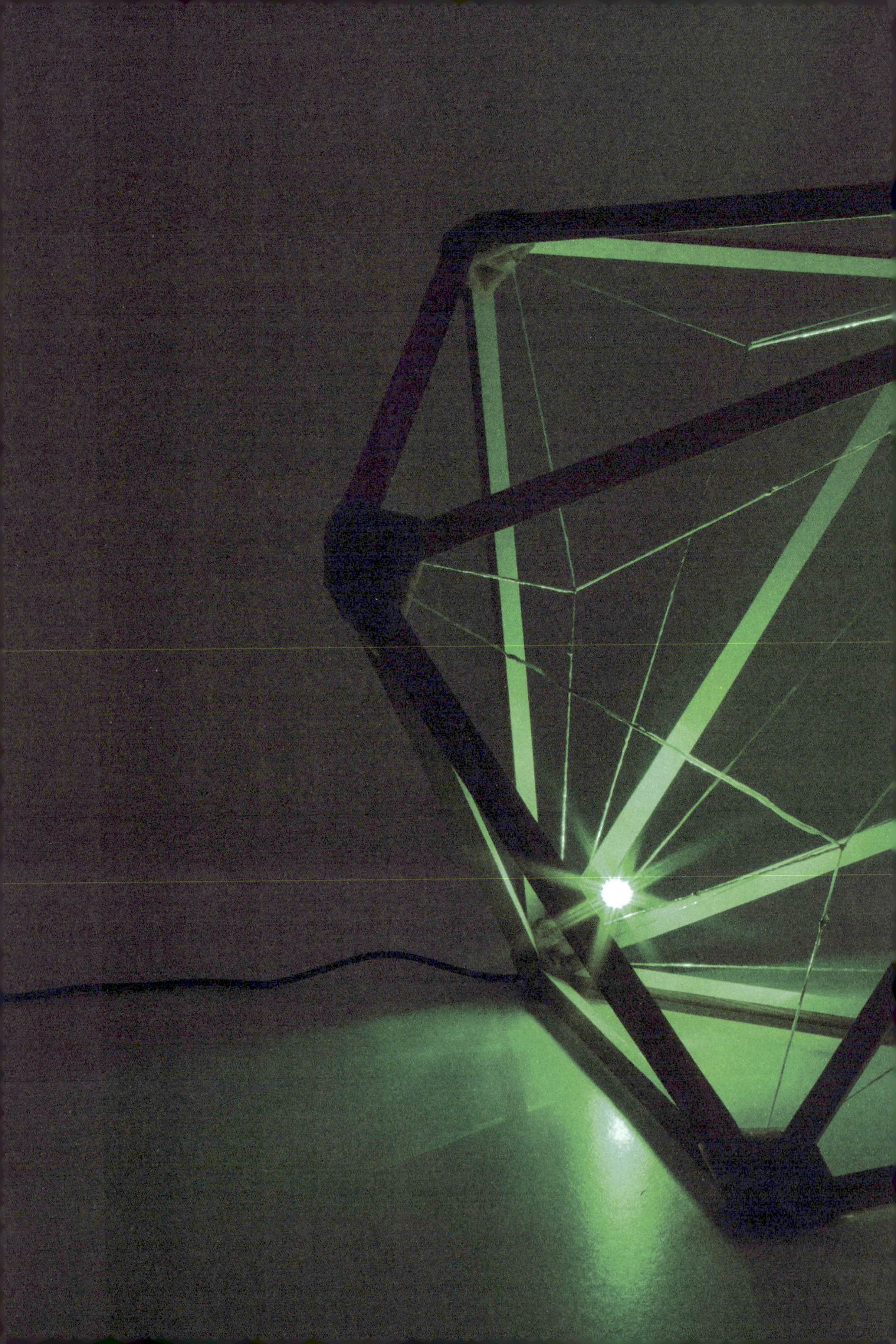

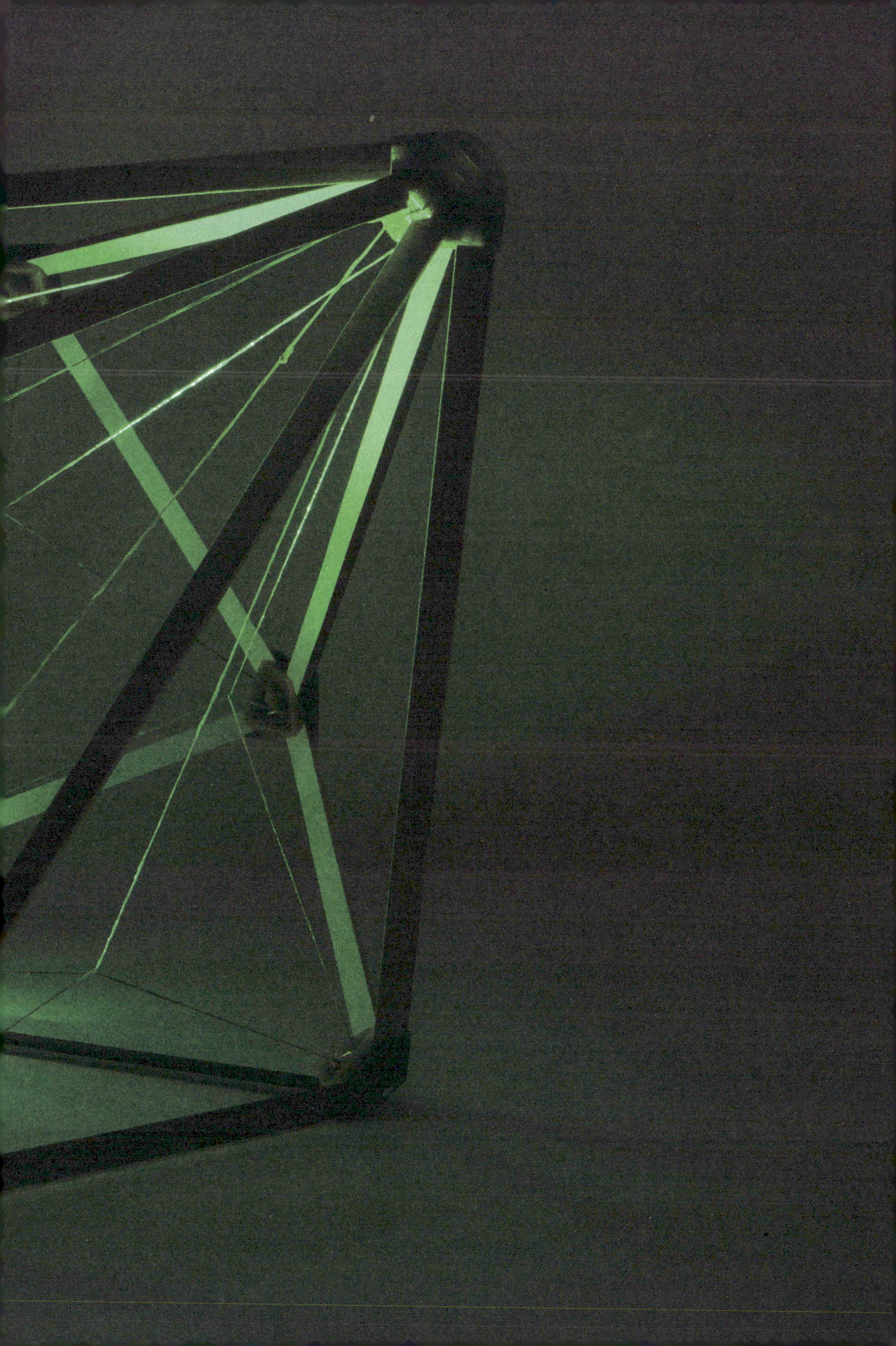

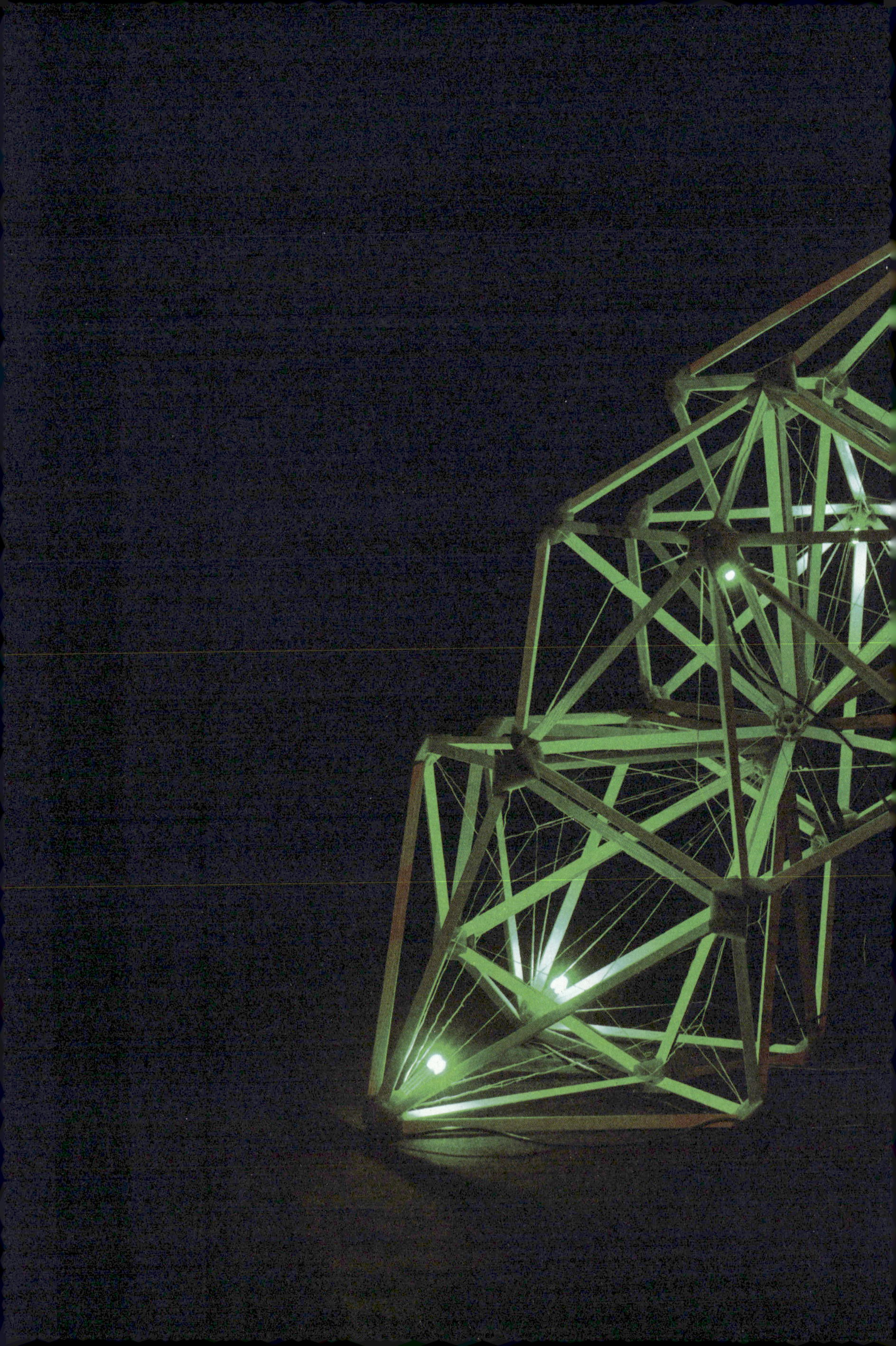

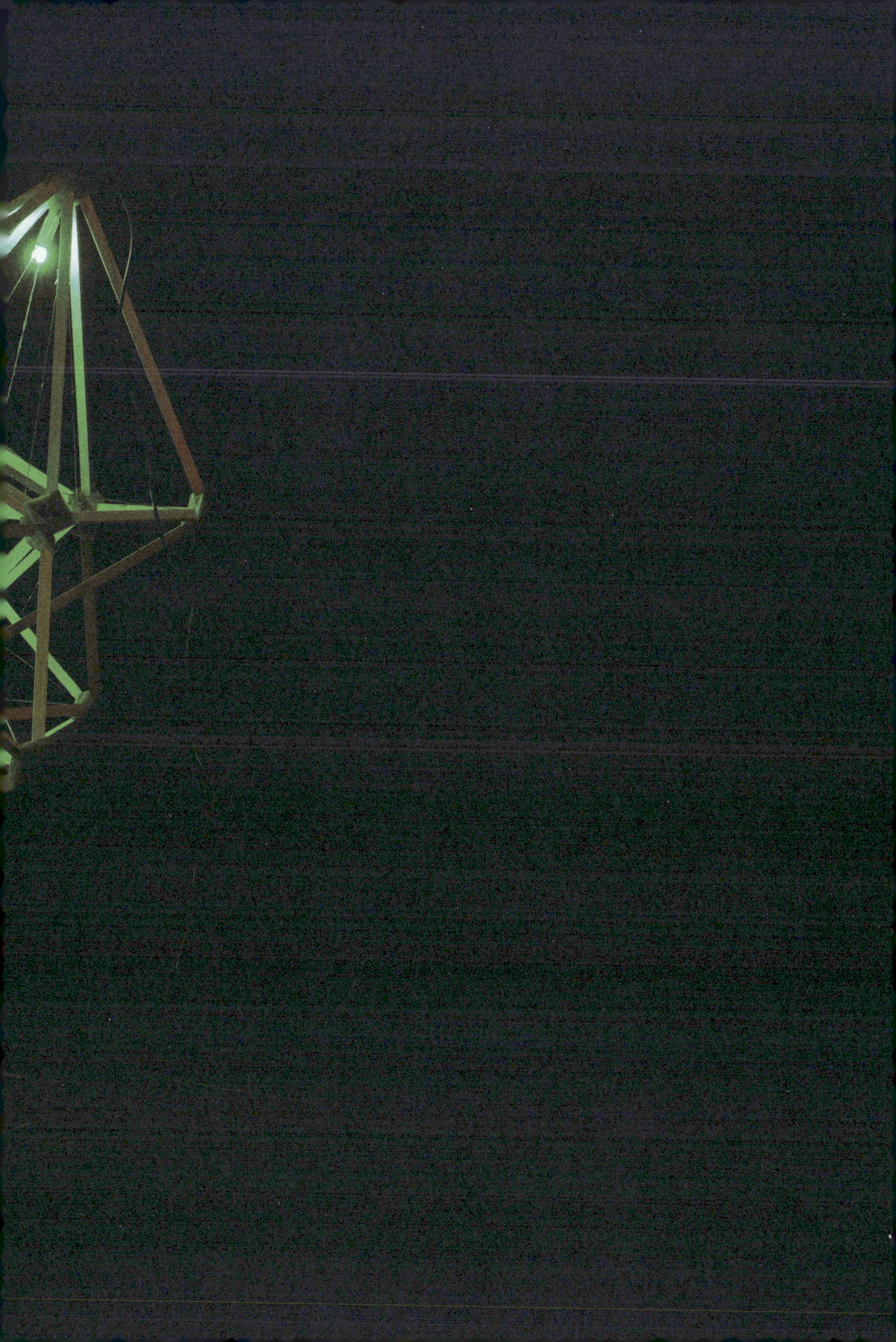

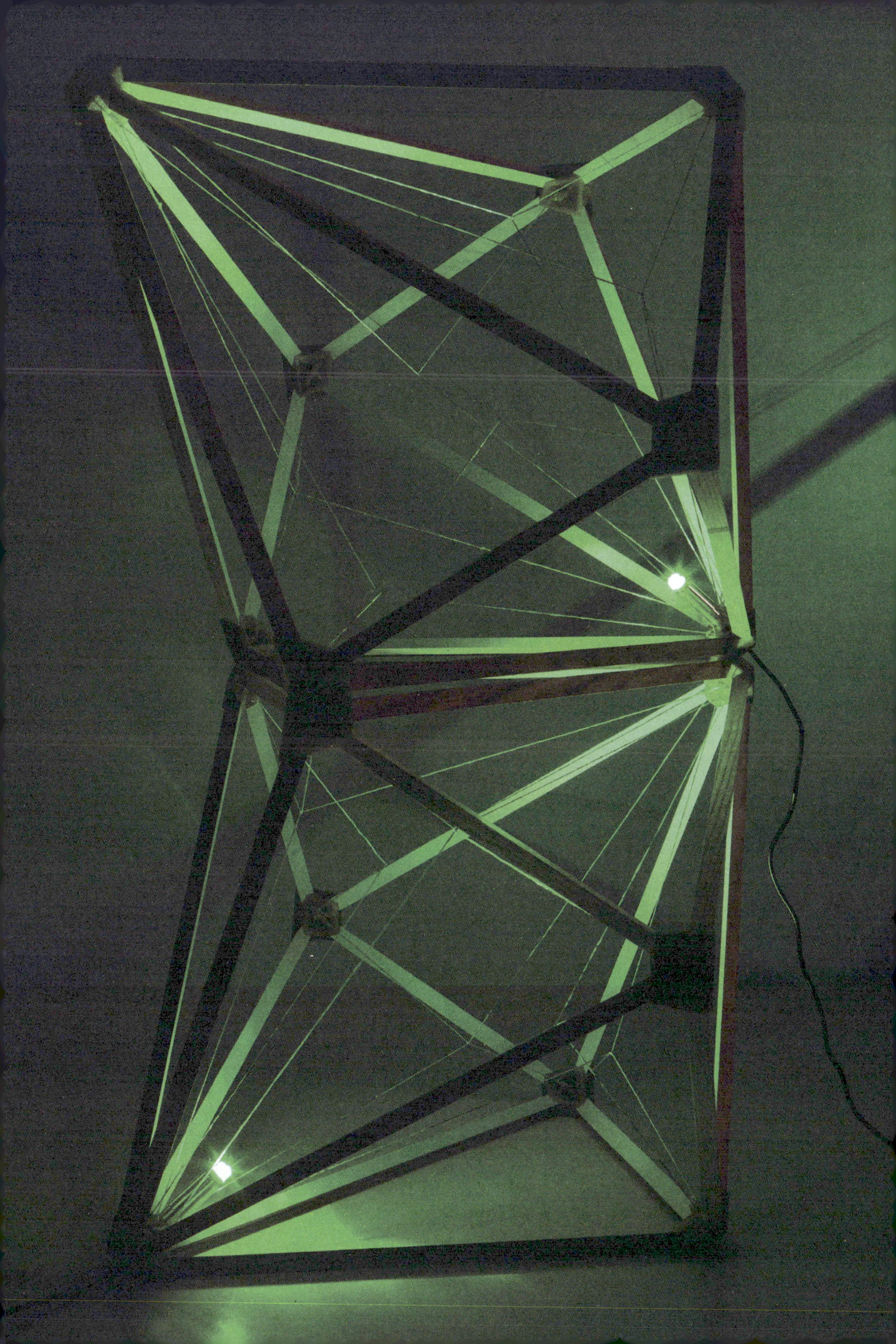

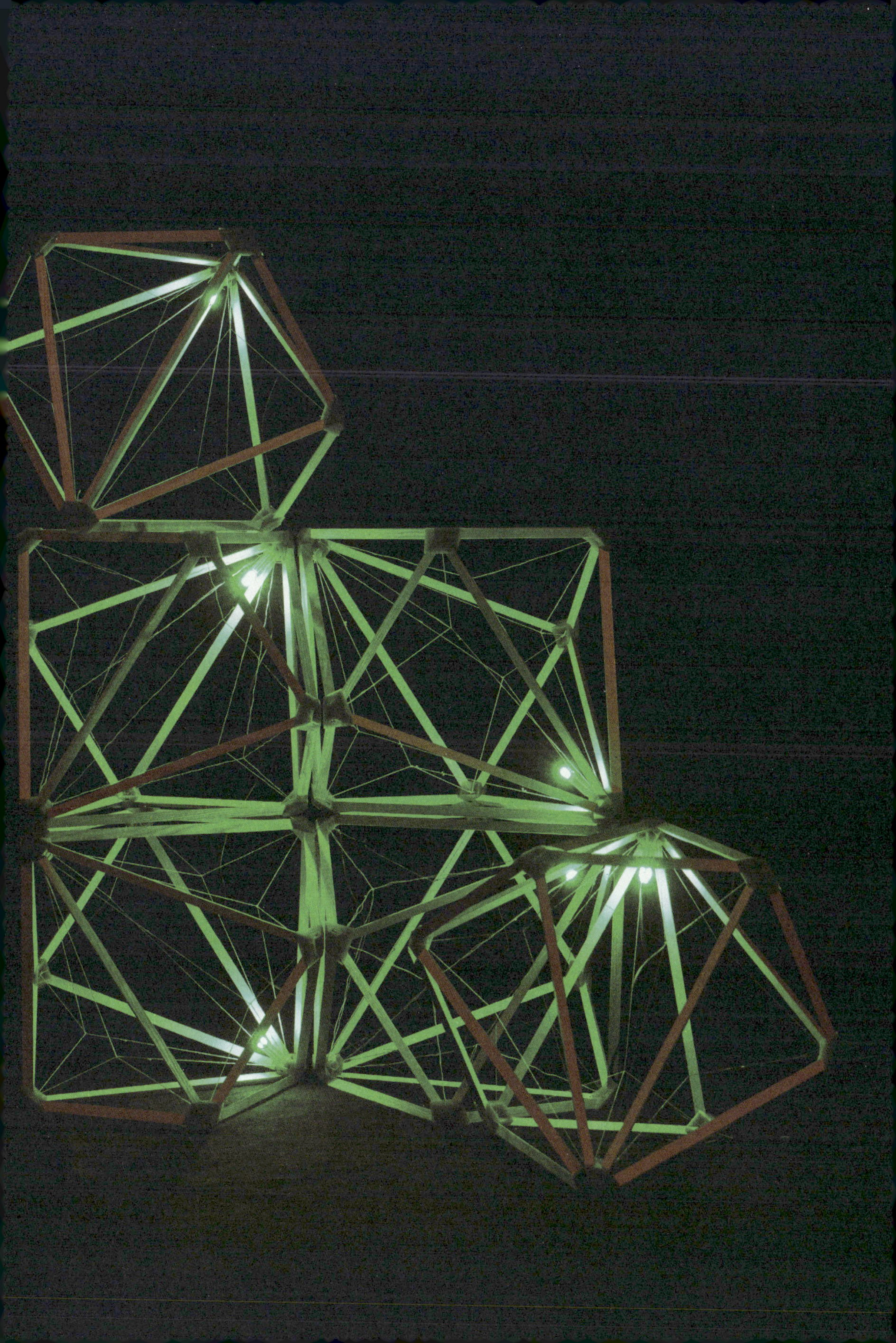

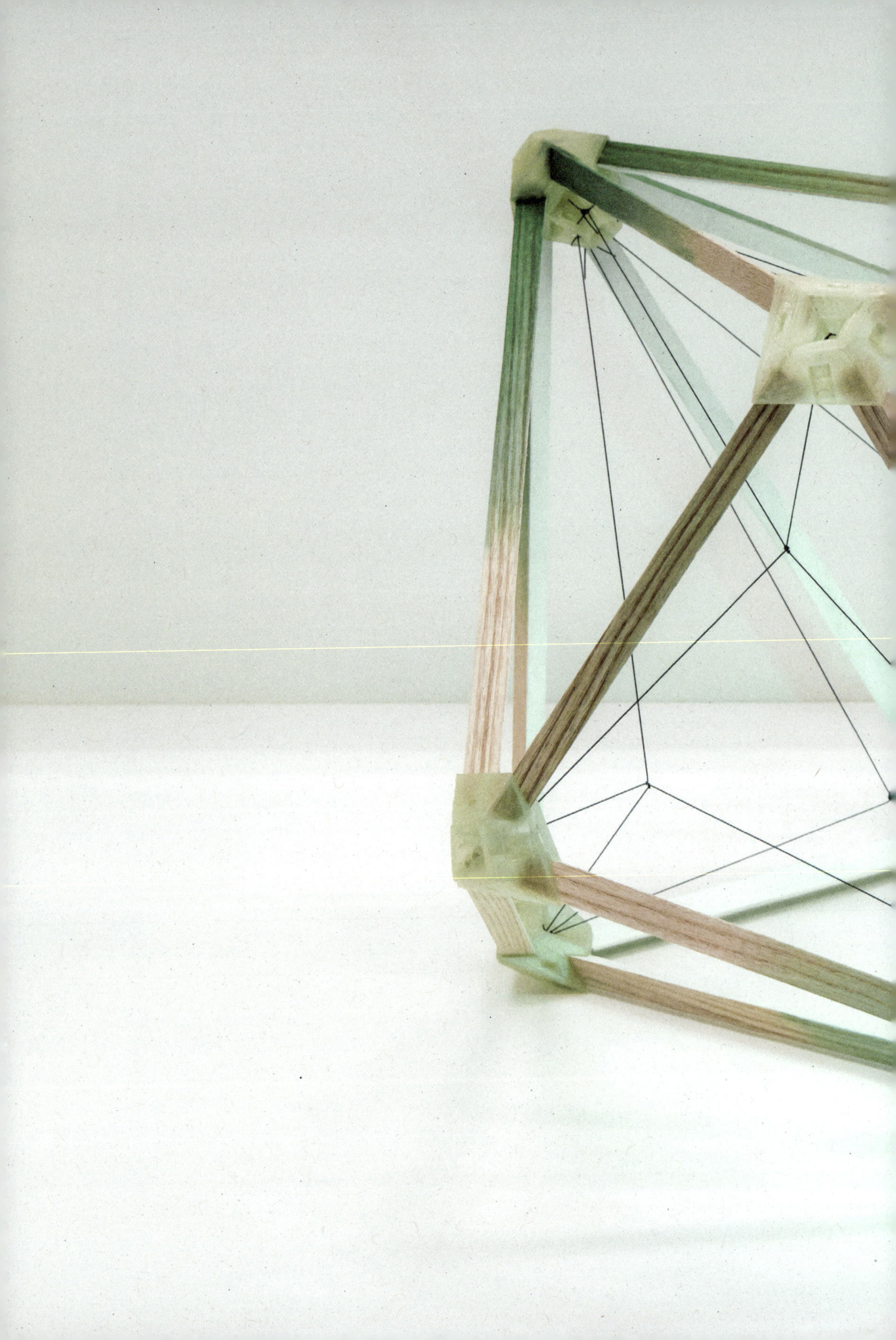

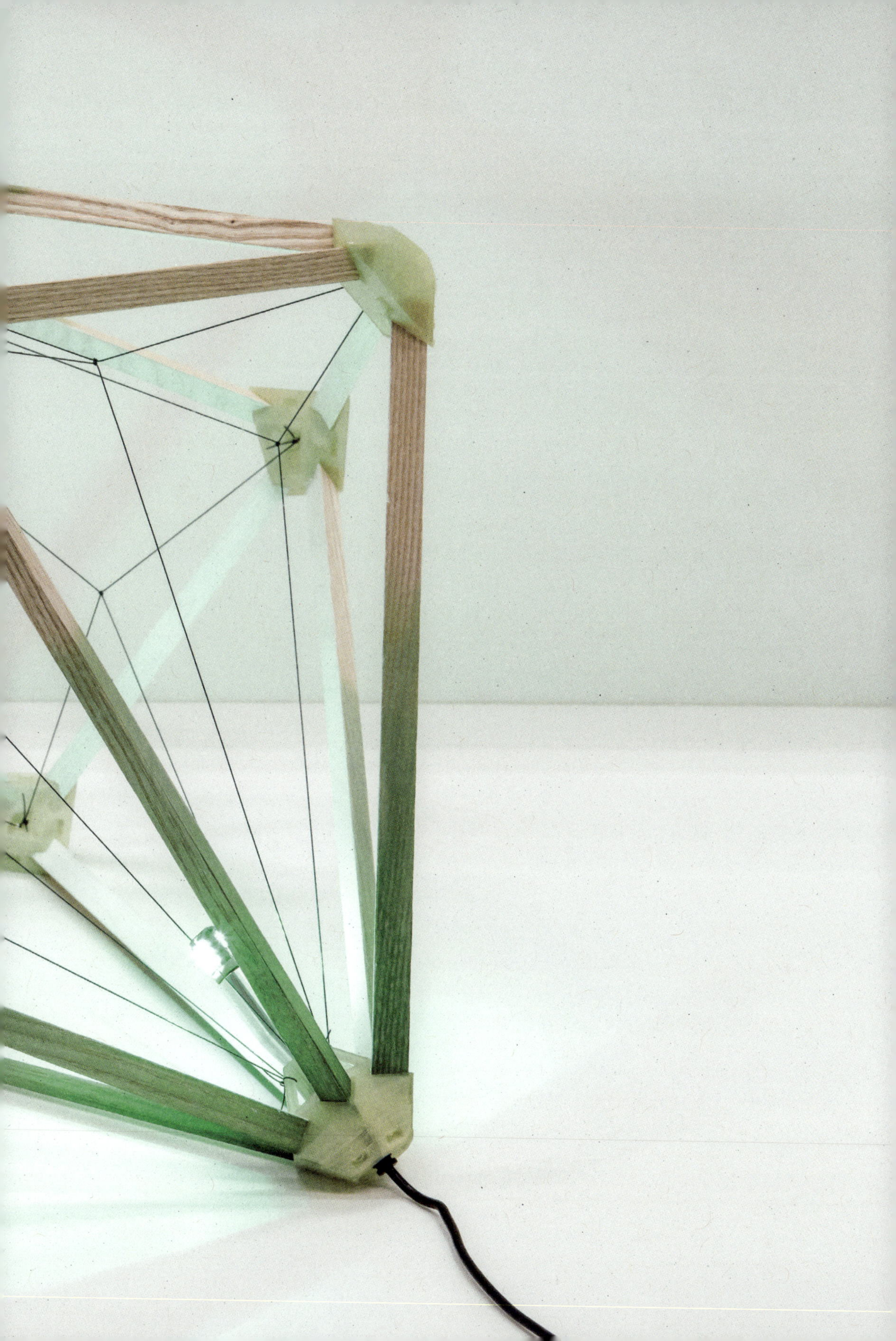

Shifting Agencies

Daniela Zyman

The intolerable, quasi-unthinkable is in the process of creeping into habits.—Isabelle Stengers[1]

On August 31, 2015, German chancellor Angela Merkel announced a "heroic" decision to receive about ten thousand refugees stranded at Budapest's Keleti train station or en route toward Hegyeshalom, on Hungary's border with Austria.[2] While millions of individuals had departed from their embattled and war-ravaged homelands during the conflict in Syria in search of stability, justice, and a livable future, it was the lone figure seen in a photograph of a drowned three-year-old Syrian boy washed up on the shore near Bodrum, Turkey, on September 2 that seemingly transfigured the emotional landscape of Western Europe. This deeply unsettling image, transcending the politics of bordering, led people to rally, however briefly, around a communal dream of being in the world. The unexpected opening of borders to Europe on September 5 set in motion a spontaneous

1 Isabelle Stengers, *In Catastrophic Times: Resisting the Coming Barbarism*, trans. Andrew Godfrey (London: Open Humanities Press, 2015), 22.

2 As we know today, Angela Merkel announced that she would "open the borders" only a few short hours after the Hungarian prime minister, Viktor Orbán, unilaterally decided to allow and facilitate the march of a small group of the 150,000 individuals registered in Hungary by August 2015 toward the Austrian borders. Merkel's lapidary statement, "Wir schaffen das!" (We will manage it), doesn't fully translate the heroic potential of this moment, as it generated at the time both a strong positive signal for German and European civil society but also led to great bewilderment within her own government, as Merkel was lacking the support of other European leaders. Clearly no one had foreseen that borders, once opened, would not close for a long while and that Germany would remain rather solitary in accommodating the newly arrived. One year later, in September 2016, Merkel would rescind her own dictum.

and unprecedented movement of people, mostly along the so-called Balkan route, lasting about six months and accompanied by the spectral euphoria of unprecedented generosity and acts of welcome.[3] Tens of thousands of "people on the move" entered the well-guarded territories of Europe, flows of individuals and families moving from south to north, on foot, trains, buses, taxis, or makeshift vessels. The transitory excitement of welcoming undercut for a brief moment the latent and volatile crisis in the global present. In these months, solidarity and compassion but also engaged activist voluntarism generated localized forces that pushed down walls, frontiers, civil order, and the regulatory systems of the nation-state and the European Union.

What was being tested, perhaps, in these short months was the humanitarian sense of social justice and ethics against the slow abrasion of civic values and the toughening social defense systems triggered by the rising tides of autochthonic politics, a phenomenon examined by Nira Yuval-Davis in this volume. The transformation of Europe (and subsequently of the United States in the aftermath of the presidential elections in November 2016) into sharply divided spaces of belonging and bordering was foreshadowed by the formation of the European Union in 1993. The fortress, established first as a protection against economically disadvantaged inner European neighbors, soon metamorphosed into a highly regulated and defensive apparatus targeted at the ethnically, socially, religiously, and culturally other. It also ended the short-lived idea of a European multiculturalism and the conception of a new form of communality. Further migrational thrusts after the Arab Spring of the early 2010s led to the buttressing of the southern borders and the formation of a new alliance of the (relatively) affluent (the Club Med states) against the new zones of destabilization along the Mediterranean.

These months of hyperactivity and acts of solidarity, signaling hope and the triumph of social justice, foretold a soon-to-come closure, a swift and sharply waged attack against the specter of the stranger, the other, the refugee, represented and stereotyped as an intruder and unmasked as a foreign offense against inherent, local-

3 A significant increase in asylum applications started in June 2015, peaking between August 2015 and January 2016. These six months represent the so-called migration crisis of 2015. By February the movement was ebbing to very modest, pre-2015 levels.

ized cultural values.[4] Culture, embodied in the European system of values, was soon placed in the service of those hegemonic majorities defending access to privileges and resources. Perhaps because cultural values were called to testify against those seeking refuge amid our lives, a plethora of artistic and cultural initiatives sought forms of articulation countering the discourses of repulsion and exclusion. Who else, if not artists and cultural practitioners, possesses the expertise and authority to test definitions of identity against the asserted normalizations of certain autochthonous signifiers of we-ness? What if artists and the artistic imagination claim a voice in the political processes of belonging and devise other, novel ways of envisioning hybrid and pluralistic forms of collectivity and communality within today's experiences of statehood? Is it not, as numerous voices have aptly described, the very moment when alternative practices of we-ness have to be imagined and put to the test, perhaps not so much to counter the existing conditions as to propose fundamental forms of difference?

Parallel Frequencies

From March to July 2016 visitors, students, and artists from Vienna and around the world came together with thirty-four participants who had arrived in Austria over the previous twelve months from Afghanistan, Syria, Iraq, Eritrea, Somalia, Tajikistan, and Nigeria to collaboratively transform TBA21–Augarten in Vienna into a space of multiple narratives, experiences, and knowledges. Seen from the perspective of visitors, *Green light* emits two interrelated frequencies. One frequency, publicly visible, involves the production of *Green light* lamps under the artistic guidance of Studio Olafur Eliasson. During set hours, *Green lights* were assembled from materials and components that were made available in an ongoing workshop. The crystalline lanterns are polyhedral units fitted with small, green-tinted light fixtures. They are made primarily from recycled and sustainable

4 The Paris attacks of November 13, 2015, only made the shifting popular goodwill toward migration recede even more. After a (fake) Syrian passport was found at one of the attack sites and it became known that several of the perpetrators had exploited Europe's immigration crisis to enter the continent undetected on the so-called Balkan route, migrants from Muslim countries became further marginalized and were increasingly seen as a potentially dangerous flood.

materials and are designed to be stackable (and scalable), functioning as single objects or assembled into a variety of architectural or sculptural configurations. As a proposition for a modular space of congregation, built around nested functions (working, being, and learning together) that are participatory and shaped in collaboration, the *Green lights*—which theoretically can be used to build entire cities—are characterized by a fixed unit structure and can sprawl into complexly configured environments. The generative potential of the *Green light* geometries is reflected in the workshop spaces proposed for the Venice Biennale. Modular elements allow the project to evolve in response to what happens within the space.

The other, quieter, more introverted frequency of the project draws from and builds on critical pedagogic ideas, as developed by artists and engaged educators. This informal pedagogic production, called *Green light—Shared learning*, embraces forms of learning that create multidirectional and collaborative processes of exchange. Engaging educators, artists, language teachers, and cultural practitioners as well as vocational training, shared learning activates the needs, talents, desires, and imaginaries of its participants. The shared-learning "school," located in the center of the Green light space, metabolizes the exchanges between the participants; mobilizes their experiences, languages, and areas of expertise; and activates the nexus of encounters between "visitors" and "students."[5]

The most vivid testimonies from participants in Vienna and subsequently in Houston, Texas, attest to the central dimension of learning from one another, with another, and with the other. For the participants, sharing an intimate space of multiple (social) productions over the course of several months led them to embrace difference in terms of cultures, languages, food habits, skills, and interests and to create through the experience of difference an expression of collectivity and communality. Together they forged a space of comfort (and conflict at times) in which they could find and cocreate tools and languages for expressing their experiences, their distress, and the imaginaries of arrival.

5 In Vienna the *Shared learning* program led to the creation of Talent Space, a platform for migrants and asylum seekers to express and employ their creative talents. Meeting weekly at TBA21–Augarten, Talent Space gathers about twenty participants and has led to a number of ongoing initiatives.

Relation, as Édouard Glissant has written, is not that which bridges one thing to the other but rather that which connects everything with everything in a "consciousness of Relation."[6] The "archipelagic" intertwining of individuals demonstrates the potentials of communal production that endorses the idea of the utopian experiment, creating a model situation of difference. Glissant, however, sees differences as pointers not toward irreconcilability but rather toward what relates us, making our being together both complex and creative.

The *Green light* Communities

We are making art, lamps, and sculptures together and have German classes. We are a community, like a family. People can get to know each other, and learn from each other. It is a collective creation, it is more than a workshop.
—Husseyin Haj Hassan, *Green light* participant at TBA21, Vienna

Green light—An artistic workshop was developed with the intention of devising a viable infrastructure that can be conceived of as a replicable, sustainable, alternative communal blueprint. The overall design of the project emerges, as discussed, from two models, the workshop and the school, and proposes a somewhat unorthodox alternative to the kinds of administrative regulations and protocols promoted by European governments as "aid work" (or rather imposed as migration policies). While the publicly visible structure of the project tests the fields of artistic and curatorial expertise, the "invisible" challenges require the astute maneuvering of engaged lawyers, partnering NGOs, and a motivated community to mobilize goodwill, to uncover loopholes, and to bend the rules within this overregulated field.

In the face of growing desires to foreclose migrational movements and the legal and social obstacles that prevent refugees and asylum seekers from accessing education, work, and therefore social life in their new environments, Green light presents both a comment and a precisely drafted, active response. While immigration quotas are being discussed and strict policies of exclusion made palatable to the electorate, the project takes shape amid a field of multiple impulses of production and mutual learning, catalyzing exchanges and encoun-

6 Édouard Glissant, *Poetics of Relation*, trans. Betsy Wing (Ann Arbor: University of Michigan Press, 1997), 27.

ters surrounding the fabrication of an unlimited edition of Green light lamps. Rather than centering on an individual artistic vision, it is a platform for multiple participants to partake of shared processes of production, informal exchanges, coexistence, and process-based contributions.

The *Green light* project was conceived by an artist (Olafur Eliasson) in collaboration with an institution (TBA21), its founder (Francesca von Habsburg), and its agents (curators, associated individuals), who collectively manifest a symbolic and economic potency and are thus able to use their public position to bring visibility to the project and to take a stand vis-à-vis the politics of migration. These circumstances accentuate issues of fund-raising, of economic self-sustainability, and of cause-related campaigning. The lamps are offered for sale in the exhibition space and through the Internet for a donation of, respectively, 250 or 300 euros. The proceeds generated by the fund-raising campaign are made available to the participating NGOs and support the shared learning platforms of the project. While the lamps are being produced in a workshop setting, their dissemination and display in the public and private realms by engaged supporters signal a welcoming green light to refugees and migrants wherever they appear. It is an active response, by means of art and culture, to the ongoing movement of individuals, families, and entire communities and to the precarious processes of displacement and asylum.

The "reclaiming" of the pragmatic field of "refugee work"—and I use these terms very much in quotation marks—leads not only to a highly elaborate project structure but also to a sensitivity to the question of scale and scalability. *Green light* not only claims to develop an engaged model of collective work, first with a nuclear group of individuals, but also addresses the need for replicability and flexible scalability in different, larger social, artistic, and humanitarian contexts. Developed in Vienna as a pilot project, *Green light* is thus conceived with the aim to be replicated and to migrate to other institutions or contexts in Europe and beyond, offering in its future incarnations new forms of interaction and the possibility to host more platforms of discussion and relationality. After the initial iteration in Vienna, the workshop migrated to the Moody Art Center in Houston (March to May 2017, with twenty participants) and the 57th Venice Biennale (May to November 2017, with around eighty participants). With smaller teaching seminars led by former participants throughout 2016, during Art Basel; at the International Peace Institute's Annual Conference in

Salzburg, Austria; and at the National Gallery Prague, the *Green light* formula has as of early 2017 started to live up to its ambition to spur critical moments of transformation.

Seeking Asylum

Green light is designed to engage asylum seekers, individuals who have fled their home countries and are applying for international protection (asylum) in a host country. Whereas the rights of asylum are defined by international law, the specific circumstances of application and the bureaucratic processes of assessing an applicant's rights to protection are overseen by national immigration authorities. Currently the average duration of assessment in Austria is about nine months and can lead to the following outcomes: the granting of asylum (at which point the asylum seeker becomes a legal refugee), refusal (thus making the individual into an illegal immigrant, a sans papiers), and deportation or expulsion according to the Dublin Regulation (under which asylum seekers are returned to the place of entry into the EU).

During the lengthy process of application and evaluation by the authorities, asylum seekers in many countries, specifically in Austria in early 2016, are hosted by humanitarian NGOs or government agencies in "camps" (their organization often outsourced to profit-making corporations) or private homes, where they are fed and provided with health insurance. They are, however, denied the right to work and to benefit from language classes or any other form of education, and they are immobilized and somewhat segregated from civic life as they are denied free public transportation and are placed in homes remote from dense social and urban spaces and may be transferred between homes against their will.[7] This life on pause is a situation of great

7 The approximately three-month-long Refugee Protest Camp Vienna, held in the Sigmund Freud Park and in the Votivkirche in 2012, is a vivid testimony to the inherent injustice and oppression experienced by most asylum seekers in Austria. The protesters, leading a one-month hunger strike by about forty individuals, issued six brief demands on December 18, 2012. These included the demand for basic social services (lodging and food) for all asylum seekers as long as they reside in Austria, irrespective of their legal status; the free choice of their location of residence in Austria and access to public housing, with no relocations against the wishes of the people concerned; access to employment, educational institutions, and social security for all migrants residing in Austria;

 distress und uncertainty. It is the first encounter with a new hosting country (and a potential home) but also one marked by hostility and aggression, at best by neglect. Young people aged sixteen to eighteen are highly vulnerable in this situation. Too old to be given the right to schooling, they are granted special protection until they reach the age of eighteen. For two full years they face stasis, exclusion, isolation, and at times racist stigmatization.

Against this backdrop and driven by the uncertainties of the winter months of 2015–16, *Green light* specifically set out to devise sustainable modes for engaging asylum seekers in practices that can be described as manual activities, offering them basic services (public transportation, food, classes) and finding means of compensation that would not put them at risk. Metamorphosing to accommodate the legal frameworks in each location where it takes place, the overall structure of the project and the legal conditions under which it is hosted have changed significantly as it has traveled to the United States and Italy.

Engaged Withdrawal

In light of the immensity of the processes of transformation that we are undergoing in the global present, some public representatives have symptomatized and stigmatized the so-called migration crisis as "the great evil." The resulting rhetoric of alienation, combined with the growing pauperization of large parts of societies, have led to mounting borders of fear and to the political exploitation of such uncertainties. The policies that are being drawn up and incrementally implemented are only "symbols of the coming barbarism," to somewhat polemicize with Isabelle Stengers.[8] The lack of alternatives and alternative politics in the present offers no respite. The short-lived moments of public solidarity in 2015 are minoritarian imaginaries, refuted in many places by the electorate. Where can we thus situate a project like *Green light*? What political ambitions and visions does it carry, beyond the pragma of momentary relief? Critical authors such as Stengers, Giorgio Agamben, Michel Feher, and Paolo Virno have pointed to the necessity to build, ever so silently, new communities

and the stop of all deportations to Hungary and of deportations associated with the Dublin Regulation.

8 See Stengers, *In Catastrophic Times*.

to come. Rather than thinking #opposition, engaging with protest and the short-lived magma of revolt, they all propose in one way or another the organization of social bodies around different ethics of social and environmental justice. The heterogeneous fields of experience on every individual constitutive level, however—age, nation, education, social status, language, and so on—beg the question: how can we establish systems of collectivity that transgress these markers of identity?

Virno proposes the slightly contradictory but nonetheless highly productive notion of "engaged withdrawal" when addressing the question of how to act.[9] How can we use this figure? On the one hand, it contains a certain form of political mapping of the present condition through engagement, thereby extrapolating the main structural tendencies we find in the current moment. As a critique it is a form of articulation. On the other hand, it sympathizes with the idea of radical politics as exile and withdrawal. But in what ways can those take part in this critique "who don't have part"? How can their articulation be articulated? How can an arts institution bypass a legal apparatus that excludes those seeking refuge from civic processes of civil society? Can asylum seekers be engaged in any form of social abstraction here and now?

What Virno perhaps suggests, shortcutting more complex debates, is to address and engage antagonistically, creatively, and collectively with the existing institutions and the status quo. He emphasizes our own capacities to imagine and build autonomous, DIY forms of community, thereby seizing agency rather than expecting the political will to change. As Daniël de Zeeuw observes in his analysis of the Occupy movement of 2011, such a movement "starts from its own qualities and potentials, instead of demanding an external agency to compensate for what it perceives to be its own lack, as if something were owed to it (e.g. a right). This implies that by engaging in the construction of new forms of being-together indifferent to, and withdrawing from, the political rationality of the existing institutions, it presupposes not scarcity, but plenitude."[10]

9 Paolo Virno, "Virtuosity and Revolution: The Political Theory of Exodus," http://www.generation-online.org/c/fcmultitude2.html.

10 Daniël de Zeeuw, "Engaged Withdrawal: Occupying Politics beyond Politics," *Krisis*, no. 1 (2014): 75, http://krisis.eu/engaged-withdrawal-occupying-politics-beyond-politics/.

Creating new communities beyond the signifiers of traditional identities is a central ambition of the *Green light* project. And yet *Green light* also contains an outward-directed demand, directed at everyone who solidarizes with its ambitions, for the necessity of change, for together fabricating alternatives to the prevailing status quo. Difference and the constitution of multi-identitarian societies are our greatest challenges. This represents much more than building lamps together. And yet the *Green light* lamps, as solitary and complex "speaking objects," carry many of the narratives their makers wish to express. They allow us to reflect on and to share the personal experience of migration, departure, and arrival that the participants have experienced and to find and reinterpret together with them what they have left behind but also what they are finding in the moments of arrival. Their exodus from their homes and communities is a very present memory in their lives, but through the day-to-day realities of the workshop they encounter the possibility of building new communities and new families in which they can express and share their skills, wisdom, and experiences.

I would like to join again

Emran Ali Rahimi (16) is an Afghan citizen who was born in a refugee camp in Iran. He is passionate about hip-hop. He arrived in Austria in summer 2015. His current whereabouts are unknown.

Emran, where are you from?
I am from Afghanistan, but I was born in Iran. I've been living in Austria for two years.

How long did it take you to travel from Iran to Austria?
I travelled for three months. I also stayed in Turkey for a year and a half, where I also worked. I don't want to tell what kind of work I had to do, but there were several types of jobs.

Why did you come to Austria?
When I was eight years old, I watched football on the Internet and I knew I wanted to come to Austria. But sometimes I mixed Austria and Australia up. When I told my dad that I wanted to go to Europe he knew why, he could understand why I wanted to come to Austria. I explained it to him, and he said okay, it's your life, so do it if you wish. But he told me to go to Sweden, because Sweden would be better for me. And for two months I pondered about which country I would go to. But then I decided on Austria. I like playing football, and I like to rap, and I like music, so I wanted to come to Austria.

How did you hear about the *Green light* project?
Marianne at Georg Danzer Haus told us about the project, that we could work and learn German, and she thought it would be good for me. So I came to you guys. I liked the atmosphere at the *Green light* workshop. I got to meet so many different people. I didn't have any problems here. The only problems I sometimes had were with myself.

***Green light* was a working place, but it was a lot of things: a place, a school, a group. But there is also the whole life all around the project at the same time.**
You sent me a certificate. With that certificate I can go to McDonald's for example, and apply for a job, and tell them that I already did something in another project.

So the certificate was helpful then?
Yes, of course. Though during the last months of the project I didn't come as regularly.

***Green light* was about using art, or using the production of the lamps, to become one group. What do you think about that idea of bringing people together through one task?**
I think it's a wonderful idea. I like it very much. You got to learn the Afghan culture, the Persian culture, this is a very good idea.

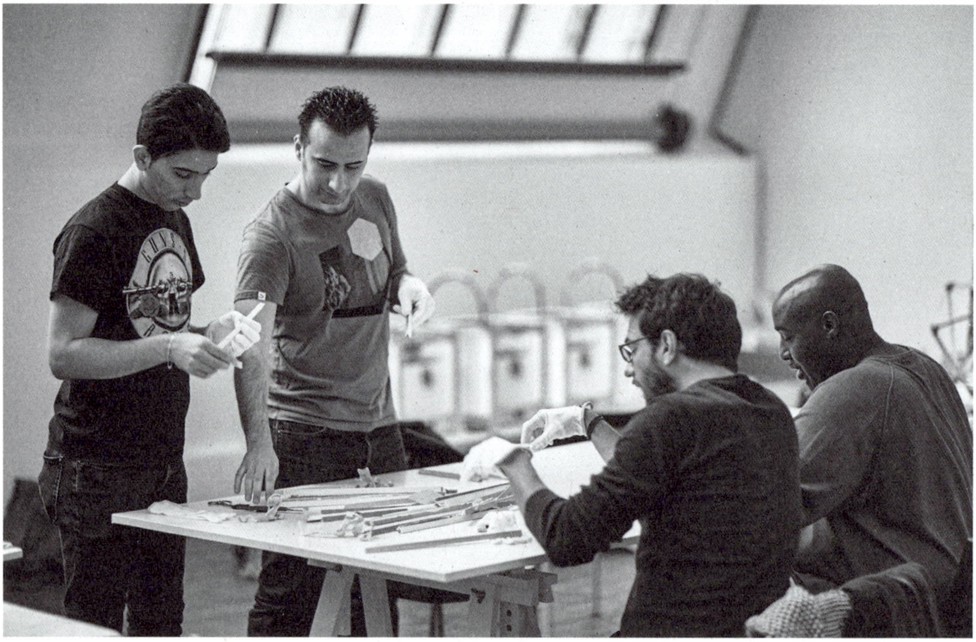

Green light graduates Husseyin Haj Hassan, Ghifar Al Darkazanly, David Weidinger, Yusuf Haibeh Said

Yes, it's right. We all learned a lot of things about different cultures, but the thing I remember are individuals.
Yes, everyone is a human being, but there is also a culture. Because when a man from Afghanistan does something silly, it doesn't mean that every Afghan is like that. Respect responds to respect.

This is right, and we have to take responsibility for our own actions. We cannot take responsibility for the actions of others.

That's right.

Is there something you would want to say in the end?
If you ever do the project again, please contact me. I really hope to participate again. I would like to join again.

This interview was conducted by Anahita Tabrizi on October 16, 2016.

The meaning of friendship

My name is Husseyin Haj Hassan. I come from Aleppo, Syria. I was born in 1995 and am twenty-one years old. The worst day of my life was in June 2012. That day, when I woke up, I saw fighter jets, helicopters, and the police shooting people. My family and I drove to our native village, where it wasn't as bad as in Aleppo yet. We left everything we had as it was, left everything behind. In the village, we had to start from scratch, we built a room where we could sleep. That lasted a month, and during that time we lived at my grandmother's. Afterward, we were out of money, and had to borrow a lot of money from people we knew. At that time, I decided that I had to do something to ensure my family's survival. I went to Istanbul to work. I wanted my family to join me there later on, so they could live safely, away from war. In Istanbul I worked two and a half years without a break: during the week as a tailor in a textile factory, and over the weekends in a restaurant, sometimes as a dishwasher and other times as waiting tables. After that I had enough money to rent an apartment for my family. I worked for six or seven months with my two brothers, and then I decided to go to Austria.

In Syria, I worked at a shoe factory in 2011. I injured my hand there, and went through two operations. Unfortunately, neither one went well, and so I wanted to come to Austria to have my hand operated on. I drove from Istanbul to Izmir, and from there travelled to a Greek island with forty other people on a rubber dinghy. I was in prison there. Two days later, they gave me a note on which was written that I had to leave the country within six months. From Athens, I then walked to Austria; the journey took twenty-one days. In Austria I had to spend two days in prison, as I had entered the country without a passport. Then I was sent to Traiskirchen, where I spent six days, and there I met Marianne Engelmann from the Georg Danzer Haus. I was sent to Graz to build a life there. I lived in a one-room apartment with ten other people. Marianne and I corresponded at that period. I told her that things were not good for me there, and she really helped me return to Vienna.

Until I was granted asylum, I was able to live in the Georg Danzer Haus for a while. In this period, I learned German and took part in many courses, including the *Green light* project. There I not only met new people, but I also realized you can have fun in life, and spend time in a meaningful and joyous way. I thank the *Green light* team, who received me so warmly and showed me the meaning of friendship. We were like a family and for that I am truly grateful. Thank you for this wonderful time. I will never forget it.

Is a Pluralist Society Yet to Come? Art against the Administration of Stasis

Angela Dimitrakaki

On the Production of Global Space

Published in French in 1974, the landmark book *The Production of Space* by the Marxist philosopher Henri Lefebvre appeared in English translation in 1991, the year of the end of the Soviet Union. One feels compelled to say that it is too bad that Lefebvre, who died during this point-of-no-return year, was unable to examine the new production of space undertaken with rigor since 1991 by capital in the hour of its global victory. It has been a lasting hour, interpreted as a dialectic of biopolitics and necropolitics (one wonders which of the two terms is more appropriate). Yet such a choice is becoming increasingly meaningless, contained as it is within a planetary politics of administration: the administration of ecological catastrophe, the administration of debt (the IMF estimated that global debt reached $152 trillion in 2016), the administration of precarity and people seen as redundant production units, and, of course, the administration of borders regulating the administration of everything else. And so, counter-intuitively perhaps for some, the manufacture of global space came to be synonymous with the intensification of practices of keeping apart.

"Globalization," it's worth reminding, came together with "alter-globalization," "anti-globalization," "de-globalization," and it may be surprising to some that the anti-globalization movement would be the place to look for the demand for open borders. In short, the production of global space has also been a time of ideological destabilization: critical concepts such as "identity politics," which left their mark on the histories of the contemporary (including of art) since the date when *The Production of Space* appeared in French, were appropriated and counter-appropriated all the way to white supremacy politics going mainstream in 2016. The production of global space became thus something more than the administration of an extractive economy operating from mines to banks. It became the administration of terrifying waves of discontent and of generalized conflict, the significance of which is always underplayed as site-specific. During these times, the chief insight of theoretical poetics possibly comes from Tiqqun. "Empire," Tiqqun offered in 2009, "is not the enemy, it is the hostis," which needs to be "annihilated" rather than merely "defeated."[1] Global space, realized as capital's empire, should cease to exist or else we should accept a way of life where every stranger is turned into an adversary.

Meanwhile, in Art

In the course of these developments, art historians and theorists were taking notes that still inform our understanding of the complex place that art has come to occupy, and in relation to the administration of global space as the matrix of hostis. Benjamin Buchloh published "Conceptual Art 1962–1969: From the Aesthetics of Administration to the Critique of Institutions" in 1990.[2] In 2002, Boris Groys was also interested in administration, in an essay titled "Art in the Age of Biopolitics: From Artwork to Art Documentation."[3] The "from this to that" format of analysis evident in both essay titles, as in many others, betrays the attachment of art discourse to elucidating change, mobility, even evolution. A sense of movement is anticipated, sought, taken for granted as necessary proof that art has a history. A history that is marked in temporal shifts rather than in and through spatial connections. We surely have art histories that seek out the links of unevenness of a global art world as well as art histories that embed artworks (and art documentation) in spatial and geopolitical arguments, but typically the sense of an evolving paradigm is not lost. But what if the production of global space is about stasis rather than this old idea, the dynamism of capital in always moving things forward?

1 Tiqqun, *Introduction to Civil War*, translated by Alexander R. Galloway and Jason E. Smith (Los Angeles: Semiotext(e), 2009), 191.

2 Benjamin H. D. Buchloh, "Conceptual Art 1962–1969: From the Aesthetics of Administration to the Critique of Institutions," *October* Vol. 55 (Winter 1990): 105–143.

3 Boris Groys, "Art in the Age of Biopolitics: From Artwork to Art Documentation," in Okwui Enwezor et al, eds., *Platform 5_ Documenta 11* (Ostfildern-Ruit: Hatje Cantz, 2002).

With few exceptions, art discourse has not given much thought to this.[4] Rather, art discourse has noted the frenetic sequence of time-based "turns," that is, the frenetic move "from this to that." The memorable opening lines of Lars Bang Larsen's essay "Turn! Turn! Turn!":

> *The Linguistic Turn! The Cultural Turn! The Social Turn! The Spatial Turn! The Ethical Turn! The Historiographic Turn! The Affective Turn! The Narrative Turn! The Educational Turn! The Emotional Turn! The Aesthetic Turn! The Locational Turn!*
>
> *The headlines! The shows! The essays! The conferences! The anthologies! The panels! The theme issues of art mags! Feel the tectonic plates shift under your feet, the seismic rumble of the curatorial stampede! It began as a whisper, a Geheimtipp in a late night conversation deep inside a global city, where the innermost insiders pick up the first fragile ripples of the most promising trends of greatest potential. Now it's a comet, a blizzard, irresistible, a law of nature ... Forget what you have read and nix what you know because from this very minute that is all obliterated by a new Turn!*[5]

Is it possible that the accelerated pace of turning conceals the fact that ultimately the administration of global space is the administration of stasis? In other words, has art discourse's attachment to the aesthetics of obsolescence been instrumental (or even instrumentalized) in covering the stationary impulses and outcomes of capital committed to its own reproduction? These questions are not raised in "Turn, Turn, Turn!" but they are worth considering, not least because *Green light—An artistic workshop*, as with many other works, is imbued with a sense of social urgency associated with, well, a turn. Claire Bishop's concerns over ethics replacing aesthetics in her widely discussed article, "The Social Turn: Collaboration and Its Discontents," are already eleven years old. But despite her concerns, what she dubbed "the social turn" did not cease to exist while artists' collaborations with multiple agents yet especially with those who are constantly pushed to non-agency continues with fervor.[6] Appearing

4 Sven Lütticken, "The Coming Exception: Art and the Crisis of Value," *New Left Review* 99 (May–June 2016): 111–136.

5 Lars Bang Larsen, "Turn! Turn! Turn!," *Mousse* 35 (October–November 2012), http://moussemagazine.it/lars-bang-larsen-turn-turn-turn-2012/.

6 Claire Bishop, "The Social Turn: Collaboration and Its Discontents," *Artforum* (February 2006): 178–183.

 on the long list of "turns" in Larsen's essay, the so-called social turn is drawn into the vortex of art historical accelerationism, suggesting that artists' involvement with what surrounds them as social beings has been but a theme. Inadvertently perhaps, Larsen's ironic demotion of the social (forget the "turn" part) reveals the first attack the social receives in Bishop's title, in being seen precisely as a "turn" in some internal and self-referential history of art. In answering Grant Kester's multi-layered criticism of her position, Bishop resorted to the authority of Jacques Rancière, according to whom: "Suitable political art would ensure, at one and the same time, the production of a double effect: the readability of a political signification and a sensible or perceptual shock caused, conversely, by the uncanny, by that which resists signification."[7]

It is perhaps tempting to take the easy path to redemption here and say that the sculptural elements of *Green light*, "which resist signification," alongside "the readability of a political signification" (that is, the slow, collaborative process of production, engaging, among others, socially abjected human beings) fulfil Rancière's "double effect" requirement. But I won't succumb to the temptation. Rather, I will ask: Where does this axiomatic double requirement arise? Where is the prescription of what "suitable political art" ought to do established and legitimized? And, especially, for how long is that prescription valid? Is it meant to cover what "suitable art" is in all places at all times? It is hard to think of an emancipatory aesthetics under the hegemony of the bourgeoisie, the consciousness of which is dedicated both to the reproduction of the status quo and the pretension that its reign (the reign of capital) is one of dynamic evolution. The bourgeoisie does not wish to perceive an interregnum, despite the proliferation of relevant signs.[8] Or perhaps it wishes to absorb the interregnum and rescue its reign by severing the ties of capitalism to democracy and liberalism (an issue to which I shall return). Under its hegemony, it is much easier to think through the abstraction of "political art," forgetting that politics is also done by racism and fascism, and not least by capital. The challenge is then perhaps to not proffer proscriptions about a blanket politics of aesthetics but in dislodging

7 Jacques Rancière, *The Politics of Aesthetics*, translated by Gabriel Rockhill (London: Bloomsbury, 2004), 59, as quoted in Claire Bishop, "Letter to the Editor: Claire Bishop Responds," *Artforum* Vol. 44 No. 9 (May 2006): 24.

8 See Zygmunt Bauman, "Times of Interregnum," *Ethics and Global Politics* Vol. 5 No. 1 (2012): 49–56.

the aesthetic from performing, repeatedly, a known hegemony as a social blindfold.[9]

An Aesthetic of Persistence and the "Labor of History"

How can we move against, and beyond, the ongoing aestheticization of critique as "turns" in the spectacle-commodity nexus or the disciplining of aesthetics under the rule of the "suitable" in its guise as critique? The aesthetic has been a problem for art. It has been a problem for art that is committed to critique, and, within that framework, to critical praxis- either because of the banalization of aesthetics as a discourse on beauty or because of the reduction of aesthetics to a discourse on "form" or "good" versus "bad" art. In its etymological definition, the aesthetic is always found to be relating to the perception of the senses with the implicit assumption that the senses are exempted from the touch of history. There is an alternative view, however, in Karl Marx's words: "the *forming* of the five senses is a labour of the entire history of the world down to the present."[10] We may want to give some thought to this if we are not to limit our exasperation to parody exclaiming with Larsen in his "Turn, Turn, Turn!" article "I have sensed the distribution of the sensible," alluding to Rancière's take on aesthetics,[11] and "I have authored a turn!", alluding to the authorship curse of modern and contemporary art—a curse which, in its tenacity, suggests that the distinction between modern and contemporary is highly questionable and that we are in fact locked into the regime of the extensive modern as the canon of "the first time." Postmodernism's assumed departure from the cult of the new proved to be a mere postmodern parenthesis, now on display in the very institutions whose attachment to the new some strands of postmodern art had wished to query. Hal Foster's appeal

9 Bishop closes her response to Kester arguing that "we can no longer speak of old-fashioned autonomy versus radical engagement, since a dialectical pull between autonomy and heteronomy is itself constitutive of the aesthetic. Good art would therefore sustain this antinomy in the simultaneous impulse to preserve itself from instrumentality and to self-dissolve in social praxis." Bishop, "Letter to the Editor."

10 Karl Marx, "Private Property and Communism," *Economic and Philosophic Manuscripts of 1844*, https://www.marxists.org/archive/marx/works/1844/manuscripts/comm.htm. Emphasis in the original.

11 Rancière, *The Politics of Aesthetics*.

to an "anti-aesthetic" proved an impossibility,[12] and postmodernism's lasting lesson has been that any further association of the aesthetic with form would have to confront the historical fact that "form," in capitalism, belongs to the commodity-form as the mediator of vastly different categories of things that are nevertheless joined by capital as a social relation.

Bearing the above in mind, *Green light* appears to be less of a social experiment and more of an experiment on the possibility of disentangling the aesthetic from the ideology that the senses have no history, that they are somehow placed outside the realm of a historical script, which, as we know, tends to be written by the winner. If anything, artists' and cultural workers' continuous engagement with social agency for over a decade since the "social turn" entered art's vocabulary suggests a disregard for yet another new, for yet another turn. Although these efforts have not overcome the structural condition of authorship, we are witnessing at the very least a refusal to pretend that global space is developing in terms that might curb the constant production of dispossession. These efforts have a cumulative effect that suppresses the art world's urge to sniff out "the distribution of the sensible" to come, prioritizing instead an inquiry into the immediate configuration of the social. It is not an anti-aesthetic stance, but rather one that does not accept the aesthetic as the prerogative of a "sector" rife with contradictions (not unrelated to the commodity-form and the current regime of production).

In its very persistence and duration then, the "social turn" practices a more humble authorship, implicitly or at times explicitly admitting that the urgency of the social has the upper hand. Once this has been asserted, once dispossession and displacement are secured as the repetitive, daily outcome of a global economy and its wars built around scarcity, art self-consciously assumes the position of a respondent. This art knows that the "perceptual shock" comes from the biopolitics-necropolitics dialectic. The perceptual shock belongs to the refugees of war and poverty at the moment their boat capsizes in the Mediterranean and they are about to drown. If they are rescued and later on encounter structures that re-humanize them, they may have a second perceptual, as well as cognitive, shock. Maybe the exchange between someone whose life has made her take the risk of

12 Hal Foster, ed., *The Anti-aesthetic: Essays on Postmodern Culture* (Port Townsend, WA: Bay Press, 1983).

drowning and someone who saves her exceeds the grasp of "signification." How many of those who will read this text have experienced the excess of this exchange? Should this excess be named political, ethical, or aesthetic? This art acknowledges what the defenders of "autonomy" (not all of them grouped under the political right) have feared the most: that heteronomy is proved to be as much of an illusion as autonomy, and that both terms suppress the possibility and potential of exchanges that are not fully submerged in capital's logic of exchange. In any event, this is where the labor of history has brought us.

On the Guiding Question

Yet you may ask: What do you mean by "not fully submerged"? Does this suggest some partial submergence? The short answer is yes. Insofar as art cannot but be contemporary, it cannot extricate itself fully from structures, processes, and institutions that reproduce the art field with all its contradictions. An art that through its autonomy leads to revolutionary transformation has been found to be a myth. But this hardly means that the art field is nothing more than the feminization of politics—that is, a site of a lesser politics, a designation which, of course, implies that another place of pure politics, of secured political effect, exists. If anything, art that takes social urgency as its theater of operations demonstrates its consciousness of non-exceptionalism. It functions within a framework of contribution rather than through the pretense of leadership. That art knows that what Antonio Negri and Michael Hardt called "monstrous institutions"[13]—institutions whose radical otherness could only appear as monstrous to the subjects shaped through existing administrative imperatives—are the real utopia of our times: a horizon to which we are directed but which so far proves to be an extension of the current ground of antinomies and unevenness as soon as it is reached. The guiding question—what is to be done, and how?—is the gentle, meditative battle cry of this procession. In the meantime, and even as part of this procession, it is true, as Andrea Phillips says, that "art is property," as much as anything else is property in capital's dominion and hegemony (since capital cannot be credited with inventing property).[14]

13 Michael Hardt and Antonio Negri, *Commonwealth* (Cambridge, MA: Harvard University Press, 2009).

14 Andrea Phillips, "Art Is Property," in Angela Dimitrakaki and Kirsten Lloyd, eds.,

But even an imagined abolition of property, we are told by Marx, would only be a first step: "The first positive annulment of private property—*crude* communism—is thus merely a *manifestation* of the vileness of private property, which wants to set itself up as the *positive community system.*"[15] This other exchange, in which *Green light* has situated itself, becomes possible in the course of acknowledging the interlocking limitations imposed on social actors, limitations that do not only define the present but also face the struggle for a future that is always a "first step" toward a history of breaks (a revolutionary history) that clearly exceeds the span of any singular generation.

The self-description of *Green light* through its entwined components—the shared learning and the artistic workshop—returns to Giorgio Agamben's positively inflected futurism, imagining a "community to come."[16] Indeed, it asks whether we can create our own society to come (a society may encompass or give rise to a spectrum of communities), and is orchestrated through an imagined negation of the ubiquitous border condition into a green light—an invitation to cross over, and to come as you are. *Green light* does not speak about "integration" but prefers to ask: "how can a pluralist community be imagined and lived, society re-shaped, in which singular voices are endorsed and the terms of being-together are constantly re-negotiated without being governed by one-directional ideas of culture"? But this is precisely what is being excised from the social imaginary at present, and throughout the period inaugurated by the English translation of *The Production of Space*: the apparently wild idea that pluralism might be a social principle and a living history. There is no point reiterating here the numerous announcements of the failure of pluricultural societies (what used to be called "multiculturalism"). In 2017, we have ample evidence of many societies becoming divided on this issue, and the Global North being swept by multiple contractions predicated on fascistic, collective, embattled forms of misanthropy. The transition of Eastern Europe to the perceived end of history under the auspices of global capitalism has led to a process of Orbanisation and the course of US politics is known to all, while at the time of writing I read that Canada (yes, proudly liberal Canada) has barred Antonio Negri from visiting and giving lectures

Economy: Art, Production and the Subject in the 21st Century (Liverpool: Liverpool University Press, 2015).

15 Karl Marx, "Private Property and Communism." Emphasis in the original.

16 Giorgio Agamben, *The Coming Community*, trans. by Michael Hardt (Minneapolis: University of Minnesota Press, 1993).

because of his "controversial past," as Canadian immigration becomes increasingly similar to US immigration law.[17] The border becomes a condition in divided cities and countries, with outlawing squat movements in both the Netherlands (2010) and Greece (2017), with air space given to France's "identitarians," with demonstrations against deportations in Finland, and with the language of war taking hold everywhere.[18] These are just some examples but ultimately (to repeat: insofar as history is written by the winner) these examples and many more signal the proximity not of a postcapitalist future but of a capitalism devoid of liberalism and yet continuing to be enacted as the catastrophe of neoliberalism. Can social entropy be the exodus from stasis?

The Minority Challenge

With its focus on an exchange structured around work in terms of learning, *Green light* joins forces with other platforms that test, and push, the limits of art as interventionist politics. But despite the temporal resilience of this practice, at any one time these platforms are a minority in the art field. This happens for many reasons. Activism, in art or not, is labor-intensive to begin with. Besides this, the art field has not undergone a structural change, relying still on collecting that inevitably speaks the language of assets and privilege. This is the popular perception of art. *Green light* comes at a time when art is not just subject to charges of being an elitist occupation (we are used to that) but of being the last frontier of failed liberalism, cut off from the desires and demands of "real people" (who, we are told, want misogynist racist billionaires as defenders of the working class and xenophobic nationalism as the solution to suppressed wages and unemployment). The challenge *Green light* faces is whether, and how, it can foreground a discourse on pluralism without affirming that pluralism belongs to liberalism as the discourse of the privileged. As far as challenges go, this one is big.

17 Levon Sevunts, "Firebrand Italian Philosopher Barred from Visiting Canada," *Radio Canada International,* April 6, 2017, http://www.rcinet.ca/en/2017/04/06/firebrand-italian-philosopher-barred-from-visiting-canada/.

18 See Artists against Evictions, "An Open Call to the Viewers, Participants, and Cultural Workers of Documenta 14," *e-flux conversations* (April 10, 2017), http://conversations.e-flux.com/t/open-letter-to-the-viewers-participants-and-cultural-workers-of-documenta-14/6393.

For a project like *Green light* to attach itself to progressive politics and, especially, to open borders at this moment in time means confronting a vastly complicated terrain of ideological mutations and material blockages. To give just one example, a symbolic "green light" to refugees and immigrants (a helpful distinction only at times) stands explicitly against the European Union's recent shameful pact with Turkey. The legality of this deal may be disputed but this does not mean that the deal is not being realized as the opposite of a "green light" stance. And this anti–green light stance is a complex outcome of the structural function of the modern nation-state in its alliance with capital and the power that democracy under neo-liberalism gives to populism. As Director of Migration Policy Institute Europe Elizabeth Collett writes, "The fact that a group of 28 states with increasingly divergent interests was able to find consensus speaks to the level of concern that leaders have for their own domestic political futures in a context of rising populism."[19] What we increasingly witness is that the presumed middle ground is crumbling alongside the purposeful disarticulation of the welfare state, now being relegated to a discourse of a lost past, when the argument of an "ethical capitalism" appeared plausible, at least to some. Those of us who have always seen this argument as a contradiction in terms and as failing to grasp the driving force of capital displayed by capitalism's trajectory have not been in agreement over the meaning of welfare state: some have tended to see it as gains drawn by workers' struggles while others as a short-lived peace, or rather truce, for which the working class exchanged its prospect of revolt. But whether in terms of the end of a truce or the appropriation of former gains, the loss of welfare as a political culture is the letter and substance of the populism for which "green light" politics is an anathema.

How then to sustain the minoritarian discourse of *Green light*? Where can its legitimacy be sought if not in some mythical autonomy, and thus in the very separation of this art from the ground of its articulation? If (certainly) not in majoritarian politics when democracy is increasingly a game of numbers (exemplified by the referendum frenzy)? If not in the inalienable commitment to the primacy of human life, being recently informed that such primacy was an idea of the Enlightenment when human life amounted to one billion whereas

19 Elizabeth Collett, "The Paradox of the EU-Turkey Refugee Deal," *Migration Policy Institute* (March 2016), http://www.migrationpolicy.org/news/paradox-eu-turkey-refugee-deal.

the ten billion our century might end with make this commitment unsustainable?[20] Answers to these questions cannot be given in the manner of critique as introspection, and they cannot emanate from a discussion structured around passing judgement on art's measurable "impact," yet another oppressive demand of the neoliberal cultural agenda. Then again, not all questions are meant to be answered by yet more words. Living, working, learning, and imagining with others requires an active questioning of, and at times disobedience to, the administration of stasis. And what justifies this is that such stasis is forced.

20 See Dipesh Chakrabarty in conversation with Boris Buden, "Between Globalization and Global Warming: Transitions in Political Narratives of the West and Non-West," in Maria Hlavajova and Simon Sheikh, eds., *Former West: Art and the Contemporary after 1989* (Utrecht: BAK, 2017), 256.

Schleifen

السنفرة

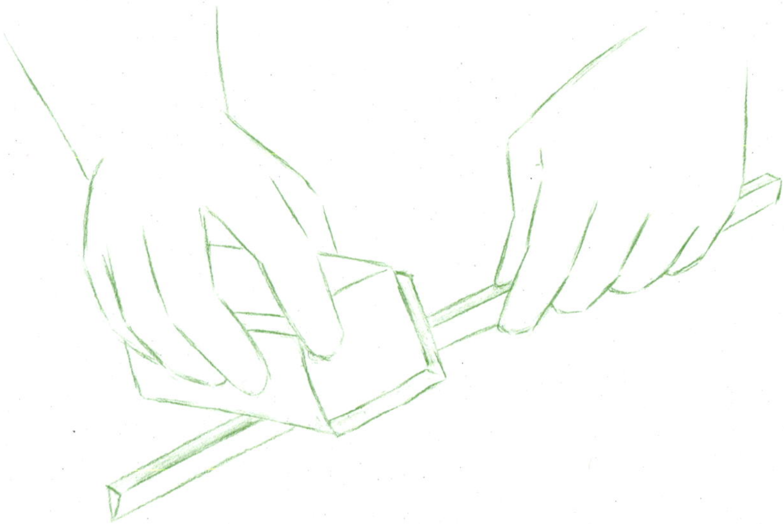

صنبل کردن

Sanding

Malen

الطلاء

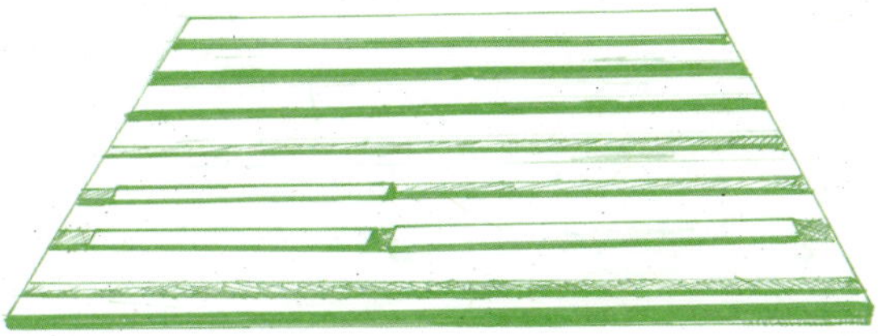

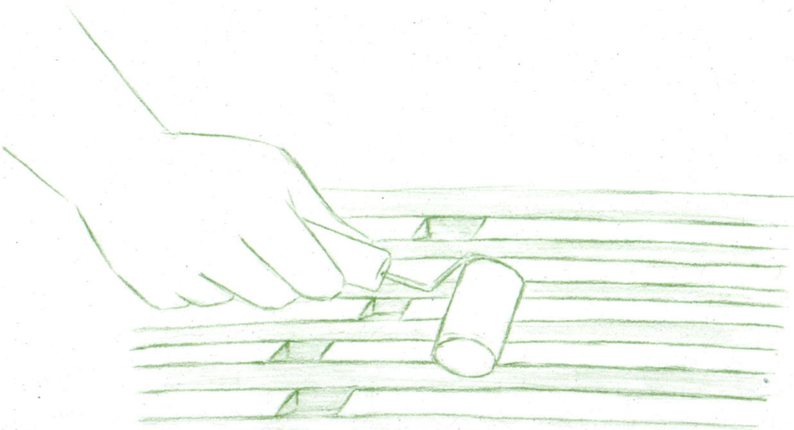

رنگ کردن

Painting

Zusammenbauen التجميع

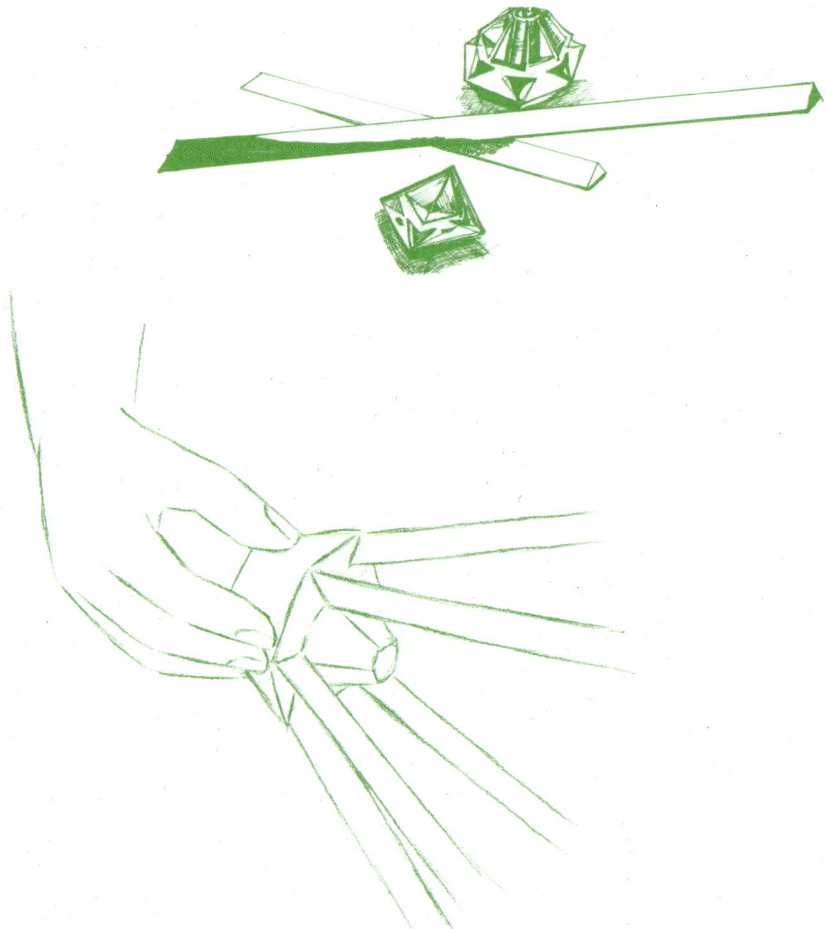

چوب وصل کردن Assembling

Knüpfen

التربيط

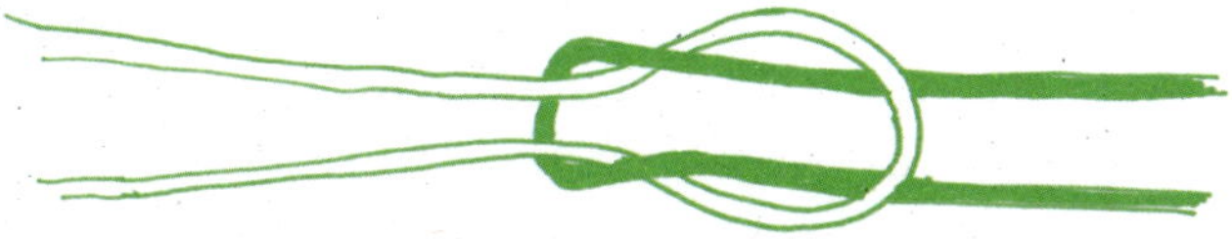

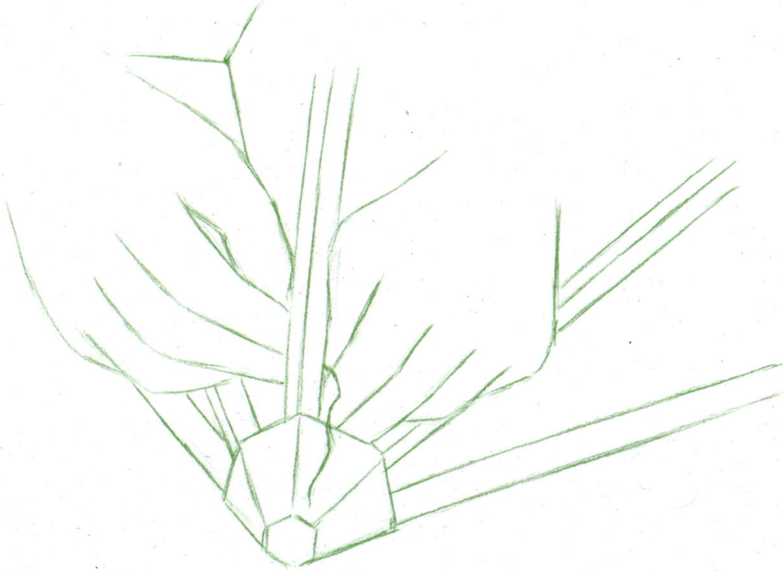

نخ بستن

Threading

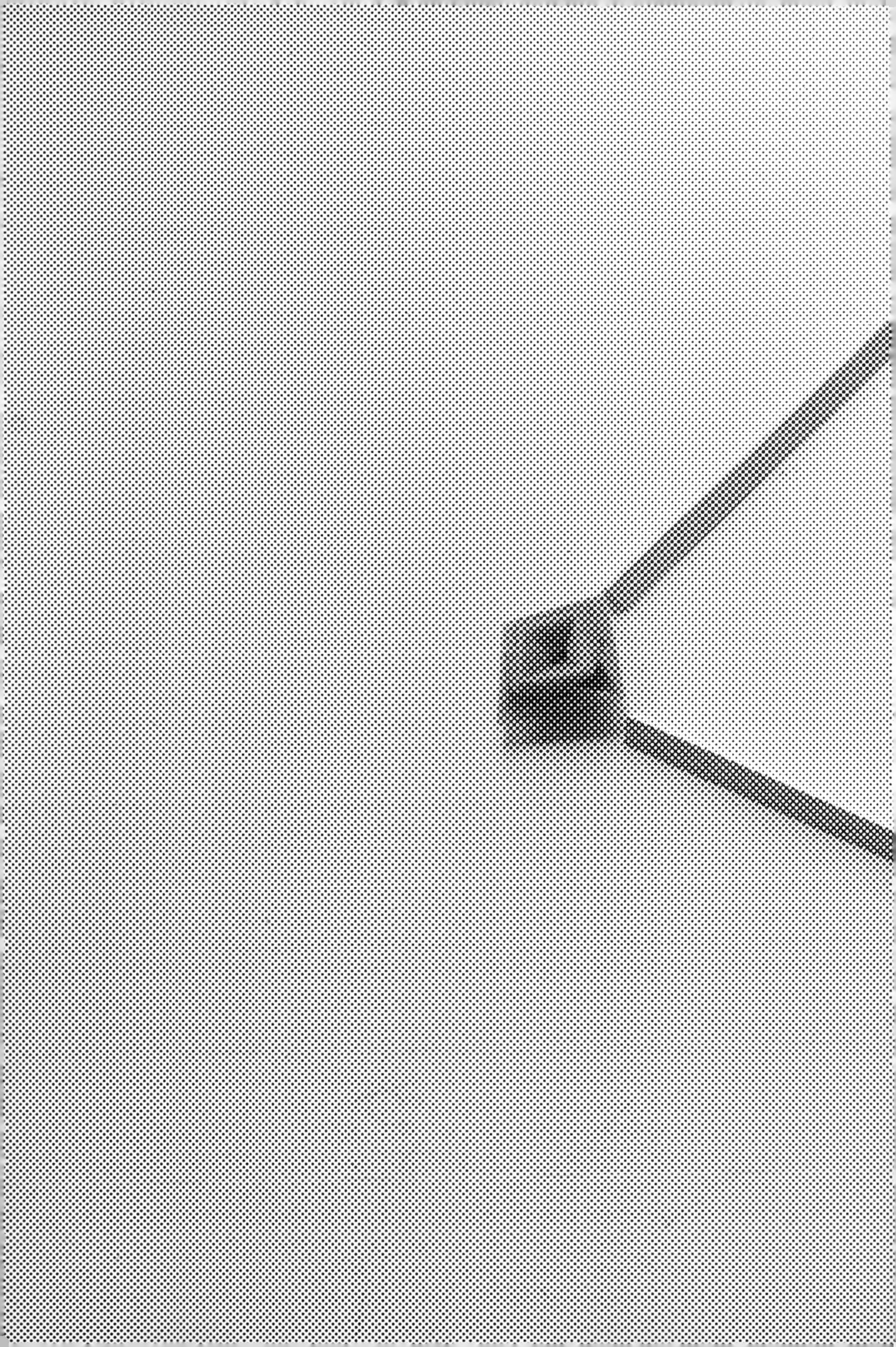

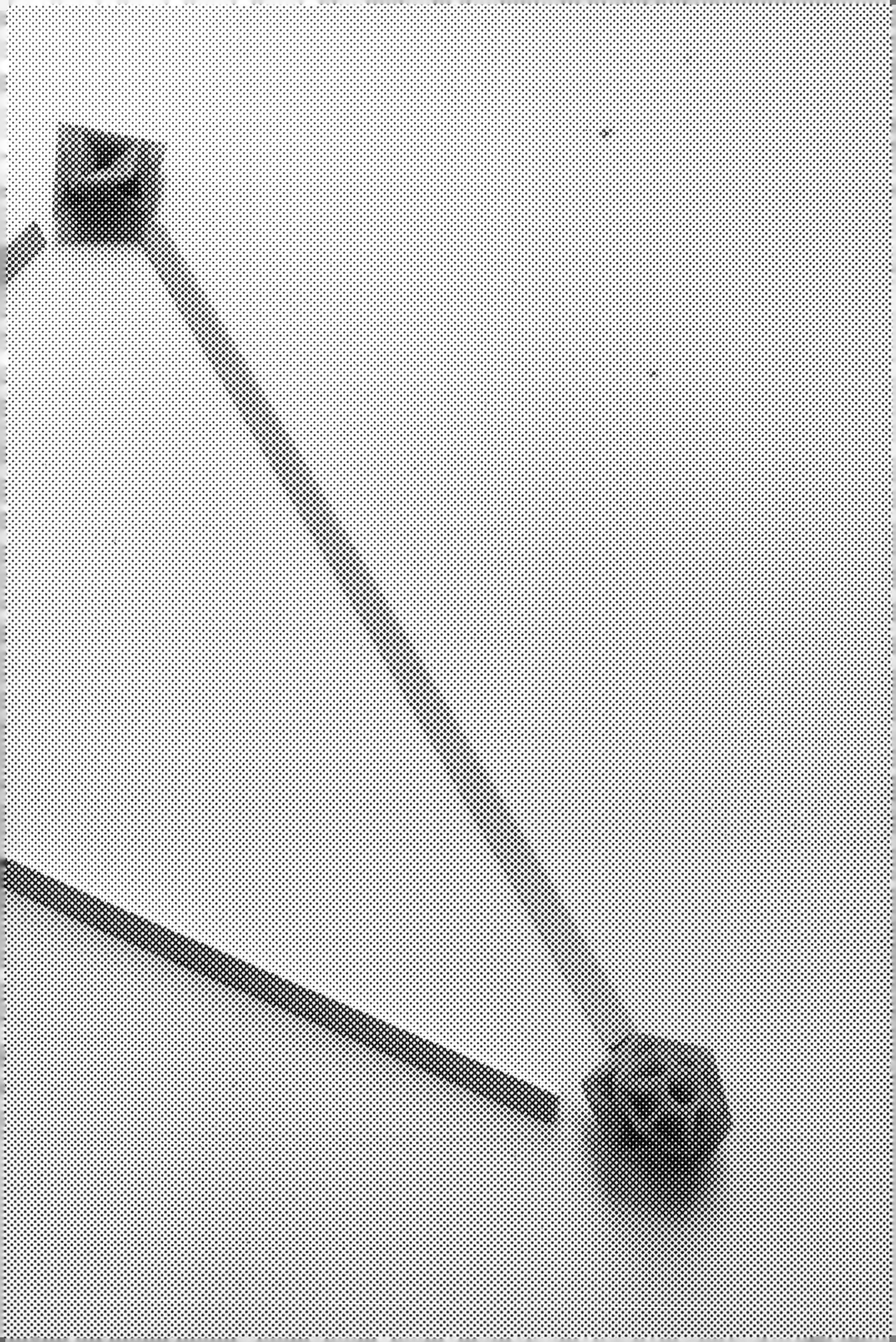

Learning is always important

Milad Amiri (17), Mohammad Amiry (18), Saber Sawari (15), Issa Shafaei (15), and Zialuhauq Oryakhel (18) are from Afghanistan and arrived in Austria in summer 2015 as unaccompanied minors. They found a home in the Georg Danzer Haus in Vienna. The Georg Danzer Haus is meant to receive and relocate minors under the age of eighteen, so at the moment they are living in different situations and are seeking educational opportunities and job training programs.

Is there something that you remember about the *Green light* project that you would like to share?
Milad. It's been a year since we were part of *Green light*. At the time, we were new in this country, we've just arrived. Most of us didn't speak any German then. When we started at *Green light*, we had a translator from Iran. I have never worked with someone from Iran that closely until then. There were different kinds of people from all around the word and we had a lot of fun together. I gained experience talking to people and interacting with them. We cooked, we ate, it was a lot of fun. It was great.
Issa. I also thought the project was very nice. I met a lot of different people and got to learn new things. Learning is always important, even if it is just in order not to stay at home doing nothing. I had to leave the project after a month, though, because I had to go to school.

What else do you remember?
Zialuhauq. I liked the celebrations. We didn't only eat together, we also danced together and celebrated. I learned a lot about cooking. I never cooked for that many people before.
Milad. We treated each other with respect, I loved it very much. We were like a family.
Mohammad. I remember learning a lot of things about the material—about wood, sanding, and painting. It was a working process and a learning process at once.
Issa. For me, the most important thing about the project was that we could say that we attended it, that we could tell people that we did something, and were not sitting around at home doing nothing. We met a lot people. We met you, and we are still in contact with you. This is so valuable.

What are you doing now?
Issa. After the project I went to Hauptschule for a few months. Now I am going to a polytechnic school. But I have to leave before the end of the year, because I turn fifteen, which is when compulsory education ends. But I want to get my certificate, the Hauptschulabschluss that proves that I finished my secondary education.
Milad. I'm in school right now. Next year I will continue, and I want to graduate

and get my Hauptschulabschluss, after which I want to do a traineeship and to graduate with a diploma. But I am still not sure what kind of traineeship I want it to be.

Most of you are still living at the Georg-Danzer-Haus in Stockerau, though some of you had to leave when you turned eighteen. How has life been in Stockerau?

Mohammad. At first the people living in Stockerau were not that open to us, but it's all changed. They say hello to us. I even went to church with a resident of Stockerau. It was interesting. I wanted to learn about the culture here in Austria and at the church I met a few people, like three or four. I went with a friend of mine. They were very polite. They said if I ever needed something, that I could tell them. I am also very interested in fitness, it keeps me healthy.

What about the Georg-Danzer-School?

Zia. The school closed down. We are not sure why, but obviously due to lack of funding. Some of the boys were not convinced at first, because of course we wanted to go to a regular school, like all the other children. We wanted to be treated like normal students. But now that the school is closed, I think it was better than no school or no education at all.

Mohammad. For two months after the project ended, I had no language classes at all. Then school at the Georg Danzer Haus started, and a short while after they shut that school down.

How about you, Zia?

Zia. Because I am over eighteen now, I had to move. My situation got much worse. Because the village where I live is quite small, I literally do nothing. I go to a German Class, but it's not very good. The people in the area are not friendly at all. I don't get out, because I can't afford transportation costs to come to Vienna or to get to the next town over. So my situation worsened since *Green light*. I don't have many contacts anymore, I am quite isolated, and I make small progress in my language skills.

Mohammad. Most of us would still need a German course.

What about you, Saber? You just arrived. You were only part of the project for a month and then you left to go to school. What about you? What are you doing now?

Saber. I go to language class in the first district of Vienna. It takes me about an hour to get to the German class. All in all, it's okay, you know. We all have to organize our own lives. Some have luck, and it works better for them, and some hopefully will have luck in the future.

This interview was conducted by Anahita Tabrizi and Clemens Rettenbacher on April 2, 2017.

Getting involved

Clemens Rettenbacher, Markus Schlüter, Philipp Bauer, Anna Schmoll, and David Weidinger are part of the TBA21 exhibition team. Working together for years, they played a crucial role in *Green light–An artistic workshop* in Vienna. Markus is a trained historian, and head of the exhibition team. Clemens is responsible for the educational programs at TBA21, whereas Philipp, Anna, and David are responsible for various aspects of visitor services, exhibition maintenance, and event organization.

Clemens Rettenbacher. **We faced many challenges while working on *Green light*, from the new format of the project and its complexity to language barriers and certain contingencies in the planning process. What experience could we draw on in that situation? I, for example, learned an enormous amount from going to the St. Marx Migrants' Society (MigrantInnenverein St. Marx) and seeing files stacked up to the ceiling, 20,000 cases for twenty-five civil servants. Austria is confronted with a real issue. What does it mean for the state or the nonprofit organizations to "take care of it"? If the state takes a backseat and everything falls to let's say civil society, which certainly does not have the capacity to process it all, what can or should we do? Could we sit back and pass this work on to others?**
Philipp Bauer. We had experience dealing with ways how to engage visitors in complex artistic projects, yes, but running a workshop with asylum seekers and those seeking a new homeland, turned out to be totally different.
Anna Schmoll. After all, we were dealing with traumatized people, who have no idea what their future holds.

David Weidinger. **The language barrier was also an issue.**
Clemens Rettenbacher. So how does one communicate in this situation?
David Weidinger. Some participants already spoke some German, others English; they could then be drawn upon to help communicate with the others.
Philipp Bauer. There were also the classic solutions—hands, feet, French, Italian. We knew that we were dealing with people from completely different cultures, but we still could not know in advance what it would be like and how the participants would act.

Markus Schlüter. Even though as a team we have known each other a long time and already worked together for many years, at times we reached our limit. Working so closely with asylum seekers and refugees, there were a lot of unpredictable situations, which meshed with

one another, making it difficult to deal with everybody and everything that the project was about.
David Weidinger. Of course, but it was also essential to see the challenges facing asylum seekers firsthand. As the project proceeded, to support them better, we gathered information on the participants' legal situations, the various stages of appeal, legal means available, and the practice of deportation.

Anna Schmoll. **I found it difficult to combine the social aspect of the project, which is about communicating and getting to know each other—*Green light* is ultimately based on participants volunteering to be involved, after all—and at the same time ensuring that the project remains within a certain logic of production. It was hard to experience this contradiction: to feel solidarity with the participants and then have to point out their mistakes and inaccuracies while working.**
David Weidinger. I feel similarly. Apart from the fact, of course, that the donations were indirectly in aid of the refugees, the central pillars of the project were the communicative and social aspects, the creation of a space where points of contact and interaction could be offered between visitors and refugees.

Markus Schlüter. **The *Shared learning* program and the interventions by various artists within the framework of the workshop—all those elements were not always helpful in working toward that actual goal that David has just described, and ultimately unhelpful with regard to the production figures we had to achieve. We needed time to develop a daily rhythm and a feel for the process.**
Philipp Bauer. And of course, we needed to respond to the different qualifications people had. We found it important to more or less guide each individual participant at every stage of the work, if necessary.
Markus Schlüter. Exactly, different qualifications, different motivations, different ages, too, with the level of maturity that came with that.
Clemens Rettenbacher. Though this heterogeneity was part of the concept, too.

David Weidinger. One of our responsibilities was to keep the workshop together. My impression was that the participants' interest faded as the production demands increased. The manufacturing process did become less exciting as time passed, and if, on top of that, the process then shifted time and again, seemingly arbitrarily, and the number of lamps produced had to be increased, not all participants understood why they had to carry on doing that. Under these circumstances, it wasn't as fun working in the workshop. This sometimes led to a certain split between us and the participants. But *Green light* is inconceivable without social relations between these groups.
Markus Schlüter. Within the participants group there was also a split between those who wanted to work, and were able to do so, and those who were unable to work as well, or didn't understand it, and so soon didn't feel like participating anymore.
Clemens Rettenbacher. That's also the key criticism that came up time and again in individual interviews with the participants, the difference between the people who gave their everything and those who held back, or lost interest, which definitely damaged the project in their eyes.

Philipp Bauer. **But we had to realize we had neither the means nor a method to really counter this, all we could do was try and reach the people and address the problems, always try to connect.**
Clemens Rettenbacher. I was changed by *Green light*. I don't mean permanently, but there was a point during the project at which I was almost broken: due to the complex situation, with only few chances to plan efficiently and proactively, the extreme flexibility that was required, the continuous mobilization of all resources—not only ours, but also the participants'—and the tensions within the team due to over-stress.

Markus Schlüter. Our working days were much longer than usual, too. We were here earlier, and after the participants left in the evening, we stayed and tried in the follow-up sessions to pull ourselves together once again, with an eye to the next day—and then it was already 10:00 pm. You go home, sleep a bit, and soon enough you're off to the workshop again. Often we felt a certain helplessness, because you don't know what to say when confronted by that kind of experiences of war, flight, and loss our participants had to go through.
Philipp Bauer. I couldn't decide whether to take that home with me or not.

Clemens Rettenbacher. I find the aspect of cultural learning particularly striking—on the one hand, the process of reaching one's limits and growing beyond oneself, and on the other hand, encountering strange worlds and problems utterly outside one's own experience. That's why I would advise everyone to get involved, to seek out contact with migrants, and to activate this immersive learning process themselves.

What came up in individual interviews with participants was that people were full of gratitude for being able to switch off during the project, for the new space that was created, in which it was possible to make a first step toward a new life. People also talked again and again about family-like structures in the workshop, and that participants still feel connected with the project and their colleagues.
Anna Schmoll. It was lovely to see visitors, who initially were quite afraid of coming into contact, eventually manage to sit down at one of the tables and converse with participants.

David Weidinger. **At a time when racism is once again visible on the streets, as well as in the media and even as a strategy of the political mainstream, it was wonderful to experience that our mutual strangeness and otherness is ultimately always overlaid by our commonalities; to find out that the possibility of coexistence is less culturally specific than one might think; to recognize that humor and goofing around doesn't have to be linked to specific languages. What's more, in my case, I joined *Green light* straight after a language trip to Jordan, so I was able to enjoy some moments of success with the Arab-speaking part of the group, and some disenchanting moments, too.**
Philipp Bauer. We invested a massive effort trying to meet individually with each participant every day, which is what we set out to do. We often lacked sufficient time and staff, however, to really involve everyone.

Clemens Rettenbacher. It's always worth trying. The people being looked after in Austrian asylum centers suffer regularly from

"cabin fever" and the only structure they have is the routine of three daily meals.
David Weidinger. Through *Green light* differentiation became possible. Bit by bit, the anonymous mass dissolved and the individual became visible.

Clemens Rettenbacher. How did you take it when one of the participants was deported?
Philipp Bauer. That was an extremely difficult situation, for all of us. We felt helpless and in despair. We tried to offer all kind of support, depending on the strength and capability of each one of us.

Clemens Rettenbacher. **In the course of *Green light* in the Augarten we not only built lamps, we also created a web of relationships. They were vibrant and important, and through them it was possible to support people in a thousand ways: in their dealings with authorities, in handing out information, in translating, and so on. *Green light* will continue in other places. What would you advise to future *Green light* teams? What is required to ensure that *Green light* carries on successfully, what does a person involved need to have?**
Anna Schmoll. Ideally, there should be a briefing in advance from social workers about what you're in for, and how to handle it. Support during the first phase wouldn't be bad, either.
Markus Schlüter. What you need is social skills and a lot of patience.
David Weidinger. I wish them manageable expectations with regards to production, so that the social aspect of the project doesn't suffer.
Philipp Bauer. Buckets full of patience—over and above the respect and all those basic principles with which one should in any case approach other people—along with a large measure of spontaneity, flexibility, and strong stress-coping mechanisms.

This conversation took place
on April 3, 2017.

The Rise of Contemporary Autochthonic Political Projects of Belonging

Nira Yuval-Davis

The radical changes that we have seen not only in Britain, with the Brexit referendum, and on the European continent but also in other places are the result of interacting processes that are happening all over the globe. There are local as well as more general conditions that are contributing to these developments. To analyze this, I would like to introduce the term autochthony, which Peter Geschiere defines as the global "return of the local."[1] While the "old" racism basically constructed the Other as essentially racially different and the "new" racism constructed her/him as essentially culturally different, autochthony is a racializing discourse that, like other forms of racism, uses origin, culture, and religion as signifiers of immutable boundaries. Its focus, however, is on spatial and territorial belonging, the building of communities based on what Manuel Castells called "defensive identity," except that these days it often applies to majoritarian as well as minoritarian community discourses.[2]

Autochthonic Politics

Some of the politics that we see now in Europe and on the other side of the globe, which can be called autochthonic politics, are different from other extreme-right politics. One of the interesting things is that many of these autochthonic political organizations take pride in telling us that they are not racist. Indeed, rather than

1 Peter Geschiere, *The Perils of Belonging: Autochthony, Citizenship, and Exclusion in Africa and Europe* (Chicago: University of Chicago Press, 2009), 1; see also Nira Yuval-Davis, *The Politics of Belonging: Intersectional Contestations* (London: Sage, 2011).

2 Manuel Castells, *The Power of Identity* (Oxford: Blackwell, 1997), 9.

 using notions of "race," as earlier forms of racist ideology did during the nineteenth and twentieth centuries, these movements construct racialized boundaries that differentiate people according to those who belong and those who do not, using a wide variety of boundary signifiers, including origin, religious affiliation, and citizenship status.

Autochthonic politics are thus very elastic. The only common message is, "We were here before you, and therefore we belong and you do not!" Adherents to these kinds of politics can pretend that they are not racist, and their ranks can indeed include people who are themselves from racial or sexual minorities and other groups traditionally excluded by other racist ideologies: for example, the British Defense League has had Jewish, Irish, and even Afro-Caribbean members.

Autochthonic politics are a particular type of political project of belonging. As I argued in my 2011 book *The Politics of Belonging: Intersectional Contestations*, there is a need to differentiate between "belonging" and the "politics of belonging." While belonging is about feeling safe, feeling entitled to particular rights and roles, it is composed of emotional, cognitive, and normative dimensions. The politics of belonging are the political project, which constructs these feelings of belonging around particular collectivities and around particular signifiers of belonging. Within this project, political actors construct the boundaries, reproduce them, and maintain them, and of course they also contest them. These contestations can, for example, include questioning whether a Jewish person can be a German, a black person can be British, or a Muslim person can be European. And of course some political projects of belonging can have more permeable boundaries than others. For example, when the British politician Enoch Powell declared in 1968 that a West Indian baby born in London does not become English, this was an absolute, impermeable boundary that depended on racial origin, on skin color. But then there is a different kind of an assimilatory political project of belonging that says, "You can belong to us if you forget that you have a different culture, a different religion, or a different language." This is also a political project of belonging that differentiates between those who belong and those who do not, but it is more permeable because people come to be seen as part of the local community even when they retain elements of their different identities and cultural practices.

I would argue that the recent rise of autochthonic politics of belonging that is affecting so much of global, European, and local politics relates to what I have called the double crisis of governability and governmentality.[3] The "crisis of governability" refers to the extent to which and the form in which governments can rule since the rise of neoliberal globalization.

There has been plenty of discussion about the effects of neoliberal globalization on the increase in economic polarization, or income inequality. There is a lot of talk about the 1 percent versus the rest. How is it possible that neoliberal globalization and deregulation have brought about so much accumulation that 1 percent can control most of the resources in the world? What is less talked about is the distribution of wealth between states and multinationals. If you combine the economic power of all the states in the world and their resources, already a few years ago it was between $60 and $70 trillion. If you combine the economic resources of all the multinationals, the total is $600 to $700 trillion. In other words, the economic power of multinationals is about ten times more than that of all the governments of all the states in the world, which includes the United States, China, Great Britain, Germany, and other wealthy nations. This means that the relative power of states versus multinationals has changed enormously. Interestingly, historically this has been the result of the Limited Liability Act and the Companies Act in the US, which defines the limited company (Ltd.) and the limited liability of shareholders. Originally, when the application came before a court in the United States, there was a very small majority that agreed to this transformation. The court agreed to the proposal believing that it would facilitate economic development. Of course it has because it means that there is no personal risk for the people who run the various economic endeavors, because if they fail, it is not their liability. Moreover, if they fail and if there is a change in conditions in the local market—we are living in a time that Zygmunt Bauman called "liquid modernity"[4]—then they just move elsewhere and continue to develop their own resources and their own wealth. Meanwhile the local people and local government

3 Nira Yuval-Davis, "The Double Crisis of Governablity and Governmentality," in "Next Generation Feminism," ed. Sally Davison and Jonathan Rutherford, special issue, Soundings no. 52 (Autumn 2012): 88–99.

4 See Zygmunt Bauman, *Liquid Modernity* (Cambridge: Polity, 2000).

 are left with all the costs of the failure: whether those costs are human, ecological, environmental, or in any other form, they have to bear them!

Moreover, what has been happening as a result of governments' focus on attempting to attract and retain powerful companies in order to maintain the economic activities within the state's sovereign areas is that we now have a situation in the last decade or two in which the multinationals have turned to cash in on this surplus value that has been the state itself, the welfare state. We have seen the privatization of more and more branches of the state in more and more countries. It was like selling the collective silver of the state by privatizing many parts of the economy, giving control to companies that are not owned by people who come from the same state.

In addition to this development, you see an entanglement of the private and public domains so that it is no longer possible to separate them. This is one of the main reasons why after the crisis of 2008 the state used taxpayers' money to salvage the banks, because there was such an entanglement between the resources of the state and private resources that they could not allow the banks to fail in the way that they did in the 1920s because it would go the heart of the economic life of the state itself.

The other side effect of neoliberalism is that the governing role of the state is not to respond to citizens' needs but is about interacting with these companies as well as with other transnational and supranational organizations, like the World Bank or the International Monetary Fund, while at the same time the legislative branches of these states become less and less effective. First of all, with the privatization of the state, they have less and less to do. In a way this has created a growing distance between elected governments, especially elected parliaments, and the citizen. And this leads to the other aspect of this double crisis, which is the crisis of governmentality. Neoliberalism has attempted to create and support—and others have expanded on it—a type of governmentality in which the citizens will cease to expect their state to provide for them and will try to take responsibility for their lives. If they are not successful, it is their responsibility. If they fail, if they are unemployed, it is because something is wrong with them rather than with the system. Of course there is a pivotal point at which people stop buying this! What they come to realize is that it is the system, the government, the society, and however they vote, the government will still do more or less the same things—for the reasons already mentioned relating to the crisis of governability. So they stop voting, they stop caring about what is happening in the state, and they turn to other forms of engagement and other forms of alienation. This crisis is not happening only in Europe, and in some ways, because of its affluent societies, the effects are less manifest there than in other, non-European countries. But even within Europe there are very sharp differences between different states.

Citizenship and Belonging

The notion of "the citizen," unlike that of "the subject," is usually marked by at least a certain sense of entitlement, an important public emotion that is crucial in various political projects of belonging. There are major kinds of rights that have been commonly associated with citizenship: civil, political, social, cultural, and what I call spatial security rights.

Spatial security rights can be seen as an important bridge between those who are citizens and those who are not but who are under the control of a particular state. Spatial security rights include the right to enter the territory of a state, to remain there, to work and/or study there—in short, to plan a future in a more or less secure manner. The right to spatial security is threatened these days not only among documented or undocumented "people on the move" (to use the words of Kofi Annan, the previous secretary-general of the United Nations). Part of neoliberal governmentality is to remove from most people their expectations, let alone guarantees, of long-term employment in the same place or even in the same kind of work, having regular holidays and sufficient funds in their pension to live on when they retire. Other elements of the "risk society" follow, including housing and place of residence, networks of friends, and even membership in a family unit. All of these push people into membership in defensive identity movements, either ethnic or religious. These anxieties among majoritarian members of the society are also important for policy makers, who are using the deprivation of migrants' and refugees' rights as an easy way to appease these anxieties and to reinforce a weakening sense of national cohesion. The basic underlying political issues here, however, concern what the boundaries of belonging are and to what extent the construction of "us" versus "them" in this debate continues to be naturalized.

The politics of belonging involve not only constructions of boundaries but also the inclusion or exclusion of particular people, social categories, and groupings within these boundaries by those who have the power to control this. Symbolic powers are of crucial importance when we deal with political projects of belonging, although they are often the focus of contestation and resistance.

In order to understand some of the contestations involved in different constructions of belonging promoted by different political projects of belonging, we need to look at what is required from a specific person in order for her/him to be entitled to belong, to be considered as belonging, to the collectivity. Common descent (or rather the myth of common descent) might be demanded in some cases, while in others it might be a common culture, religion, or language.

Loyalty and solidarity, based on common values and a projected myth of common destiny, tend to become requisites for belonging in pluralistic societies. In other words, in different projects of the politics of belonging, the different facets of belonging—social locations, identities, and ethical and political values—can become the requisites of belonging and the delineation of boundaries.

Migrants, especially forced migrants, challenge the naturalized equation between people, territory, and political community. Most develop practical as well as emotional, multilayered belonging/s, claiming inclusion in the new territories and spaces to which they have migrated. Many are of course prevented from gaining spatial security rights where they live—they are denied permits to stay, to work, and to gain formal citizenship. Even if they gain these rights, however, their attachment to the societies from which they or their parents and ancestors came usually do not disappear. The communication and transport revolutions of the age of globalization have reinforced these tendencies. They have also reinforced what Michael Mann has called "the dark side of democracy"—an impetus toward ethnic cleansing and autochthonic spaces that are "otherness free."[5]

Hannah Arendt and, following her, Giorgio Agamben claimed that refugees—and, I would add, other "people on the move," especially the undocumented ones—embody the border zone between the

5 See Michael Mann, *The Dark Side of Democracy: Explaining Ethnic Cleansing* (Cambridge: Cambridge University Press, 2005).

citizen and the human.[6] All too often the human rights of people are respected only if they also have formal state citizenships, and even among this group there is local and global stratification among those who "really" belong and those who do not. Migrants, especially racialized and forced migrants, are the specter of the Other in the autochthonic dream of a "pure," otherless universe that we must confront. This border zone is our political as well as analytical challenge.

This text is an adapted version of Nira Yuval-Davis's lecture at TBA21's *ephemeroteræ* program in Vienna, July 2016, with additions from her book *The Politics of Belonging: Intersectional Contestations* and her article "The Dark Side of Democracy: Autochthony and the Radical Right," *50.50: Inclusive Democracy*, July 26, 2011, https://www.opendemocracy.net/5050/nira-yuval-davis/dark-side-of-democracy-autochthony-and-radical-right.

6 See Hannah Arendt, "We Refugees" (1943), in *The Jewish Writings*, ed. Jerome Kohn and Ron H. Feldman (New York: Schocken, 2007), 264–74; and Giorgio Agamben, "Beyond Human Rights," in *Means without End: Notes on Politics*, trans. Vincenzo Binetti and Cesare Casarino (Minneapolis: University of Minnesota Press, 2000), 14–26.

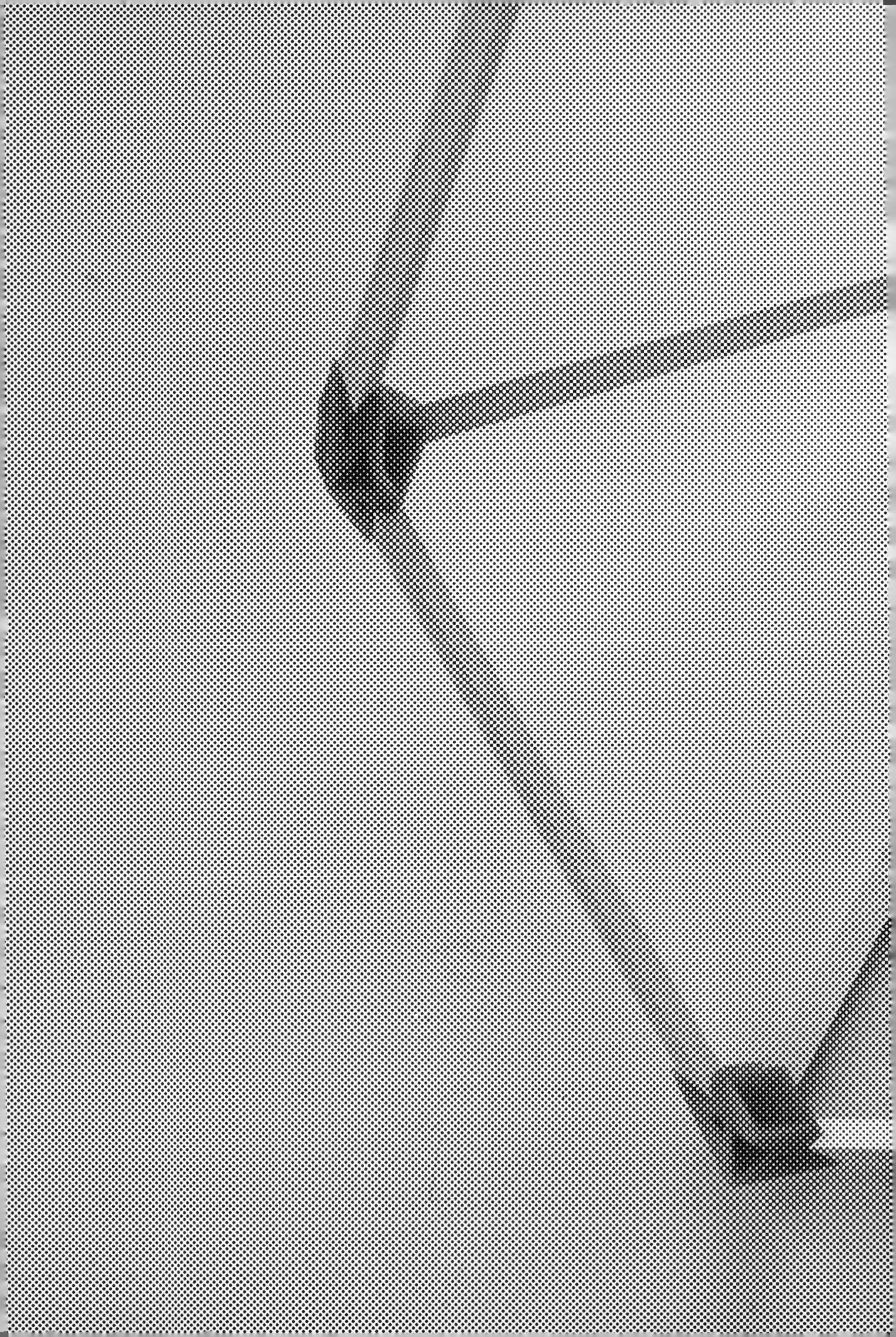

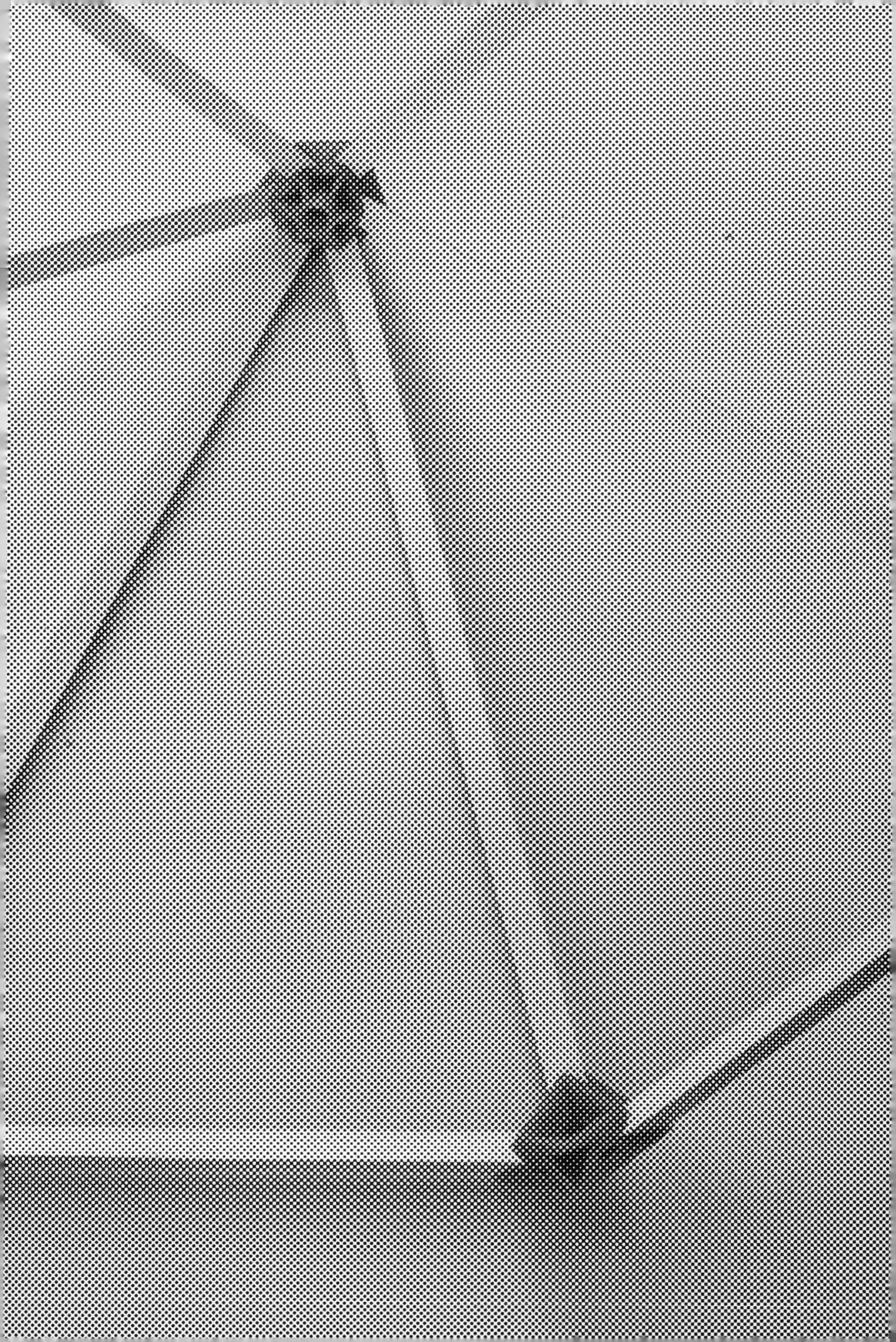

The value of helping others

Qasim Tahmasebi (16) is from Bamiyan, Afghanistan. After traveling for many years, he arrived in Austria in autumn 2015. He practices martial arts, in particular Kung fu. Today, he is living in the Georg Danzer Haus in Stockerau (Lower Austria), where he is also attending school hoping to obtain a school certificate. He has not been granted asylum yet.

Qasim, where are you from?
I am from Bamiyan, which is a province in Afghanistan.

How old were you when you left Afghanistan?
I am not so sure anymore. I would have to ask somebody to be sure. I travelled through Afghanistan for two years, then went to Iran and Turkey before arriving in Austria.

Can you tell us something about your life in Afghanistan? How was your home or your life?
Most of the time I worked. I started working when I was nine years old. I never went to school. I don't have good memories from my childhood.

Why did you choose Austria to be your home?
I knew for quite a long time that I wanted to come to Austria. I made a plan where I would want to live and chose Austria, but I don't know exactly when it was that I first heard of Austria.

You live at Georg Danzer Haus right now. What is the Georg Danzer Haus?
It is a home for refugees from Afghanistan, young men who arrived in Austria without their parents. The Georg-Danzer-Haus gives us an opportunity to go to school and take German classes.

I remember, I saw you doing Kung fu. Where or when did you learn it?
Some boys I met taught me.

The Georg Danzer Haus was also part of the *Green light* project. When did you first hear about it?
I heard about the project from our guardian Marianne. I was told it would be a good opportunity to meet people from other countries, like Syria or Iraq, that there will be a German class as well, and that we would get the chance to meet Austrian people too and it will be a lot of fun. I was excited, because I spend most of my time with Afghans. I've never spent a lot of time at a place with that many different people from different countries before.

We had a certain ambition with *Green light*. What do you think about it?
I cooked, I played football, I learned German. But the most important thing for me was that I learned about the meaning of courtesy and the value of helping others.

I understand completely. I learned about people. I learned through the project to see and to understand foreign people in a completely different way. Maybe you know what I mean.
We, or I can only speak for myself, learned and had the experience of not being perceived as dangerous. Most

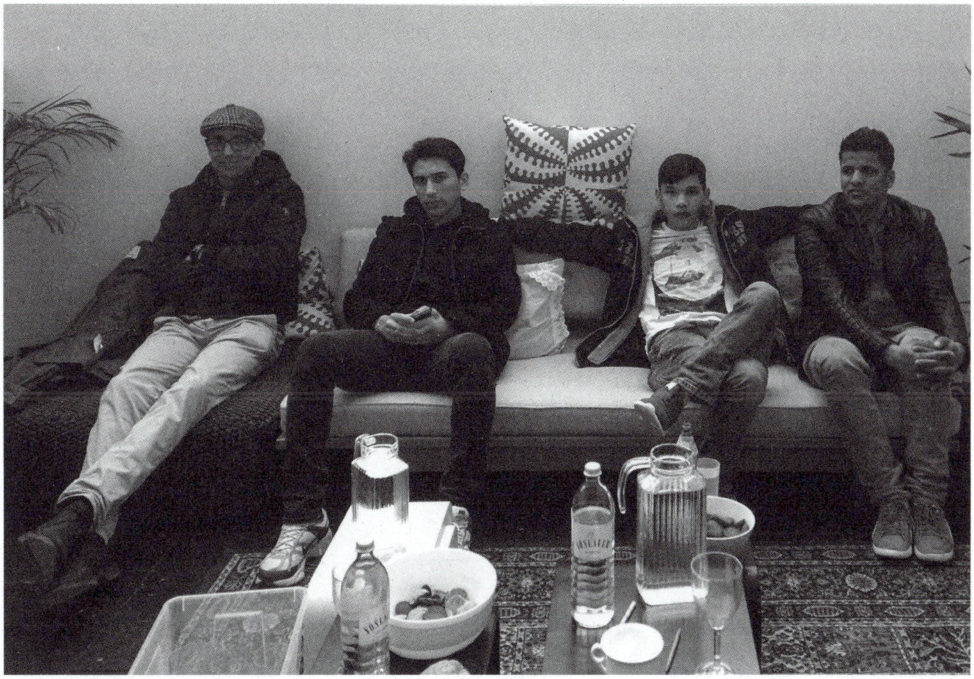

Green lighters Alarabi Raberi, Husseyin Haj Hassan, Qasim Tahmasebi, Tawab Baran during a break

people avoid us boys from the Georg Danzer Haus, or they avoid refugees in general. At the project I learned that you can share laughs and happiness with others, even if you don't share a language or a home country.

How did you like working at the *Green light* workshop? Was it boring sometimes?
No, it was not work after all. It was art. It was a project where we were supposed to learn a lot of things only by attending. So it never felt like work and was not boring at all.

Do you have memories that are special to you?
Not really. There were so many different funny situations when we laughed.

This interview was conducted by Anahita Tabrizi on October 17, 2016.

Statelessness and Reinventing the World

Rasha Salti

One of the most poignant and morbid legacies of the twentieth century is the notion of a refugee. A woman, man, or child, forced to flee from their home, village, town, city under duress, often fleeing sure death. The twentieth century's first refugees were the survivors of the genocide of the Armenian populations living in the territory that would soon become the Republic of Turkey. The campaigns of organized massacres started in 1915 and lasted until 1923, the genocide claiming the lives of approximately one and a half million people. The Ottoman army organized the deportation of those who survived massacres across the borders of modern-day Syria and Iraq. People were crammed into trains like cattle or forced to walk across the Syrian desert for weeks without water, food, or medical aid, and while they walked, they were humiliated, brutalized, and raped. The genocide was reported in the press. The survivors of the massacres and of the long march were received by international relief agencies (such as the American Committee for Relief in the Near East), a novelty at the time, in makeshift "triage" stations established in Deir ez-Zor, Aleppo and Mosul. Refugee camps were improvised in the environs of these cities in the entire region (modern-day Iraq, Syria and Lebanon), sometimes in military barracks abandoned by the Ottoman army, as in the village of Anjar in Lebanon's Beqaa Valley. In the case of Bourj Hammoud, a swampy marshland at the outskirts of Beirut, refugees were housed in tents. As the Ottoman empire collapsed, the nascent Turkish Republic expelled all the communities it defined as culturally, ethnically, and religiously "alien," and deemed potentially dissident or secessionist. The communities identified culturally as Greek were also forced to flee, but they were smaller in size and there was no large-scale organized massacre as in the case of Armenian Ottomans. Ottoman Greeks were aggressed, terrorized, and given express instructions to leave and return to "their homeland."

As colonial empires collapsed in the twentieth century, new borders were drawn in blood and fire as nation-states fought for self-rule, one of the most tragic outcomes was a sudden, large-scale forced expulsion of populations from their lands and homes and their overnight transformation into refugees. The thorough and systematic cultivation of ethnic, cultural, and religious differences among "indigenous" societies was one of the most toxic legacies of colonial rule. Moreover, the settlement of foreign populations (in some cases native to the colonizer's society, and in other cases migrants from other colonies) to whom were afforded remarkable social and economic privileges on the grounds of racial or religious "superiority," compounded the pathos of incommensurable difference. Within the wars for independence from colonial rule, whether they had been inspired by ethnic nationalisms, or less chauvinist forms of nationalist ideologies, were less visible and less understood internecine power struggles among different communities.

For instance, ruling high-ranking British colonial administrators who understood that the end of their empire was near and that they had made contradicting pledges to different social or communal groups, decided that "partitioning" a territory (that had, more often than not, been a historically coherent entity), was a solution to fulfill the jarring promises that were made to different populations. In India and Pakistan, the partition plan of 1947 spurred, a year later, a violent armed conflict and a blood-drenched population transfer of nearly 10 to 12 million people.[1] In the case of Palestine, the British covertly pledged an independent state to both the Palestinians and the Zionist settlers. As violence mounted between both communities, a partition plan of the territory was discussed at the United Nations in 1947, and resulted in a war a few months later. The outcome was the expulsion of nearly one million Palestinians into bordering Arab countries or within Palestine, outside the territory recognized by the international community as the State of Israel in 1948.

1 The Partition of British colonial India along the division of two provinces, Bengal and Punjab, based on a logic of Hindu versus Muslim majority in each province, led to the creation of two independent dominions, India and Pakistan, which eventually became the republics of India, Pakistan, and Bangladesh. The partition came into existence legally on 14–15 August 1947.

In that same year, the Universal Declaration of Human Rights, adopted by the United Nations General Assembly on December 10, 1948, in Paris, was intended to incarnate fundamental and inalienable entitlements of human beings specifically after the devastations of World War II. A few years later, the Convention Relating to the Status of Refugees (also known as the Refugee Convention) was signed by 144 countries on July 28, 1951, in Geneva. Building on Article 14 of the Universal Declaration of Human Rights, the text defined who is a refugee, and the rights entitled to people identified as such. That said, the second half of the twentieth century was far more focused on studying and celebrating the nation-state as the incarnation of political, economic, and social progress, the sole guarantee for a life with dignity and the protector of cultural identity and patrimony. Meanwhile, the millions of populations that existed under the status of refugees continued to do so, living, working, and procreating new generations of refugees, while new conflicts generated more refugees. The political science dictionary of the twentieth century was eschewed in its positive bias toward nations, state actors, and citizen because refugees were regarded as an epiphenomenon of specific conflicts, a problem at once substrate and temporary that should be resolved in the writ of eventual political truce. The "state of exception" that refugees embodied was bound to end, either in allowing the forcibly displaced to return to their homes, or to integrate into their host societies. Refugees were and continue to be quantified and qualified, indexed in all kinds of censuses and databases, but their being in the world as denizens, their subjectivity of statelessness, their experience as outside the polity and system and yet within it, have rarely instigated inquiry or analysis, and almost never in a positive light. Academics, policymakers, experts, and activists have rarely imagined learning from refugees, from the skills, wisdom, and poetics of surviving, adjusting outside and within at once.

It is an oddity when considering number of seminal figures that have made towering contributions to the western humanities (in social theory, the arts, and the belles-lettres) of the past century who had themselves endured the trials of seeking safe harbor and asylum, an experience that marked their thought and mindset. Furthermore, refugees are rarely accredited for the growth they contribute to their host countries' economies, the know-how they bring and improve, the resourcefulness that amplifies with survival skills. Those who seem to have monitored that economic angle most notably are the big capitalists and proponents of globalization, and who have notoriously negotiated the relocation of manufacturing outside countries where labor has protections. In fact, much of the conditions of "transnational" capitalist manufacturing reproduces the disenfranchisement from basic rights that refugees endure. In other words, when states deprive communities of their basic rights for whatever reason, it may be useful to regard them as "stateless" in order to imagine strategies of struggle and resistance.

When Palestinian refugees arrived in Lebanon in 1948, they were directed to sites where a few decades earlier Armenian refugees had been first directed to. And when Syrian refugees began to arrive in 2012 and 2013 they were settled on the vestiges of old refugee camps and nearby existing camps. Camps are sites or spaces compelled by a permanent, enduring impermanence. The decision to locate camps on these sites was the outcome of negotiations between various Lebanese governmental institutions and the international agencies entrusted with the mission to bring immediate assistance, relief, and protection to refugees. These international organizations have accumulated and transmitted a degree of knowledge and wisdom regarding the management of life in refugee camps. They have also created a vocabulary within the writ of international law and non-governmental humanitarian practice. For instance, refugees are "aid recipients" and "stakeholders" and programs aimed at social empowerment and nurturing skills are referred to as "capacity-building." States too have created a vocabulary to refer to the lingering traces of expelled communities. The Ottomans organized the systemic expropriation of the expelled Armenian population's properties through the establishment of the Abandoned Properties Administration Commissions and Liquidation Commissions in 1915 and 1916, that were supposedly entrusted with safeguarding them. Under the aegis of the Turkish Republic, the expropriations continued under a less veiled guise of guardianship and protection, some of the referents were altered, but essentially, not much has changed. The Israeli State refers to Palestinians displaced from their homes and who relocated elsewhere in the territory that came to be Israel (i.e. internally displaced) as "present absentees." The term is used to refer to their descendants as well. The strange semantic construction originates from the fact that the Israeli government registered them as "absent from their home," on a particular day, even if they had left involuntarily or under duress. Their homes and property were entrusted to the Custodian of Absentees' Property via legislation imparted in 1948 and 1950.

In the past two years, the large-scale influx of refugees to Europe seems to have polarized societies and flared the rise of right-wing nationalism, which has been on a rise for the past four decades. This political crisis is also related to the steep decline of the nation-state system. In his prolific reflections on statelessness, the bare life, and refugees, Italian philosopher Giorgio Agamben proposes to rethink the organization of societies from these notions, precisely because they seem to embody less and less a state of exception. If, for instance, the notion of the present absentee is explored concomitantly with its experiential "palindrome," namely the absent present, then the potentiality of repairing an injustice or suturing a wound begins to emerge as material and immaterial patrimony are placed at par. And the possibility of imagining forms of restitution of expropriated material patrimony exchanged for immaterial patrimony, or the knowledge, skills, and poetics acquired while absent from one's property.

You have to be social

Anas Aljajeh (27) is from Damascus, Syria, where he studied interior design until the Syrian civil war interrupted his education. He arrived in Austria in autumn 2015, and has been granted asylum. Today, he is living in a shared apartment in Vienna and taking care of the son of fellow *Green light* participant Ibrahim Mawazini, who is working full time as a mechanic. Anas is currently looking for a job so that he could bring his fiancée to Vienna.

The first day of the project, what was your first impression back then?
I remember that I was very happy about the artworks, the handcrafted aspect of the project, and the recycling—everything that I'm interested in could be found in this project. So, I was very happy because that's my world. The first feeling I remember was that I was very happy and very hopeful.

You just said you found your world, right? What is your world?
[laughing] Everything that includes art, handmade things, recycling, making something from nothing. You know what I mean?

The idea of the *Green light* workshop was to produce art and bring people together. What do you think about this premise?
Actually, producing art is a very important task, since it can give you new experiences and a new set of skills. And it's good to meet new people from different countries, because you will get to know each other's ideas. You will be sharing your ideas, you will be sharing your culture, and you will be learning a new culture. So I think it is a positive point in *Green light*.

Could you define any problems within the conception of the workshop? What do you think made it easier to share and collaborate on the production of the artworks? What do you think didn't work so well?
I think most things worked out fine—cooking together, eating together, sitting, talking. But the work itself, when we were working as a team, could sometimes get complicated, because not all the members of the team were working on the same level, you know? One person would make three lamps per day and three other people together make only one lamp a day. It created some complications.

Was there some kind of competition? What was the atmosphere within the group like?
Generally, it was a very friendly and very lovely situation. I didn't feel stressed, nobody was nervous and nobody was angry.

Going back to the *Green light* itself: Anas, as an interior designer, what do you think about the design?
It's very creative, maybe a bit strange. I think as an art piece it's perfect, there is nothing to change.

It's just perfect?
Yes. [Both laughing]

Did you meet some interesting people? Was it hard to become part of the group and how did you manage to find your own personal way into the project?
Almost all the people I met were interesting. I generally like to work in a group. But in *Green light* I found that I actually preferred to work a little bit by myself. Because I preferred to improve, to make more lamps every day, which I could do that better if I worked alone. I'll give you an example: sometimes, I didn't think the preparation of the wooden sticks was perfect. So I would have to redo them to my standards. Because I knew how to do it the way I wanted it to be. So that the lamps I made were perfect in my eyes, by my standards. I wanted to keep my standards.

What did this mean to you back then, do you remember? To have the opportunity to build an art piece by yourself and by your highest possible standards?
It meant everything to me. Because I am not used to being unproductive, I'm not used to being unemployed. I always worked, even when I was in university, or back when I was in school. I always used to be productive and active.

Why do you think it is so important for people—or for you—to be productive?
For me, if I want to be a creative person, I can't do it through the hands of other people. I must do it with my own hands to get ideas. Sharpening my ideas, my skills, it's not something I can do it with another person's hands. I must do it with my own hands to get the perfect result I want.

So what do you think about the situation where so many people applying for asylum are not allowed to work, that they don't have the chance to sharpen their skills, to be productive with their own hands?
Well, you are allowed to work—just not for money. I think it's important to find places like this, where you create infrastructure, where people come together with ideas, people who want to work and sharpen their skills. By now, there are other places like this. It's important to let people work and let them realize their ideas and improve their skills. With this work, they will learn German, like we did here. That way, when they get their papers, they will be more prepared: they will have both a new skill and a good understanding of German.

Was there anything that didn't work at *Green light*?
I think there were some negative things, it wasn't always perfect. The problem with translation was there, since on the one hand we had work connecting us, but we still always needed language. You need good translators. If you can't communicate to someone else the full idea in all its clarity, then they won't understand what is happening.

Thank you. That is indeed an important aspect, to get the translation right. Translation also does have a lot of meanings: there is translation between languages, and I also feel it's a translation of ideas. Do you feel like this is a "Western" project, or, if we put it another way, do you think it's difficult to translate the idea to people from Syria, Iraq, or Afghanistan?
I think it's not difficult because it's not a very strange idea to Arab people. It's simple materials.

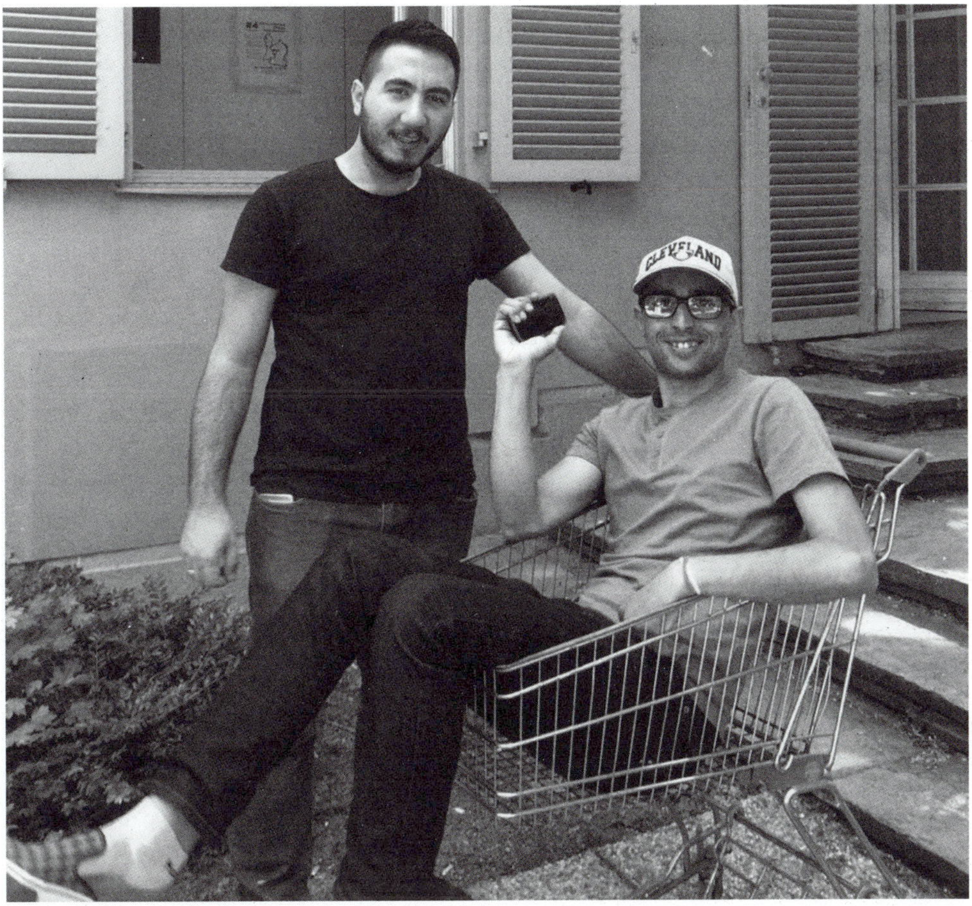

Anas Aljajeh and Alarabi Raberi

Of course, and it must seem especially simple for you as an interior designer. I mean more like the *Shared learning* workshops, which sometimes felt like an artist would come with all these questions, but when we tried to interact, it was difficult. Because the artist would probably not be able to convey what they really meant, not for lack of words, but on a conceptual level.
Maybe there were strange ideas for some people, but not the project itself as a whole. Maybe someone would say: "What is this?" Or wouldn't understand the idea, why it had to be designed that way. What the meaning of it would be. Maybe someone wouldn't understand.

Do you think the project could be universal? That it could go to different places and succeed there?
Of course. It's not a strange idea. Maybe it will be strange for some people, but for the most part, it's not that different: anybody anywhere can learn it and can do it. It's not a problem.

What do you think, what does one need in order to be a *Green light* participant, to be here and feel comfortable?
First you need to believe in this project and in this idea and to love it, to like what you do. That's the most important thing, because if you don't like what you do, you won't be doing it well.

What skills do you think you needed for making the project successful, for getting the best out for yourself?
For assembling and for making the *Green light* lamps, you don't need many skills, because it's simple. You just need to pay attention when you learn it the first time and then it will be fine. For the other parts, you have to be social, to be able to be with the other people. I think that's the most important, to be social.

This interview was conducted by Clemens Rettenbacher on November 29, 2016.

Respect for everyone

Alarabi Raberi (32) is from the territory of Western Sahara and has an Algerian passport. Born the oldest son in a family of carpenters and stone masons, Alarabi ran the family business until he decided to migrate to Europe. He arrived in Austria in October 2015. He is currently living in refugee accommodations run by the Volkshilfe Wien. While his application for asylum has not been ratified yet, he is active with various initiatives supporting and empowering refugees.

Why did you choose Vienna?
Artists from all over the world show their works in Vienna. Vienna is a large museum, a cultural capital. I am a carpenter and would like to learn something new, like new design. And I would like to show people my work and my designs. I am currently taking part in in various projects: Open Marx, Wiener Fahrradshow, Talentspace.

The *Green light* workshop is based on the idea that people can be connected, that a community can be formed, by collaborating within the framework of an art production. What do you think of that?
That's a good idea. I have always worked, I was never one for sitting around or sleeping. That is the most important point about integrating foreigners. Those fleeing their home countries need energy, positive energy, not idleness and sleep.

As a craftsman, where do you see the value of working with one's hands, of being productive, and of collaboration?
I consider working with one's hands to be most important. For myself and for

others. Because in the early years, when you're new in a place or you're simply a "foreigner," then it's hard because you're always looking for work. Whether you're an engineer or a technician, at first you'll work with your hands. And only later will you get the chance to practice the trade you learned.

What do you think about the *Green light* lamp?
I think it's good. I sometimes go on a walk in the street and see the lights installed somewhere. Last month I had an appointment with the Volkshochschule and the interviewer asked me if I had any kind of papers for the German course I took. When I showed him my documents, he said, "Ah, you were part of *Green light*, at the TBA21. That's good!" And the same thing happened to me at the AMS, the public employment service. *Green light* opens up opportunities for me, not necessarily great ones, but still. Because the revenue from the sales went to charitable institutions, and so by taking part in the project you have worked for others.

How did you find the cooperation with the people, like the TBA21 staff and the other participants?
I was able to gain a lot of experience at the Augarten. The most important thing in doing this was always respect —respect for everyone, no matter whether it's the boss or not. No matter if they were Austrian or foreign, another participant or a TBA21 team member. I was also able to gather some experience cooking with Ibrahim. I never cooked much before. It was the same with the team—no walls between us. Nor between any of the people involved.

By working together, fear and insecurity disappear. It becomes possible to put aside prejudices, and to understand the situation others are in.
For us it was possible to build respect for Austrians. And to understand and accept the rules and laws, like standing still at a red light. That worked for me and I have fewer problems with racism. Whenever you're in a new country for the first time, you don't know the rules. The first thing I learned was that smiling is very important. When you smile at people, they react differently. In another place, there is always another culture, and you have to discover it.

This interview was conducted by Clemens Rettenbacher on October 15, 2016.

The Border in Us: A Note against Indifference

Sandra Noeth

Borders are many things. Material, architectural, constructed, symbolic, felt, fictional and memorized, embodied, lived. Always already there—always yet to come. In crisis and collapse, in light of environmental calamities, war, and forced migration, but also, on a much smaller scale, when thinking of everyday experiences of exclusion, of nonrecognition and of indifference: the way in which we conceive of structures and systems, of centers and peripheries, of the local and the international is continually challenged by current realities. Driven by a catchy and intuitive rhetoric of a borderless world, of flows and fluids, and parallel and insistent discursive and visual scenarios of securitization and division, defense and accessibility, borders are commonly measured by their capacity to control and monitor human and nonhuman movement. The complicated symbolic and material acts of translation between the need for and restrictions on mobility and flexibility and the openness to exchange and a valuable reciprocity impact the field of the arts as well. They stay not without cynicism when reminding us that the hopeful and hazardous overflow of bodies in public and urban space during different revolutionary events across the world took place less than a decade ago and that border regimes have kept on being observably tightened since then.

Borders select bodies: they mark and target who is legitimate to cross, to be heard, to speak, and to move around our physical and imaginary territories. For this we have invented a multitude of strategies and protocols to choreograph the bordering body: to make it wait, linger, and dwell, to facilitate its movements or to restrict them. Borders hide some bodies while making others visible. Equipped with lines and legends and organized in color bars that in all formal clarity still carry the memory of colonialism, they paradigmatically influence how we imagine and experience the world. They remind me of the privilege of my passport with every single line placed on paper.

Borders are spaces in their own right—they are always in a state of becoming, always unfinished. Permeable and porous, visceral and felt, the border is situated in—it is part of—my body.

And I actually remember crossing the border for the first time.
Like any other time afterward.
After a while one recognizes its movements: its procedures and formalities, the preliminary establishment of a network of conditional hospitality, its manifest and immaterial infrastructure, the rhetoric, the passiveness, the waiting as well.
Sometimes the movement of the border catches you by surprise, and you don't see it coming. Usually when leaving the house to set off for a trip, sometimes already long before, in the middle of a conversation, when lingering at the supermarket checkout or when daydreaming.

And still: it always starts in the body.
There is this familiar feeling of excitement and tension, marked by contradiction.

I remember rehearsing, revisiting the physical and mental movements of the border, trying to welcome them: firmly yet cautiously navigating through space, placing the gaze, controlling the breath, listening to the sound of the body. Lowering the voice, detaching, uncoupling from any direct experience. Projecting, letting go. Not too daring, not afraid either. Disciplined, concentrated, and insecure. Ready to improvise at all times.

The movement of the border is restless, disquieting. Oftentimes it is creeping, gradual, accumulating, delayed, anonymous. Often it is perceived much later, like an echo in the rhythm of life. Like a continuous state of displacement, unfolding slowly.
Caught in a meticulously crafted texture of narratives and emotions, it feels that—in the encounter with the border—my body doesn't belong to me anymore. It is like entering an illogical reality—as if I had lost autonomy about it. Like moving back and forth between contested space: between countries and places, memories and expectations, between the unseen, the unsaid, that which I can't find words for—like traveling through interwoven, competing glimpses of thoughts and feelings while staying unrecognized—like a kind of visitor in another person's—in one's own story.

Mostly border zones are populated and inhabited by different kind of bodies: everyday bodies, disciplined and trained, absent and invisible ones, bodies in fear, broken bodies, bodies in limbo—joyful bodies as well. Bodies that witness experiences of fracturing and disorientation, in which space and material, authority, order, and meaning are redistributed. They all appear as representatives of and inscribed in an uncountable number of unnamed, silenced, or silent voices and cases. They are suspicious, hesitating bodies, suspended between action and reaction, response and responsibility: they draw us into a dispositive of concurrent and concurring, unsettling readings of what we call reality. They put us in touch with a more brittle, preliminary, unstable, and incomplete idea of the border.

When arriving at the Augarten in Vienna in April of last year for *15 Acts of Participation*—a gathering of artists and thinkers that Olafur Eliasson and TBA21 had set up in conjunction with the *Green light* workshop—they were already there.[1] Among the international crowd and random passersby who had convened on the premises, their bodies were inevitable, and it was difficult to ignore them even though they inhabited the space in a most generous way. The movements and gestures with which they arranged and put together the materials for the crystalline green lights and the words and signs that they found to explain their actions and procedures to the visitors were self-secure and skilled, patient and kind of playful. And while I was mingling with them, it became, for a moment, almost an undeniable yet unobtrusive detail that they were border crossers, carrying the experience of the border with them. They came from elsewhere, from afar: from Syria and Afghanistan, from Nigeria, Somalia, and Iraq. And in a pleasurable and at the time irritating way the bodies of the women and men who welcomed us to their workshop reminded me of the bodies that I had just left behind me. Only a few hours before, when traveling back from my regular places of research and writing and living in what we often content ourselves with calling the "Arab world." Yet what had felt so familiar and obvious there felt displaced now, and the desire to get to know them was tainted by an undefined and awkward feeling of insecurity and even shame: my encounter with

1 *15 Acts of Participation*, April 7, 2016, hosted at TBA21–Augarten, with Olafur Eliasson and Francesca von Habsburg, Atıf Akın, Gina Brandlmayr, Damian Christinger, Alexander Ehrmann, Paul Feigelfeld, Rasmus Nielsen/SUPERFLEX, Sandra Noeth, Ben Paine, Johannes Porsch, Andreas Roepstorff, Zavoloka, Daniela Zyman, members of Studio Olafur Eliasson, and the *Green light* participants.

 the bodies of the refugees had turned into an encounter with myself, an encounter with a very specific border: the border that is *us*.

In his auto-ethnography of borders, based on his own journey as well as border narratives by other people, the anthropologist Shahram Khosravi gives an account of illegal migration across Asia and Europe.[2] By reminding us that borders are zones in which meaning making and meaning breaking conflate, he points us to the polysemic nature of the border, its heterogeneity and ubiquity.[3]Among the manifold experiences of inclusion and exclusion that he describes, it is what he calls the "invisible borders" that appear to be the harshest and most invincible ones: "those in the minds of people," he writes, are "more difficult or impossible to cross ... These borders are intangible and elusive, yet powerful and deep rooted."[4] These borders are not spectacular, explosive, and not easy to detect, they are not mapped out but rather a matter of intimate politics. Gradually and with insistence they enter all textures of those who face them: our vision and imaginary, our behavior and understanding. Entangled in hardly traceable dynamics of affecting and being affected, they attack the body's integrity in a much more silent yet pertinent way. In the experience of vulnerability, the resilience of the body is on display; its capacity to accommodate different and changing environments and to threaten sovereignty while being jeopardized at its boundaries is on display, as is its ability to resist, persist, and endure and to adapt, recover (physical) shape, and reorient itself beyond positivistic ideas of flexibility, elasticity, and change and beyond biopolitical strategy. Here, in the experience of the border, the real, physical danger unfolds its epistemic violence and confronts us with the question of what it actually means for a bordering body to be safe, unharmed, intact, and sound.

Borders are a matter of performance: standing in line, removing my shoes and objects, being body-searched, placing my finger on the biometric reader ... Equipped with artifacts and objects, drawing on already lived, conveyed, or yet to be imagined aesthetics and navigating shifting modes of somatic attention, the body appears, as

2 Shahram Khosravi, *"Illegal" Traveller: An Auto-Ethnography of Borders* (London: Palgrave Macmillan, 2010).

3 See Étienne Balibar, "What Is a Border?," in *Politics and the Other Scene* (London: Verso, 2002), 75–86.

4 Khosravi, *"Illegal" Traveller*, 75.

Sophie Nield describes it, in an almost theatrical act at the border.[5] We train our movements and gestures and mimic, rehearse, and stage them; caught in a loop of deadly repetitions—rituals, arbitrary orders, contingent matters—the border addresses us with the ever-same questions: *Who are you? Where are you from?* Questions that, as Khosravi insists on pointing out, don't require an answer. Rather, unfolding their transformative potential in an almost liturgical manner, they are designed to keep the foreigner, the stranger, the border crosser not *out* but *in* place: to complete her or his otherness, ever anew,[6] and to keep the subject unstable, make it fail and ultimately keep it under control. Yet: in a never identical or in equal manner—paralyzed, in fear and anger, tired and exhausted and out of balance, full of desire and hope—sometimes our body betrays us. It disturbs and irritates our physical and material processes of assigning and asserting belonging and affiliation and exposes the border in its systemic quality—in its amplifications and intensities, in its traumatic and residual effects. At the same time, in the moment of hesitation and break-off, the body reminds us that every border carries a promise as well: the wish and the trust that it accesses, actualized and affirmed when our eyes touch, that being together can be imagined differently.

In the experience of the border, bodies are depicted as legal or illegal ones, and collectivity is evoked. Following communal stereotypes, exotic imagery or discriminatory projections, the individual body becomes representative of and caught in another, collective body when in times of catastrophe and crisis real and imagined communities enter the scene and a third body emerges: the neutralized, politicized, generalized, mimetic, expanded, forgotten, and fleshless body of the collective. The body of the Occupier, the Refugee, the Religious, the Exiled—which is the body of the Lover, of the Friend, the Caretaker and the Lost One. Thereby the border confronts us with the wish—which is often the need—to inscribe ourselves in another, in an Other's story, in order to be recognized. Wrapped in globalized and universalized notions that tell us of "waves of migration" and "the refugee crisis," the body of the border crosser seems to exist

5 Sophie Nield, "On the Border as Theatrical Space: Appearance, Dis-location, and the Production of the Refugee," in *Contemporary Theatres in Europe: A Critical Companion*, ed. Joe Kelleher and Nicolas Ridout (London: Routledge, 2006), 61–70.

6 Shahram Khosravi, "Prosopagnosia" (lecture presented as part of the project "Violence of Inscriptions" at HAU-Hebbel am Ufer, Berlin, March 5, 2016).

only in plural, that is to say, in brackets, in suspension, never fully there. Or, in Khosravi's words describing the violence linked to the consequent acts of representation: "The stereotype of 'the refugee' and what he or she 'looks like' is formed by visual representations ... A 'real' refugee is thus supposed to be a 'profound,' 'poor,' 'traumatized,' 'serious' and of course 'sad' person ... Refugees have to perform 'refugeeness.'"[7] Exposed to an active act of unseeing, the body is kept faceless and invisible. And Khosravi reminds us of the role of imagination and fiction in this visual and discursive, embodied and corporeal process of collectivization and objectification in which the border crosser—scripted by and inscribed into contested space, "is only visible in the phantasm of others."[8] Meanwhile, whereas most of the real, uncountable bordering bodies stay silent and silenced, their images, stories, or words have entered our artistic and aesthetic worlds as well. It feels trapped. How to account for the singularity of the bordering body, its suffering and joy, its hope, desires, and interests, in a competition for media-worthy attention that has gone global and provided easy access to images of suffering and disaster? How to communicate awareness and information and still trust in the agency of the body without getting lost in romanticizing its subversive potential? Where to speak from and, more importantly, whom to address? Whom to move toward?

Becoming-border: To feel it, to carry it in your body before it becomes visible. Smelling, sensing the border under your skin, before it finds an imitable and exterior form. This takes place, shapes your body. This is a physical, a visceral experience. Hidden memories that emerge, bodies that seem frozen, to have fallen out of time. Untimely encounters.

In light of the catastrophe, when becoming-border, the bodies pull back from history and tradition; they escape subjectivity and the promise of presence; they are caught in between fiction and memory. They move through contested space, expand the physicality of the body, blur chronologies, affiliations, and temporality. Facing intrusion and menace, the movements, images, and words seem to take care of one another, hiding themselves in other artworks in order to—maybe—resurrect and gain agency at some later moment in time. And yet:

7 Ibid., 73.
8 Ibid., 72.

Every movement leaves a trace
It puts us in touch with—it welcomes the wounded places in our lives.

It is like visiting any catastrophic place: harmed, left over, destroyed, seamed by bodies in contradiction, in tension, referring back to themselves, scattered, torn in responsive dynamics. Pointing us to the wounded places of our lives, the event of the border complicates the logic of cause and event, of responsibilities and obligations. It draws us to our own borders and boundaries, it readdresses the question of our individual and collective agency. It invites us to silence, listening:

To listen. To interrupt your Self and go towards the Other. To open your Self to all the possibilities that arise in you by the words of the Other, the logic of the Other, the breath of the Other.—To accept and to surrender to that which enters you, so that it settles in you and remains in you. This is what we have lost ... for our words now fall to the ground, in front of us, before they reach their target—and if they succeed, they arrive at a barren, destroyed land, like our language.[9]

These words of a friend stay with me—a soft warning and an unbearable call: a call to go to a place where the poetic hurts and to stand it. The movement of becoming-border puts us in relation to the Other, to the Other in us. It confronts us and invites us to be hand in glove with all the absent bodies that we carry in us and that are mobilized in the experience of the border. Bodies *in*, *of* and *as* evidence, that introduce an ethical dimension into our social, political, and aesthetic projects as well and allow us as well as others—like the bodies of the refugees in the *Green Light* workshop—to appear differently.

I need the bodies of the Other, their movements and eyes and gestures, their proximity and their distance, in order to learn with, through, alongside them, in order to be part, to participate in this world. In order to understand that the capacity to see from more than one perspective carries an obligation as well. Thus I propose to stay with a humble and open-ended question that might seem all too evident: a call to not mistake borders as stable, preset, and unchangeable structures. To understand that they are not primarily spatial categories but relational ones. To acknowledge that they

9 Tony Chakar, *The Dialogue That Is Us* (Sharjah, UAE: Sharjah Art Foundation, 2013).

 are not unshakeable tools of power but something that we continue weaving, that we contribute to maintaining day by day, all of us.

The border *in* us, the border that *is* us might then be exactly a way to encounter the disquieting, contradictory, and responsive movement of the border. This stirs up questions about our own involvement, participation, and responsibility in constructing and maintaining borders and calls for our individual and collective capacity for action—as artists, thinkers, and citizens. It invites us to consent to not be a single being.

This movement of becoming-border follows the movement of what seemed to be motionless. This is disquieting, yes, uneasy, and asks us to leave a safe position—and yet: there is nothing to claim, nothing to wait for.
The ghosts are already in the house for long.

An early version of this essay was presented by Sandra Noeth in the context of *15 Acts of Participation,* at TBA21 on April 7, 2016.

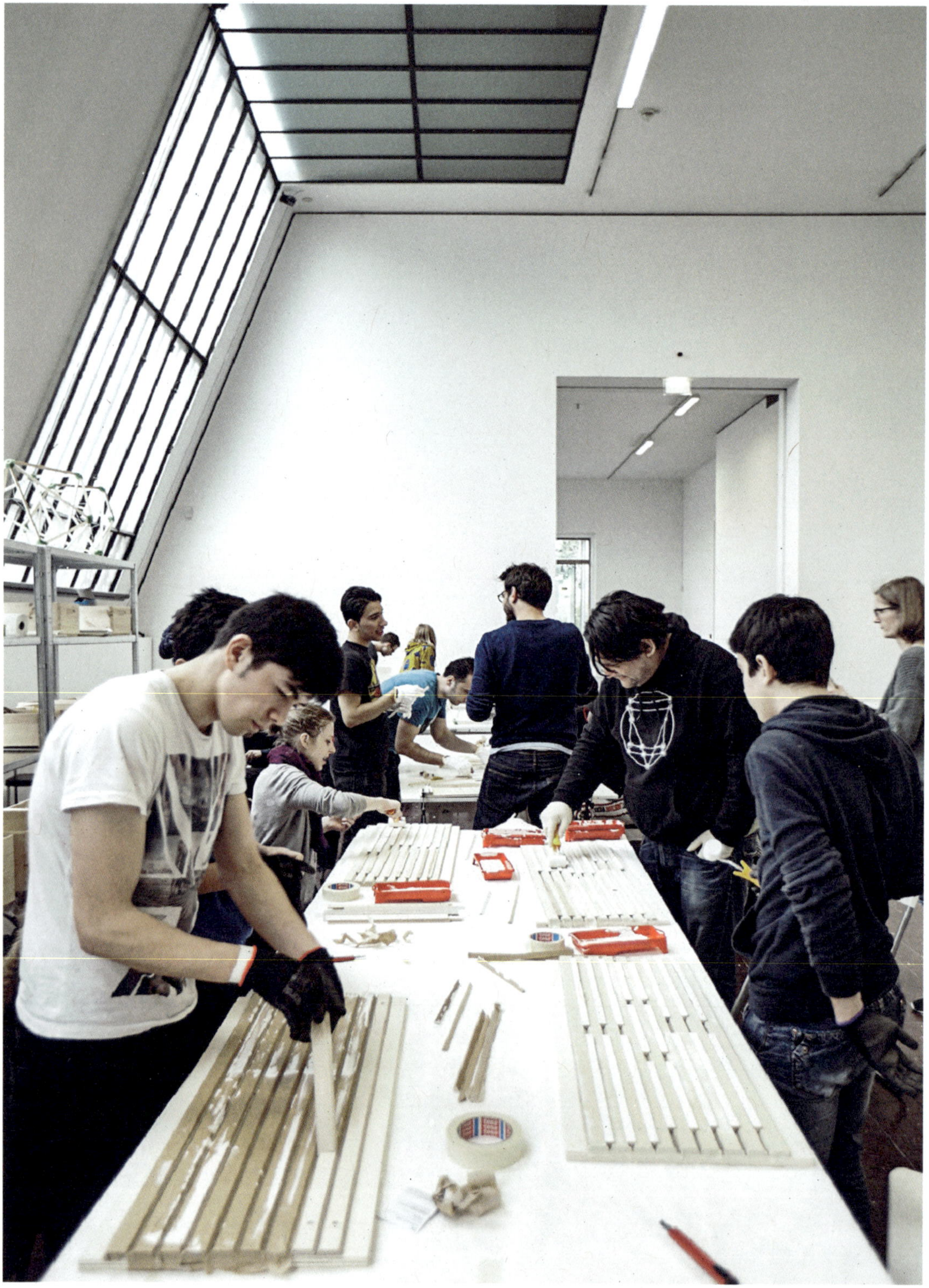

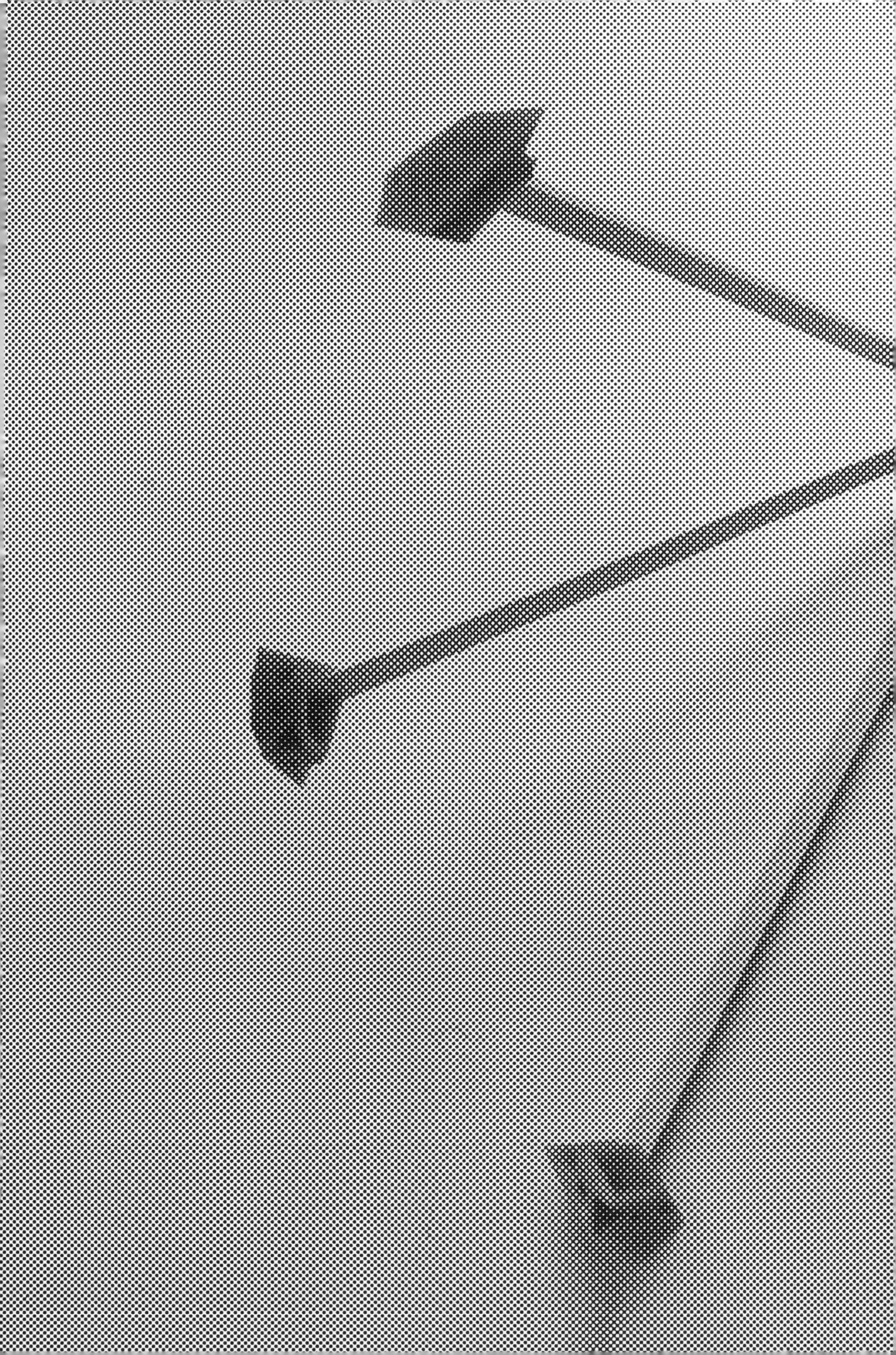

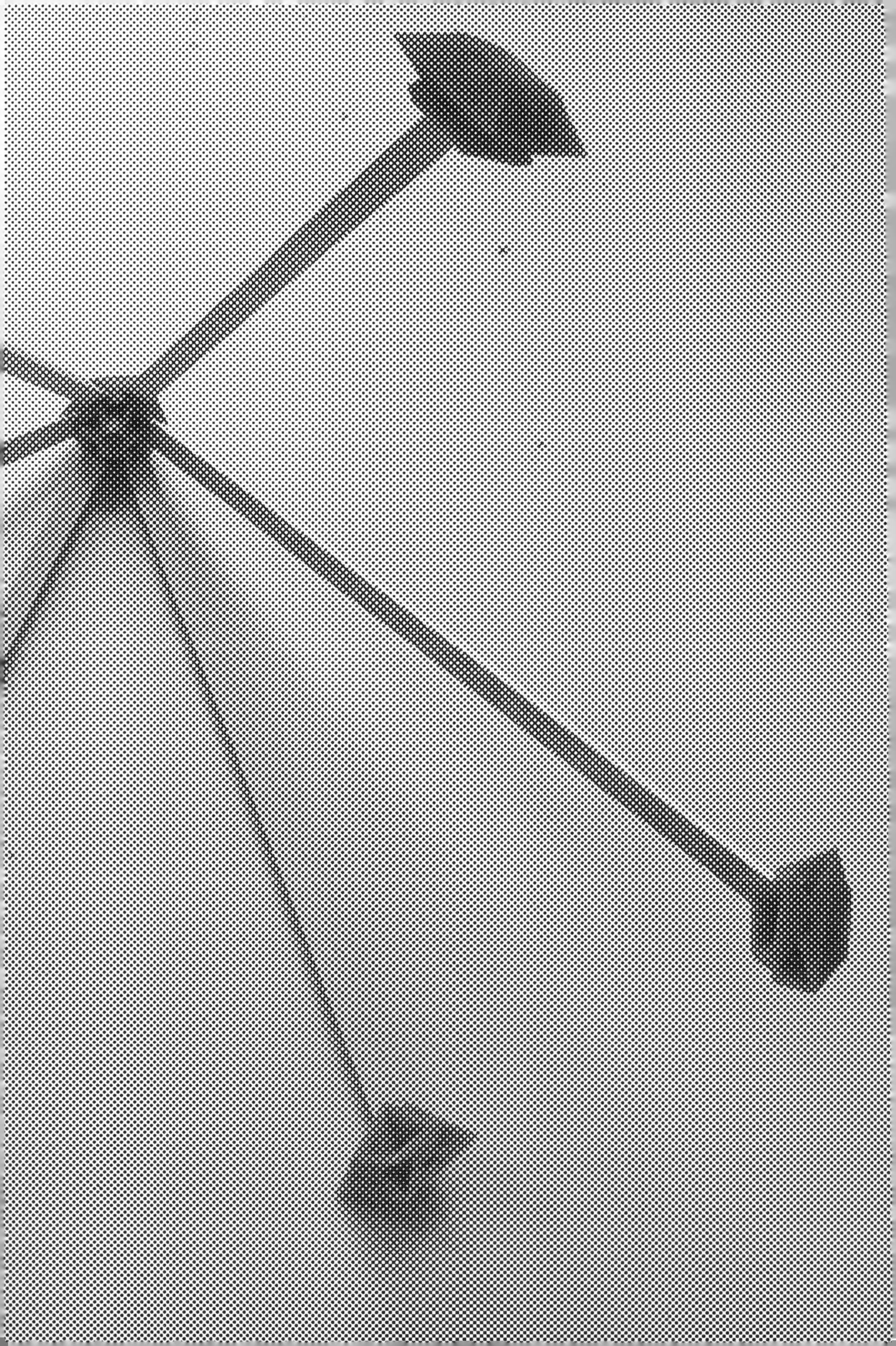

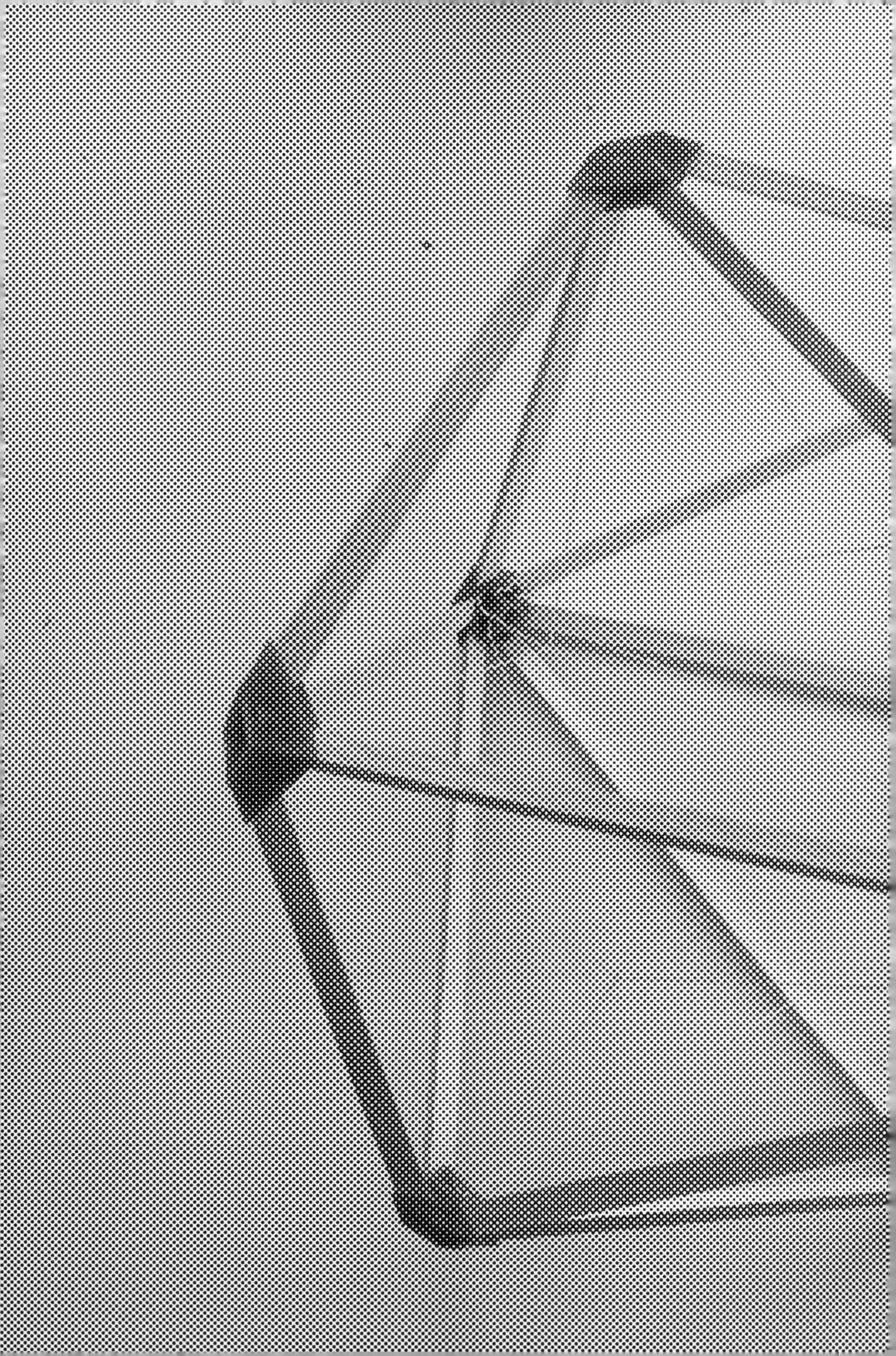

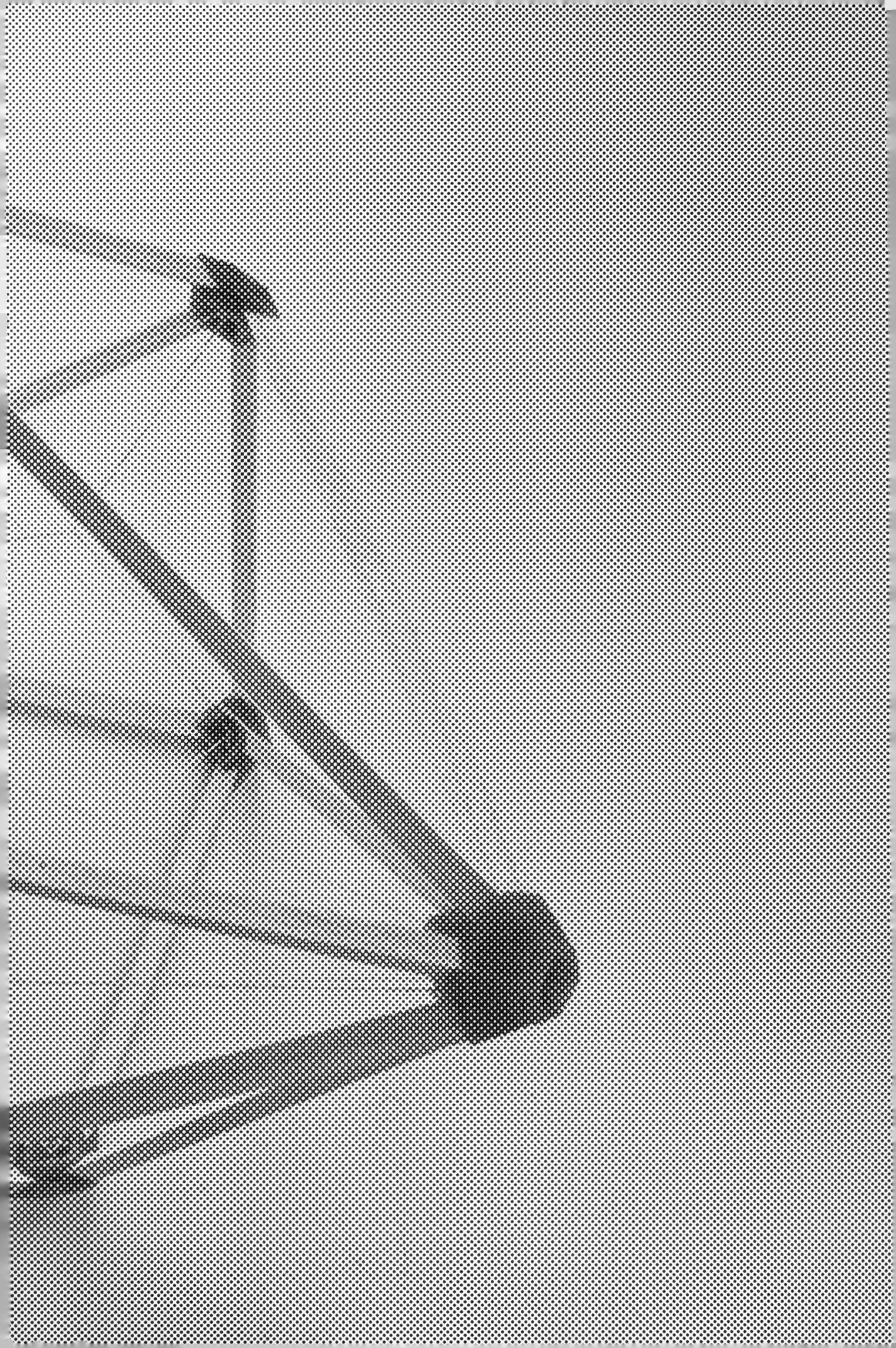

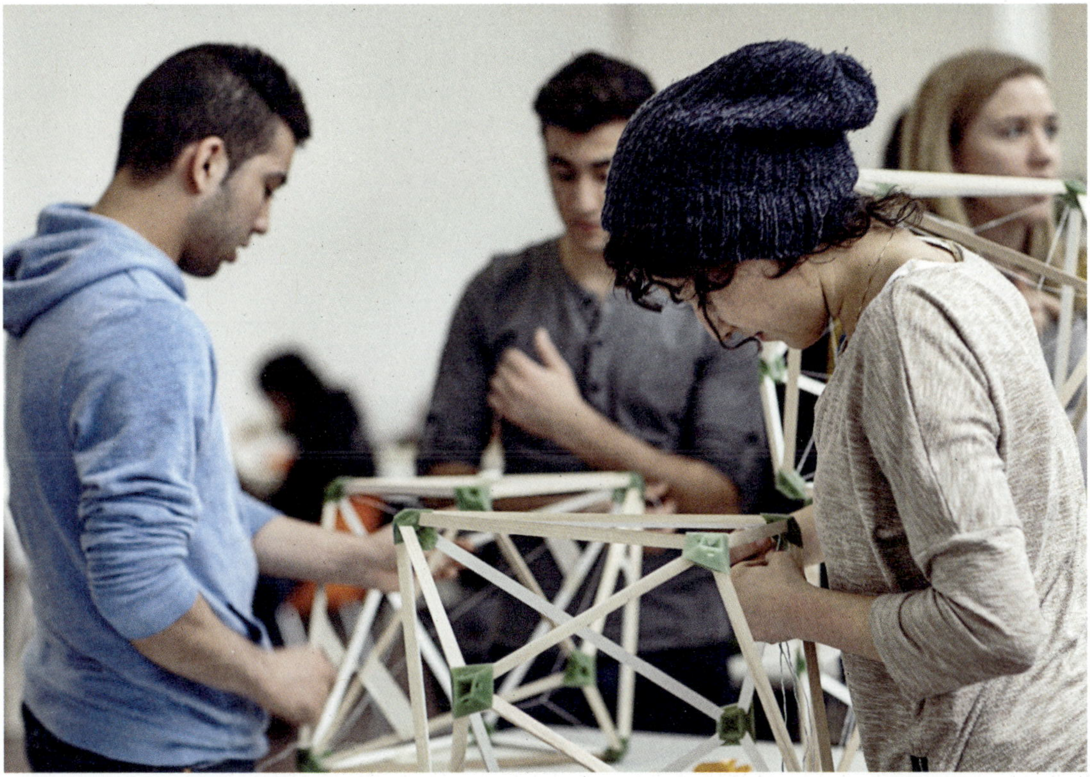

Green light experts Murtaza Azimi, Husseyin Haj Hassan, Anna Schmoll, Ghifar Al Darkazanly, David Weidinger, Markus Schlüter, Kerstin Palermo (p 136); and Milad Amiri, Milad Wasil, Anahita Tabrizi, Borghildur Indridadottir (p 137)

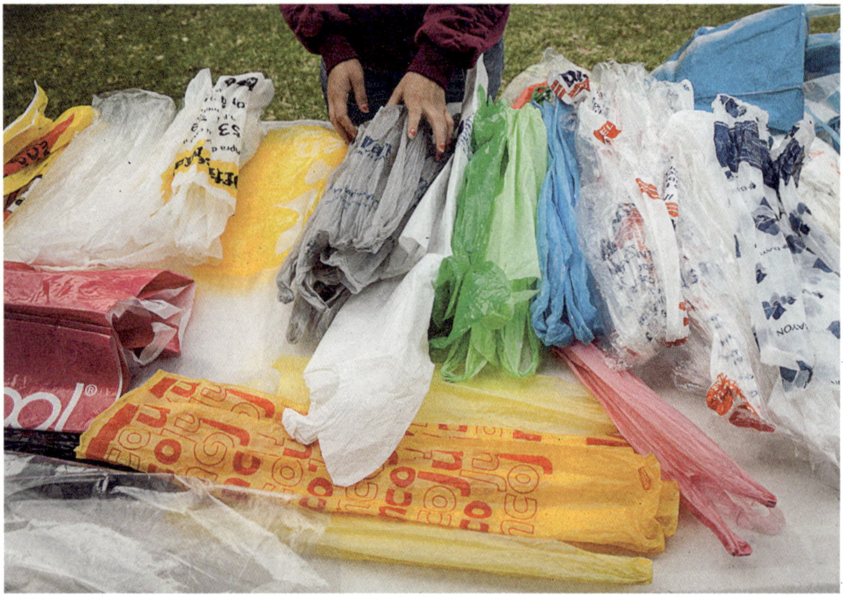

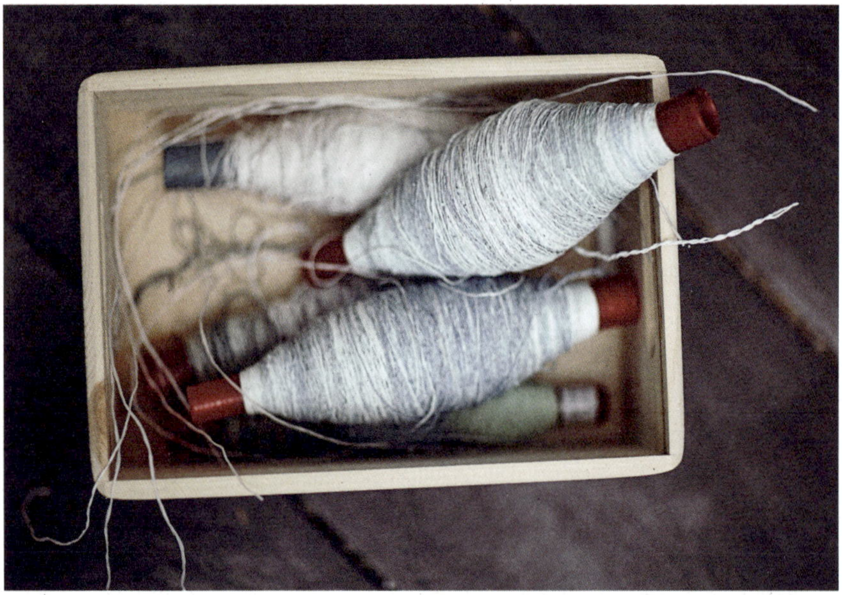

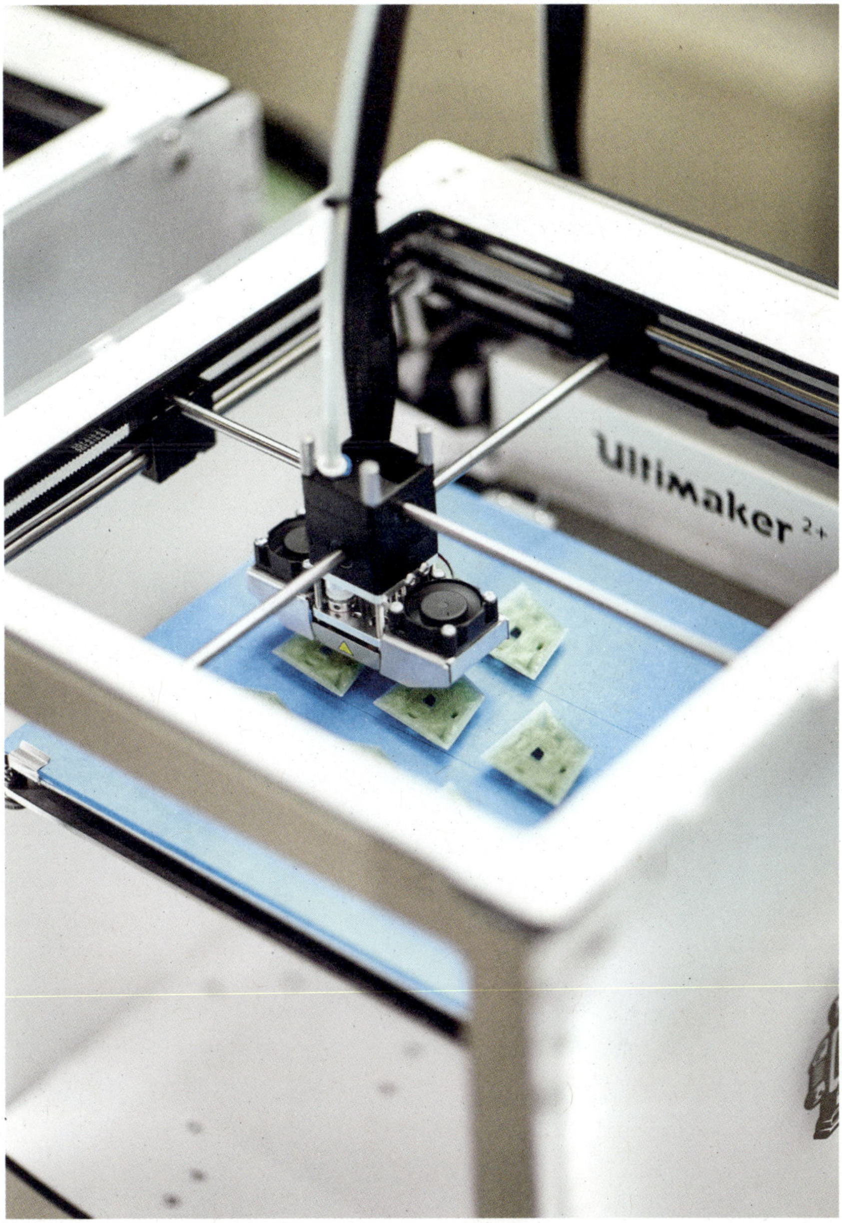
Ultimaker 2+

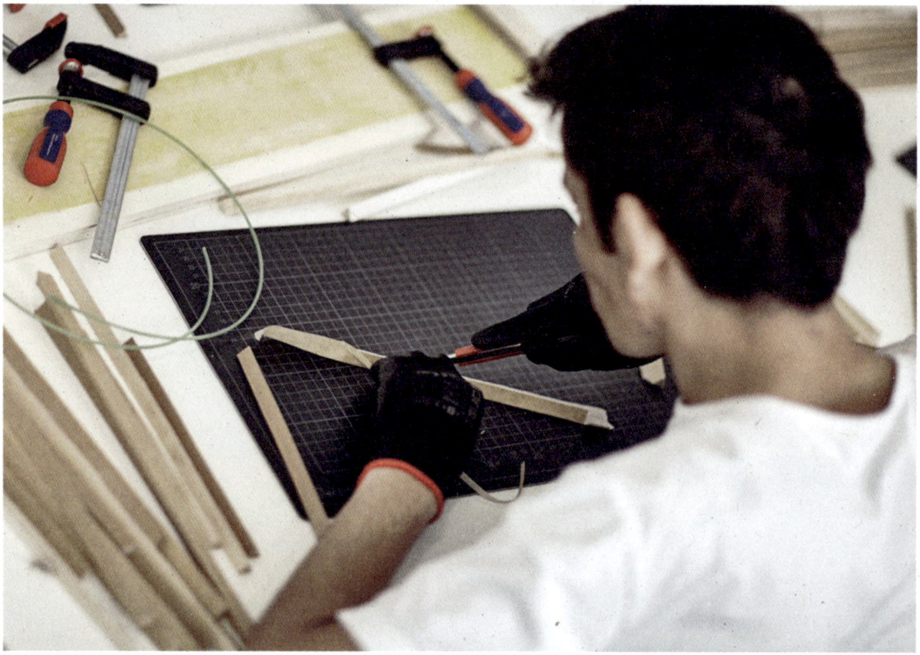

and Shamahmood Ahmadi (p 140); and Sahed Niazi, Milad Amiri, Milad Wasil (p 141)

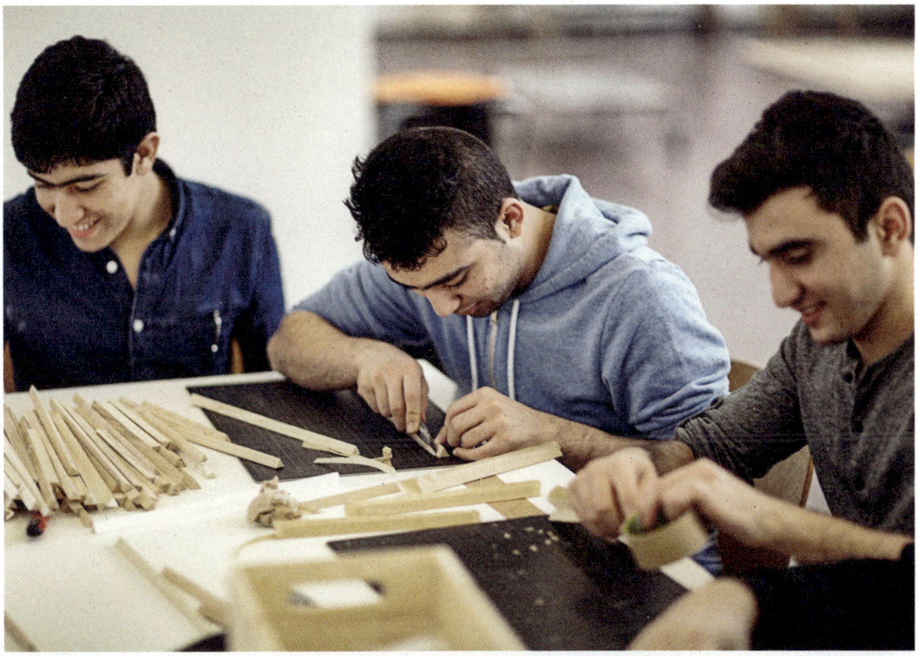

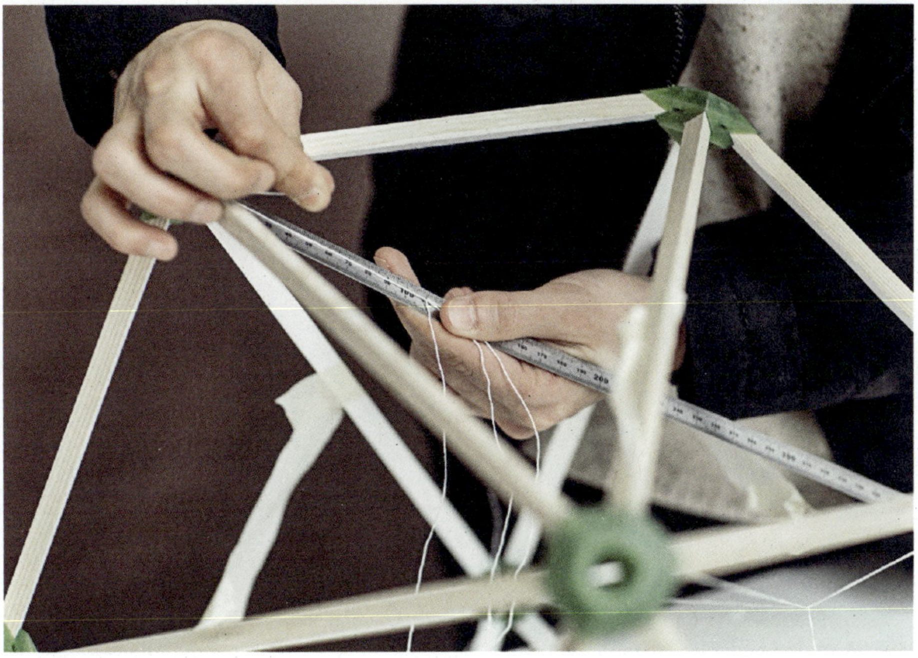

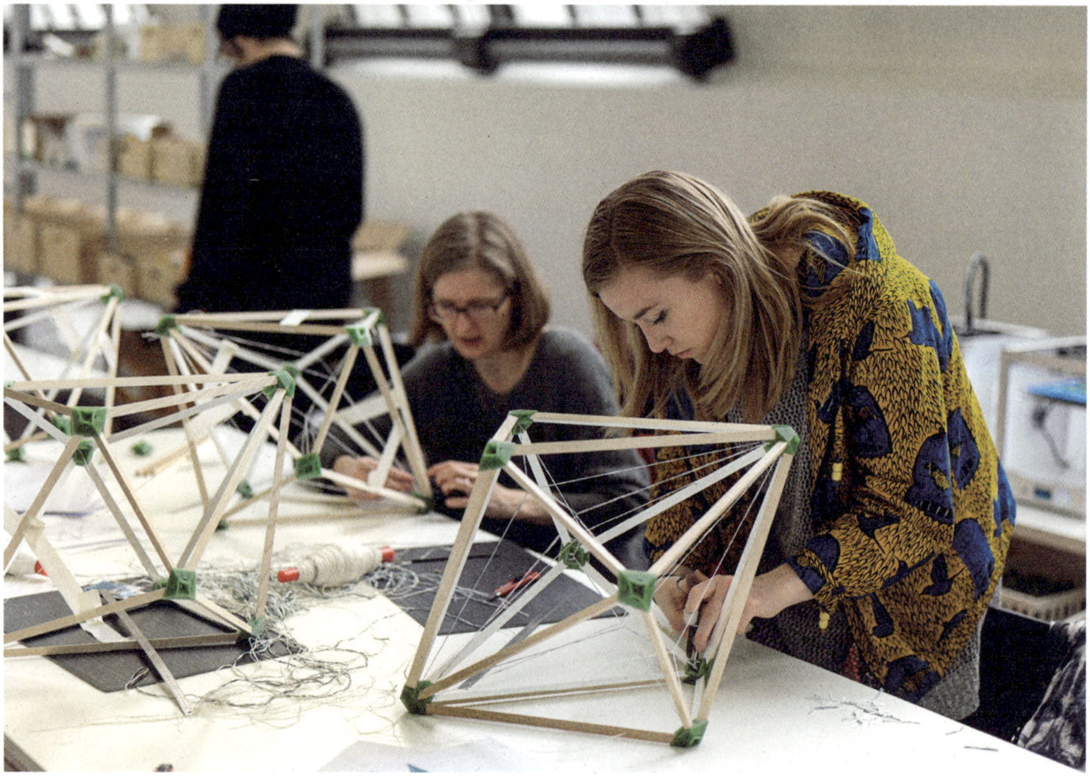

and Kerstin Palermo, Borghildur Indridadottir (p 142);
and Anahita Tabrizi, Aliakbar Ahmadi (p143)

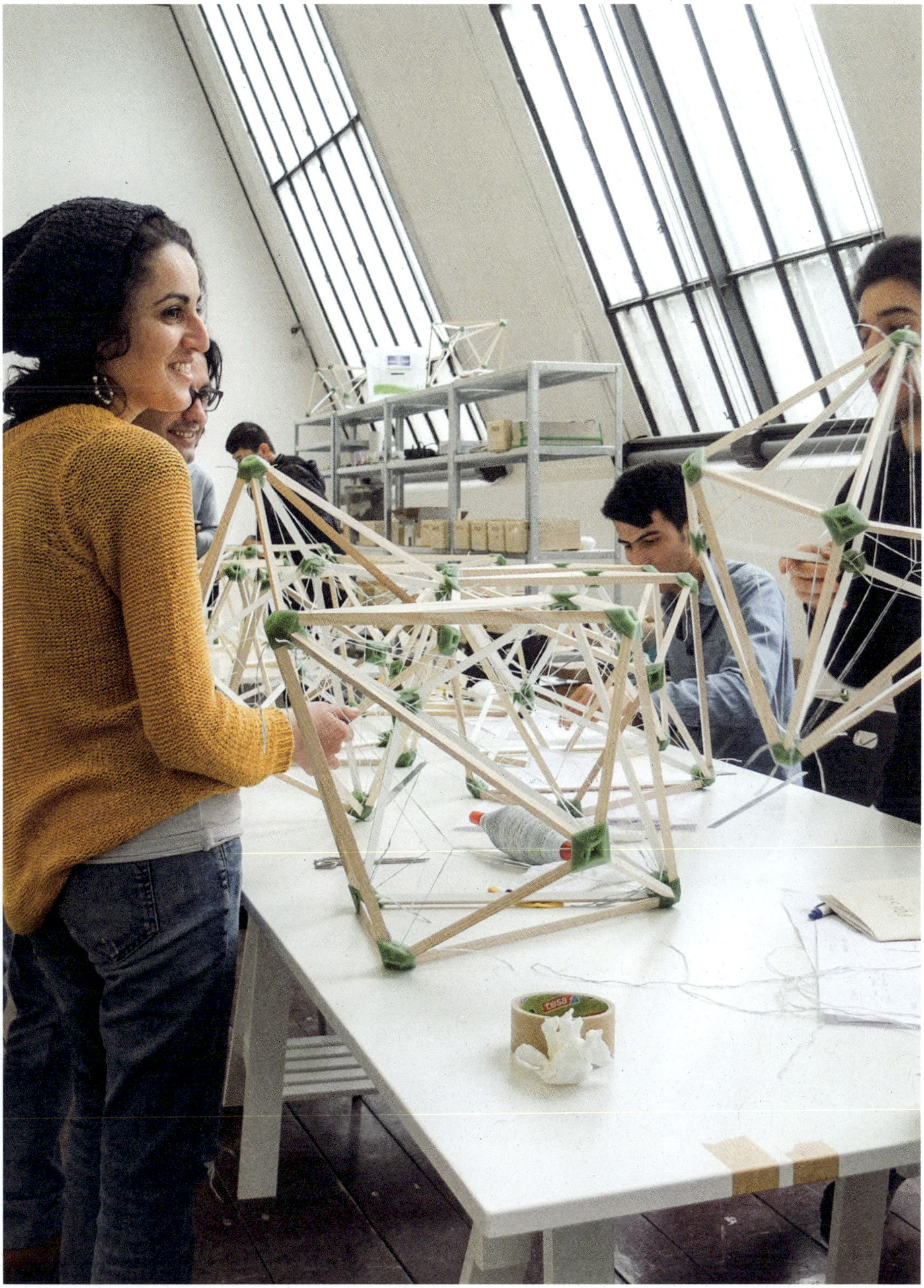
tesa

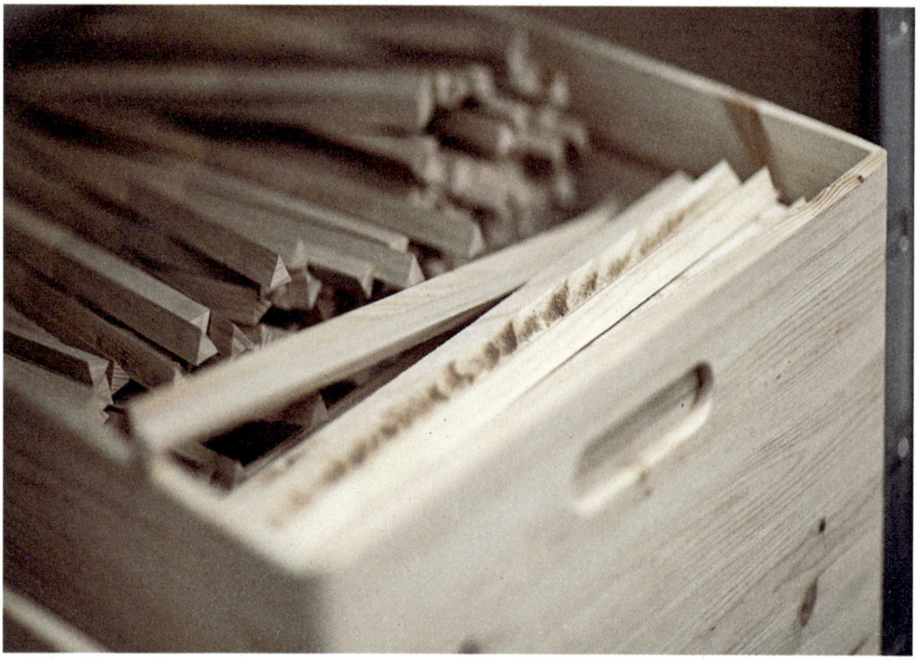

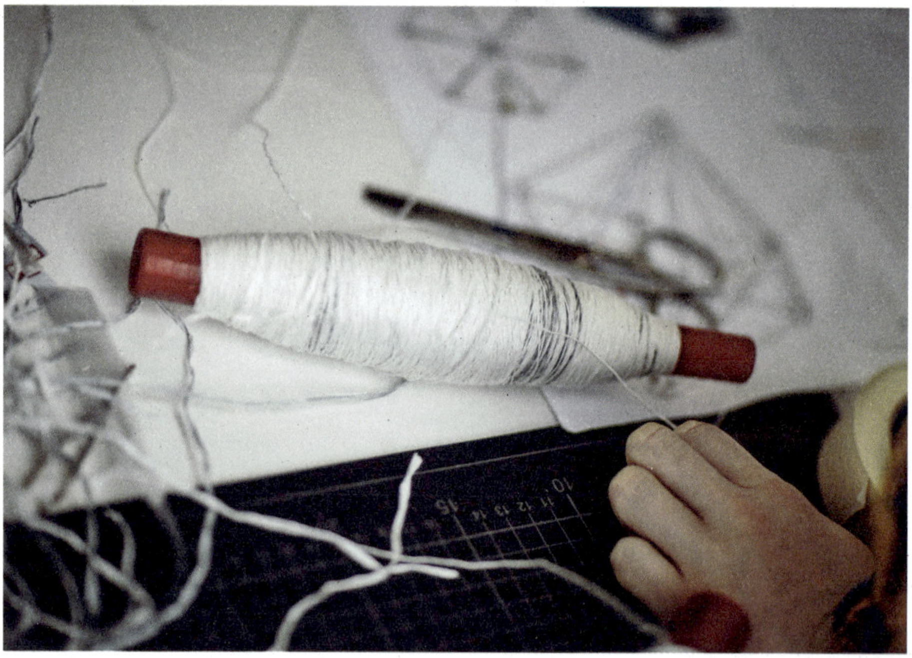

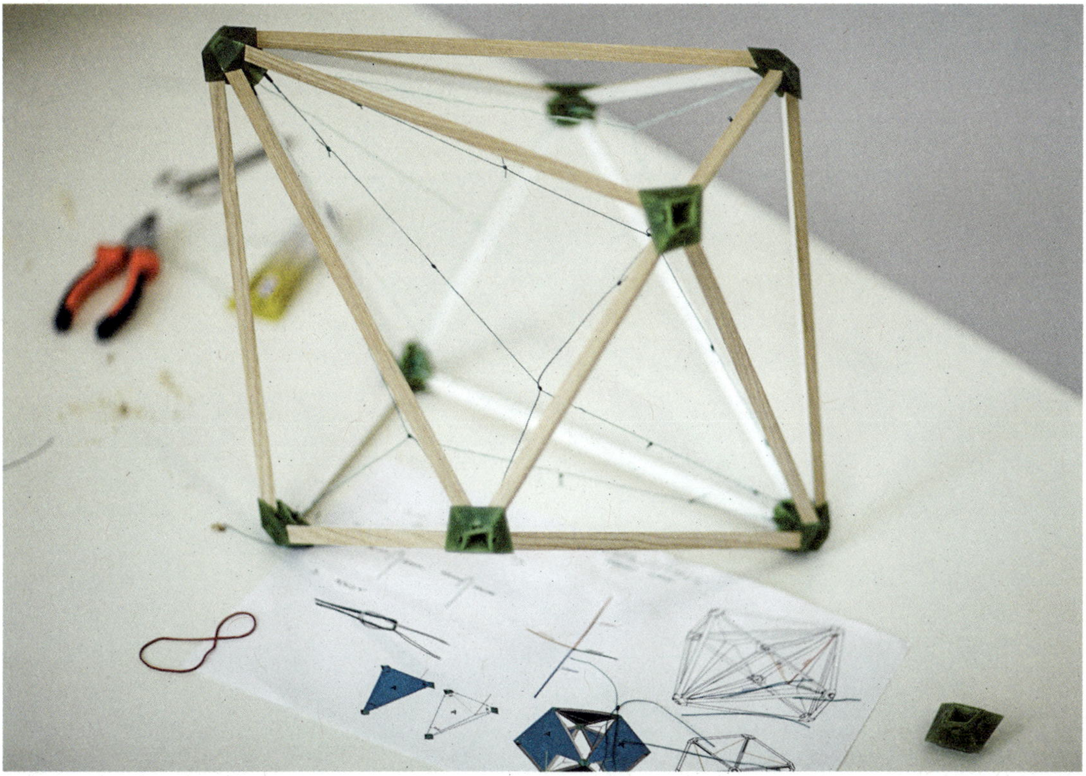

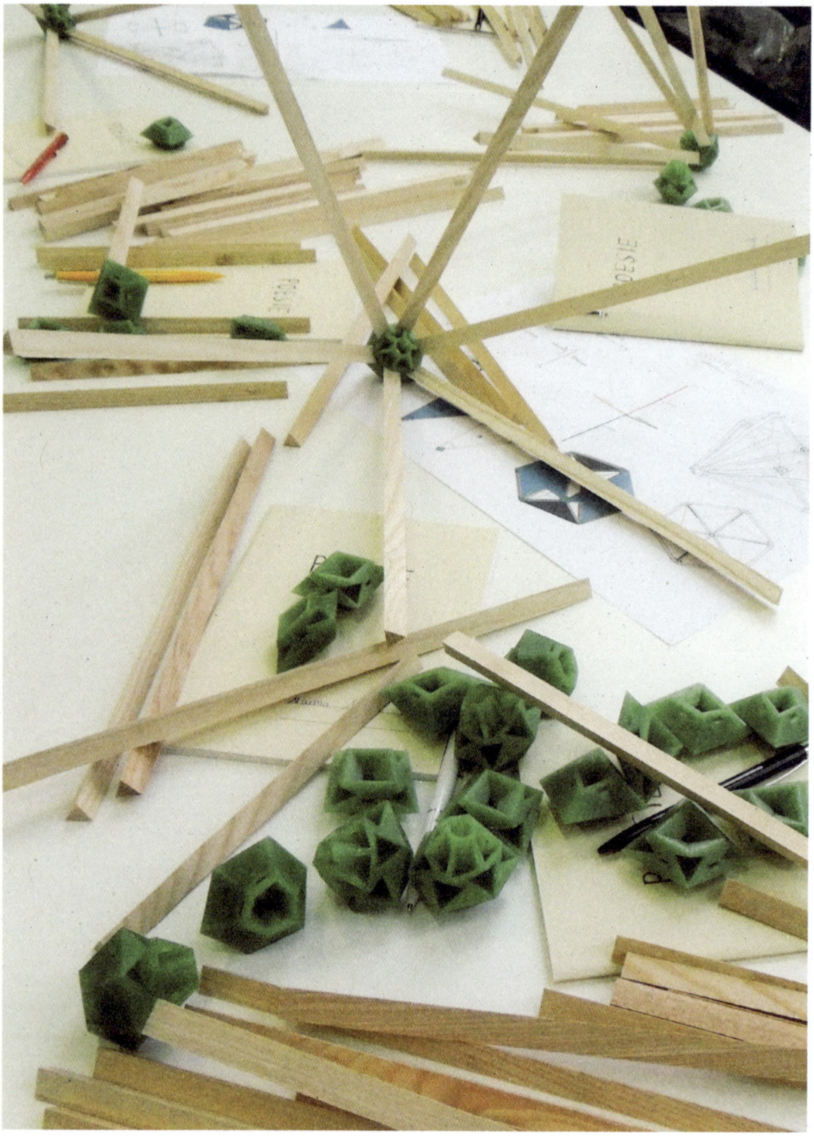

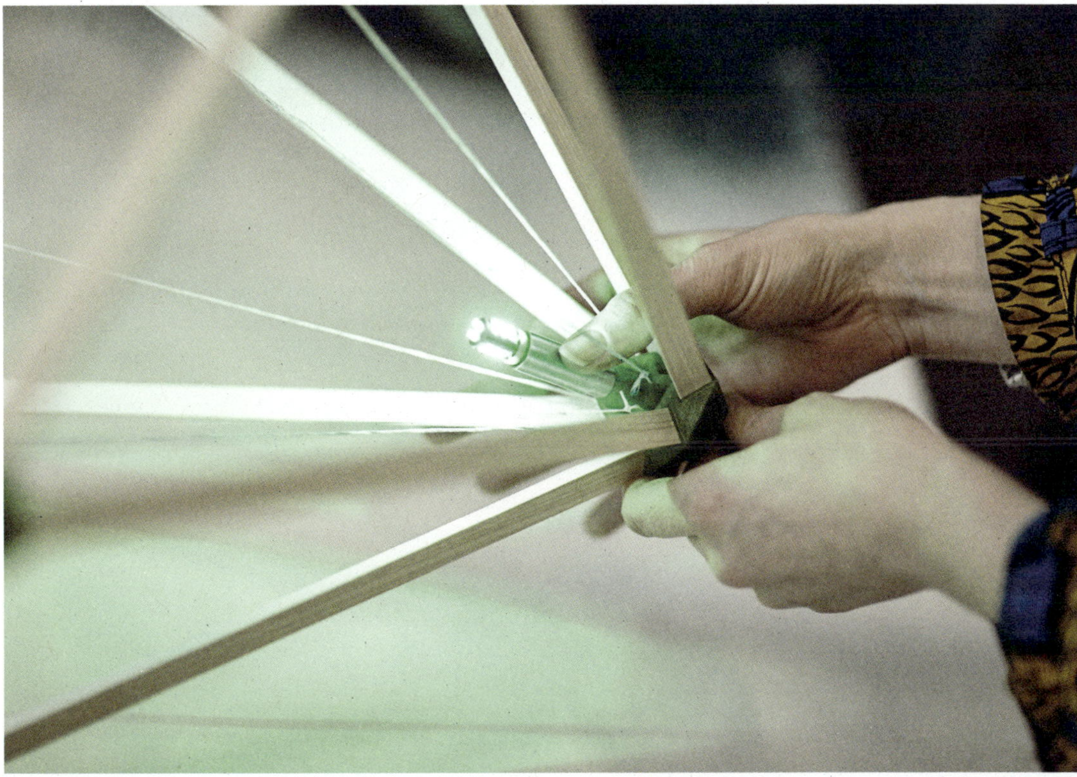

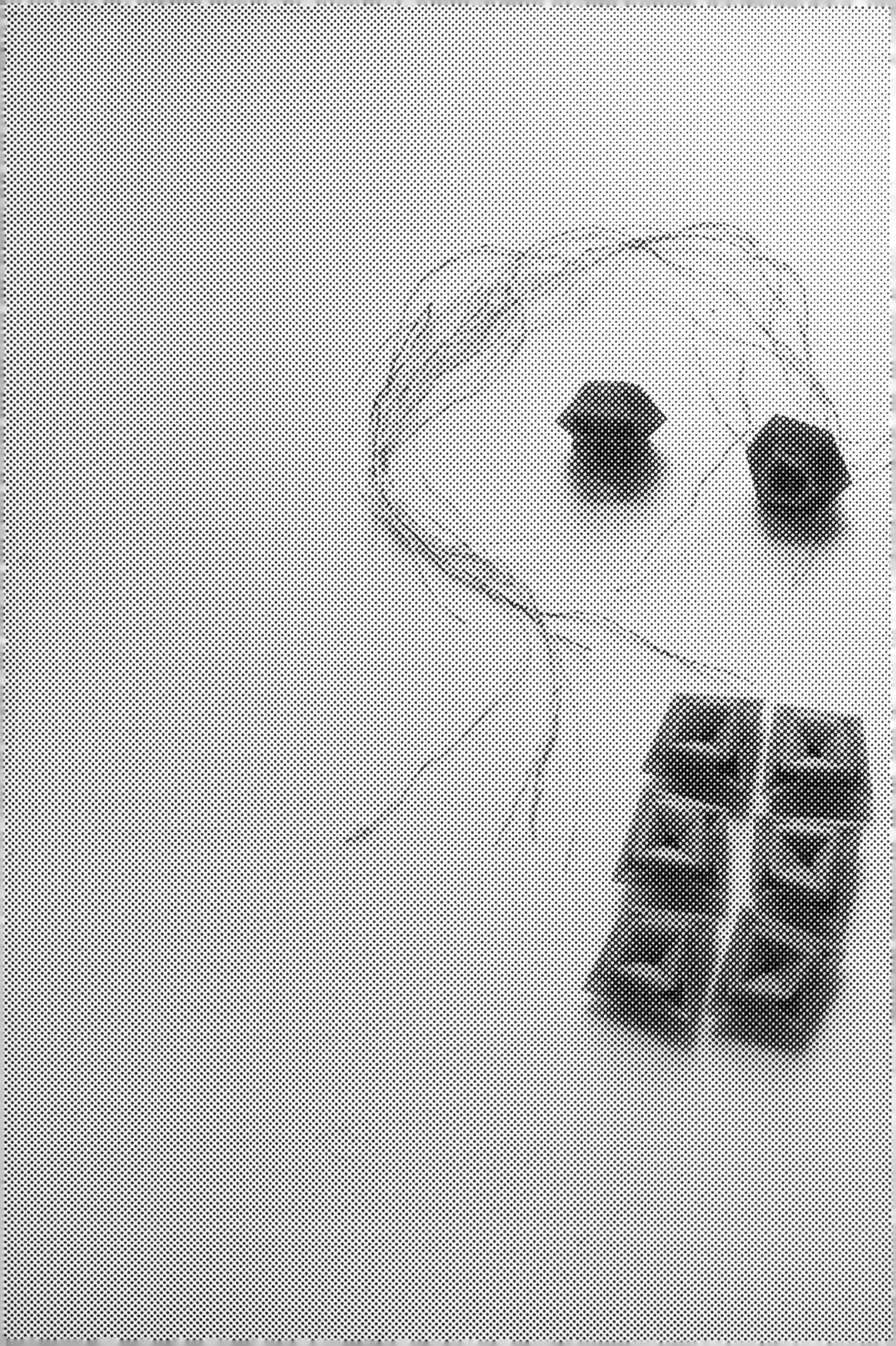

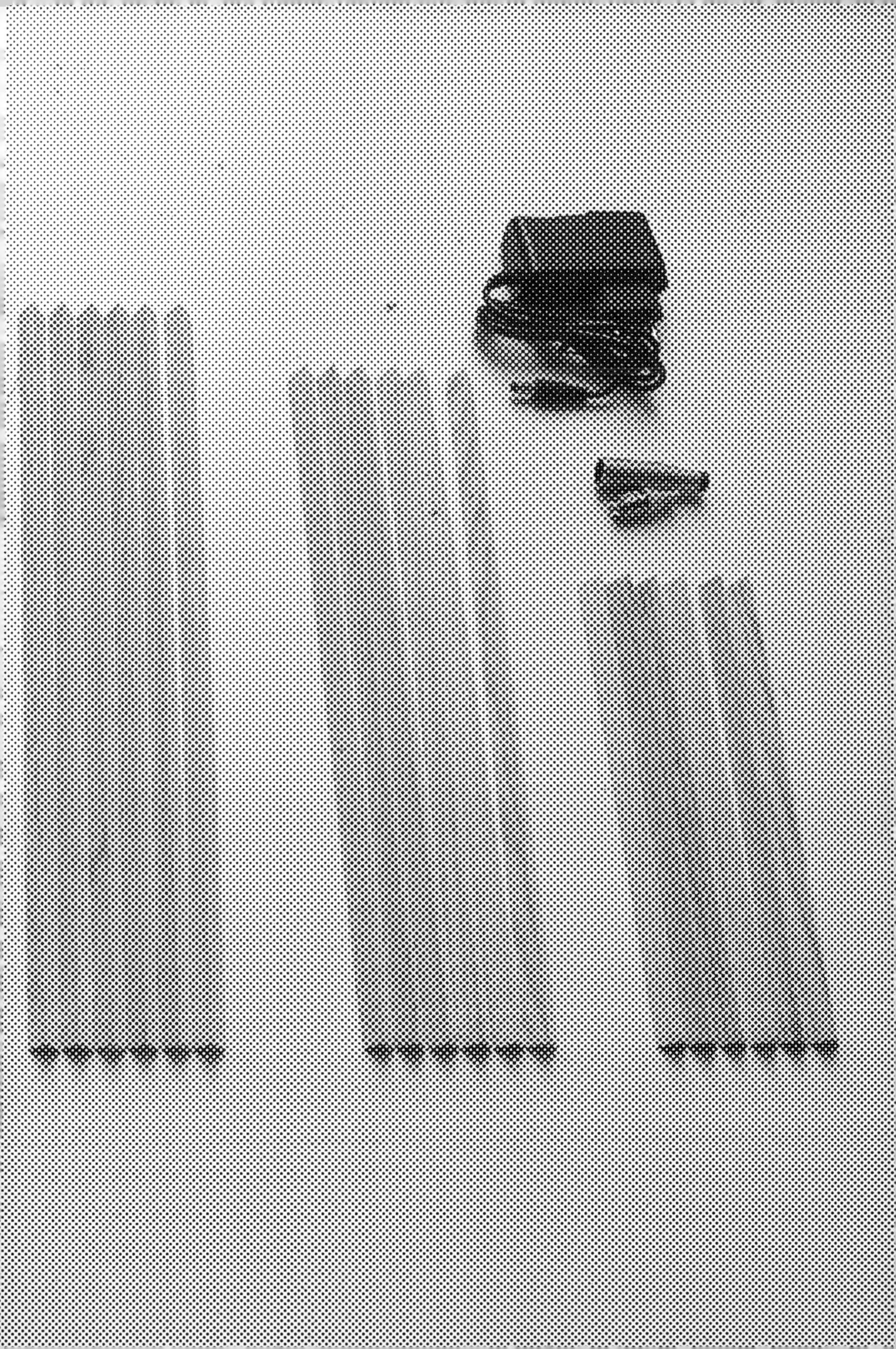

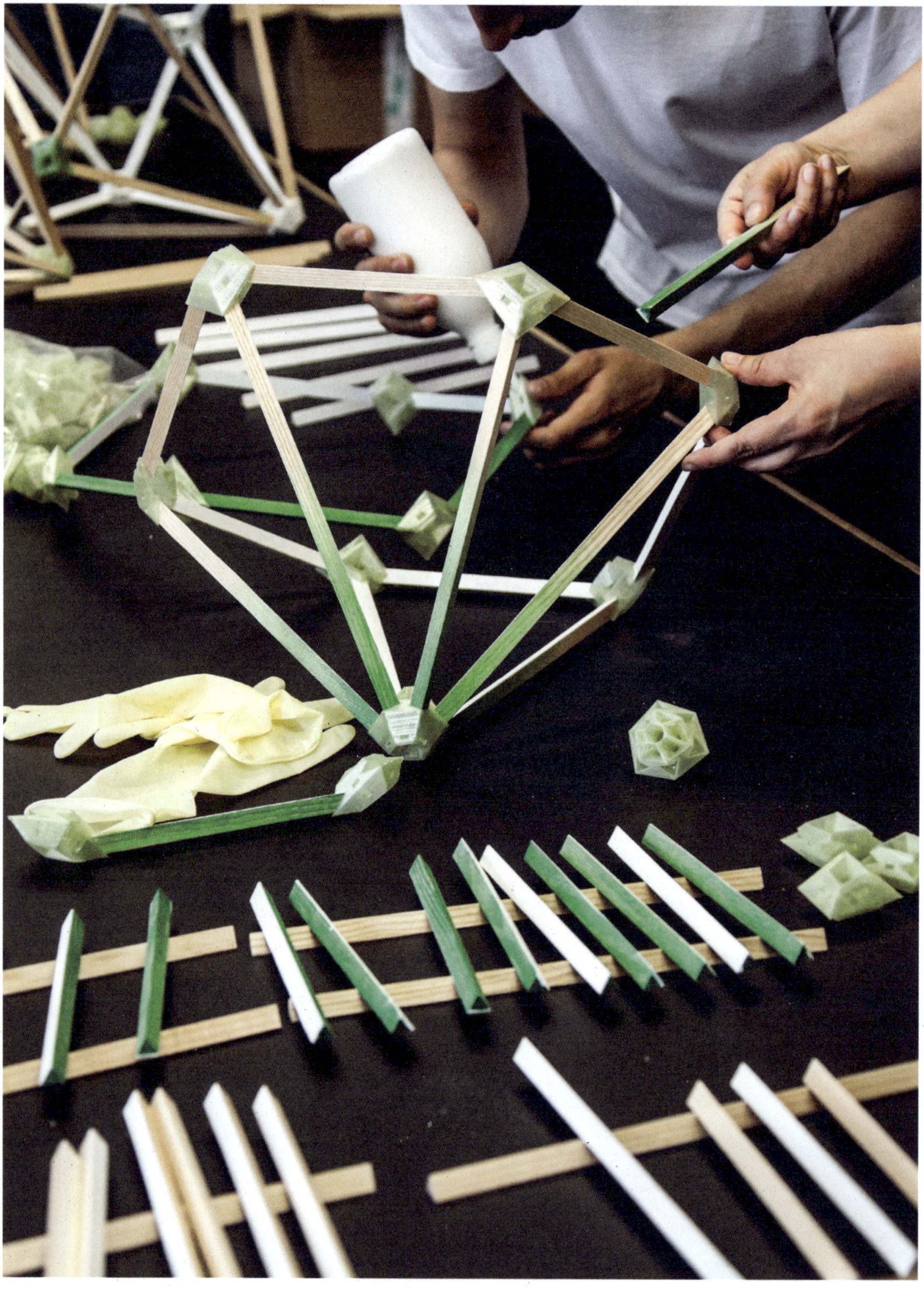

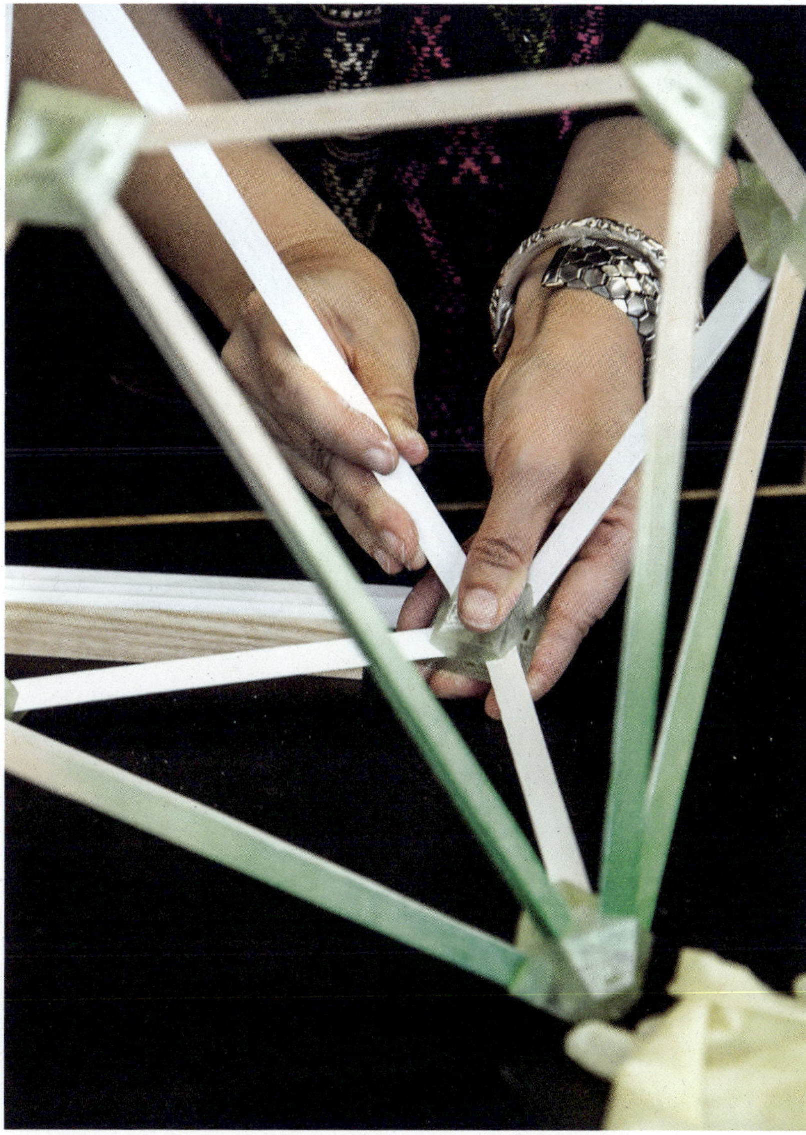

Green light workshop at Studio Olafur Eliasson, Berlin,
in preparation of the Venice Biennale, 2017

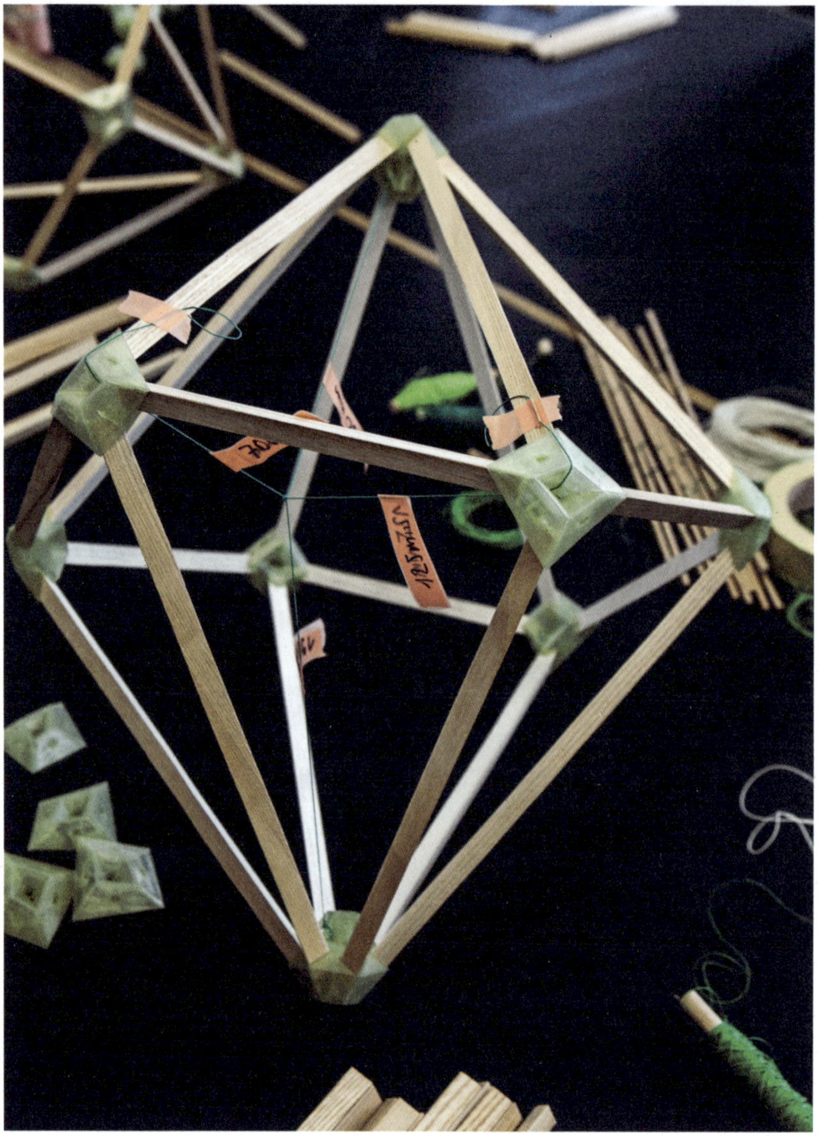

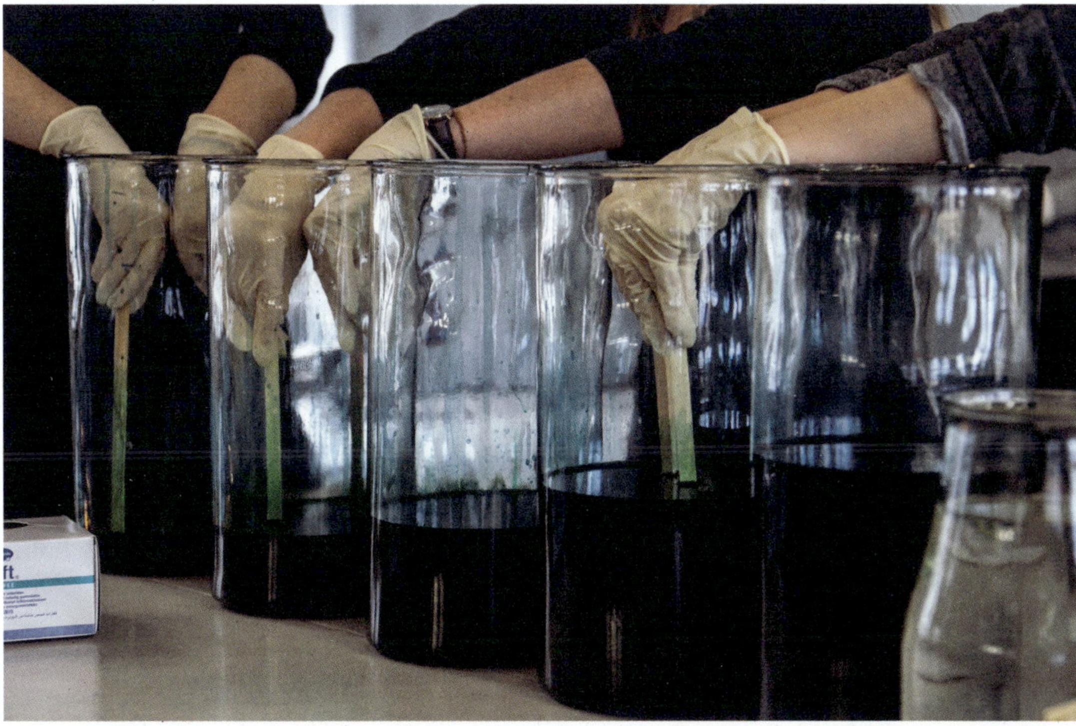

Shared Learning

Franziska Sophie Wildförster

Welcome

If you stepped into the spaces of TBA21–Augarten in Vienna from March to June of 2016, you would have been welcomed by the sound of sanding paper on wooden surfaces, wood sticks rattling, and machines printing, surrounded by a mist of chatter and laughter and music buzzing from mobile phones or the radio. You would have been invited to join the ongoing production process of the *Green light* lamp by people sitting or standing around six large worktables or, depending on the day and time, taking part in one of various activities, such as the weekly theater gatherings and seminars or daily screenings of films by Neil Beloufa, Basma Alsharif, or Marine Hugonnier. Maybe you would simply have come in for a coffee or tea and chat in one of the communal areas. If you were particularly lucky, your visit might have coincided with one of the evening dances, carried by Arabic or Persian tunes and formidable hip swings, or with lunchtime, when food from Syria, Austria, Eritrea, Germany, Iraq, Afghanistan, or Nigeria was prepared and served daily by changing self-organized groups at Augarten's Kiosk. You could have seen one half of the group attending daily German classes, sometimes held outside in the shadow of big trees in the park, or become a participant in one of the workshops initiated, for instance, by the Lebanese sound artist Tarek Atoui, the artist Ahmet Öğüt and his experiential learning platform the Silent University, or Raqs Media Collective's Shuddhabrata Sengupta and his experiments in "world making" through storytelling and video production.[1]

1 The daily German classes conducted by the dedicated Marianna Amon, a teacher at the mytraining educational center in Vienna, were a central element of the *Green light–Shared learning* program. Throughout the three months that

Green light—An artistic workshop and *Green light—Shared learning* were developed as open fields of collective production in the making, led by a group of thirty-four participants who had arrived in Austria over the previous twelve months from Afghanistan, Syria, Iraq, Eritrea, Somalia, Tajikistan, and Nigeria and open to anyone who wished to join. Surrounding the continuous *Green light* workshop as a nexus of modules and activities, *Green light—Shared learning* was conceived as an alternative educational model catering to plurality, and it posed an array of questions and propositions: What if cultural and public institutions opened themselves to interpersonal and intercultural shared learning methods? Can novel perspectives and alternatives to prevailing socio-pedagogical and integrative measures be identified that cater to a multitude of cultural, social, personal, and linguistic histories rather than squeezing them into a phantom *Leitkultur*?

The artistic and discursive expressions relating to the shifting statuses arising from *Green light* and *Green light—Shared learning* are embedded in European societies' migration politics and its shortages: thematizing migration through a "deficit approach" and discourse of problematics. The other possible approach—which supports equal opportunities; participation in terms of social, economic, political, and cultural rights; and essentially reciprocal process—is, however, hardly noticeable in this discussion.[2] The project answered to a double-bind systematic default: a lack of future possibilities for those who slip through the loopholes of the governing legal system and the construction of internal borders that enforce social, economic, cultural, spatial, and personal marginalization.

the project was held at Augarten, two levels (A1 and A2) were taught continuously. Participants who completed the class received certificates. Although this part of the curriculum was essential, given that language is the first and foremost tool to access societies, education, and work opportunities and to navigate and interact with new environments, this aspect of language skill is not the focus of this essay. In this specific line of thought, translation is, beyond linguistics, understood as shifts of perspective and changes of status—expressions of heterogeneity and plurality fostered in the artistic curriculum and defying a ruling idiom and masterful expertise.

2 See Stephan Lanz, "In unternehmerische Subjekte investieren: Integrationskonzepte im Workfare-Staat; Das Beispiel Berlin," in *No Integration!*, ed. Sabine Hess et al. (Bielefeld: Transcript, 2007), 105–22.

Endorsing the art institution as a place for critical pedagogy by, for instance, providing the democratic conditions of education, *Shared learning* asks how one could, in a collective effort, create spaces and methods that recognize non-hierarchical value systems of equal expression, argument, and knowledge. Shifting expertise from social workers and state institutions to artists and cultural stakeholders, this educational experiment's aim to establish a dynamic of sharing knowledge, which besides, or instead of, disseminating the hegemonic value system allows for a more flexible practice that also considers current issues and the needs of the participants. How do we allow for relations and understandings to *unlearn* conditionings of privileged social systems that prejudice behavior toward and expectations of the "other"?

The Plural of *We*

The modules and events of this three-month experimental curriculum were manifold. And so were the methodologies of challenging understandings of "we." Who is included, who stands outside of particular constructions of groups or communities? How can an ephemeral interaction constitute a larger disruption in internalized social and cultural habits?

Green light reimagined the rules of acting together reciprocally and through cohabitation: in the daily *Green light* workshop or in German classes and cooking sessions or in weekly initiatives. The latter included Displaced, in which students and teachers from the Faculty of Architecture at the Technical University worked with physical and process-oriented productions; History(ies) of Migration, in which members of the Department of Social Design of the University of Applied Arts organized reading and debate groups over tea and homemade sweets; and the Austrian artist Johannes Porsch's invitation to a "theater without theater," in which the participants acted without the guidance of a story but collectively worked with the given situation and circumstances.

The participating artists tried to conceive of alternative educational models and approaches to knowledge production through interpersonal activities, striving to take another subject's perspective and position through enacting, narrating, and recording. They reflected on education without an emphasis on the production of expertise. Learning from one another means believing in the arrivals as individuals and actants who can significantly shape societies and selves. It manifests itself in room for the personal element, those "unpredictable" elements that may be forces of destabilization and re-creation of systems, as Olafur Eliasson reflects in his conversation with Andreas Roepstorff.[3]

Ahmet Öğüt, to cite an example, was invited to present and activate the methodology of the Silent University, a "solidarity-based knowledge exchange platform" with curricula developed by refugees and migrants for refugees and migrants, as a means to reactivate knowledge, professions, and studies that can no longer be practiced due to the members' status. Answering to the fact that most asylum seekers are forced into inactivity and boredom and cut off from their accustomed social lives, Öğüt had planned to research and discuss alternative educational systems in Austria with the *Green light* participants. A synergy of coincidental visitors, Öğüt, and the participants resulted in a still ongoing weekly gathering known as the Talent Space, in which students at the local communications college and former *Green light* participants at Augarten share and foster talents, knowledge, and resources. Alarabi Rabhi was a carpenter back in West Sahara, and Ali Azouky worked as a book illustrator and cartoonist in Syria. More than a year after having arrived in Vienna, neither has had the chance to practice his profession, as they are held in a gray zone of legal status and social borders. The gatherings at Augarten provide one of those rare spaces in which the status of "refugee," "asylum seeker," "migrant," or "Austrian" are not of primary importance, and novel kinds of "we" can be woven beyond origins, nationalities, or religion and continue to flourish.

Translations

These novel configurations of "we" underlay subtle daily processes of translation. They are ways of finding understanding that exceed linguistics and challenge dominant idioms in a play of similarity and difference, as suggested by the Polish sociologist and philosopher Zygmunt Bauman:

> Translating is not an idle occupation for a limited circle of specialists, it is the texture of everyday life, the work that we perform

3 The events mentioned here are a necessarily abbreviated selection of a multitude of weekly changing events initiated during the fifteen weeks of *Shared learning*.

> each day and each hour of the day ... The possibility of universalism lies precisely in this common capacity to reach an effective communication without possessing in advance common meanings and interpretations. Universality is not antagonistic with differences; it does not require a "cultural homogeneity," or a "cultural purity," much less the kind of practices that are evoked by this ideological notion ... Universality is only the capacity of communication and mutual understanding, which is common to all groups, in the sense of "knowing how to proceed" reciprocally, but also knowing how to proceed when confronted with others who have the right to proceed in a different manner.[4]

Two further examples from *Shared learning* may illuminate such simultaneity of mutual understanding and the untranslatability of irreducible difference. For his workshop, the artist, composer, and musician Tarek Atoui, who has been fostering collective approaches to composition and improvisation, arrived with his self-made instruments and a couple of ideas about what could be done in a short period of time with a group that he did not know and could hardly anticipate. In a project catering to the diversity of the group, *Green lighters* and interested participants recorded their environments with microphones—the park, the city, activities within the institution, instruments, speech and chants, the making of *Green light* as well as interviews and conversations—in teams. On the second day the sounds were composed into a collective acoustic experience: a sound piece of manifold listening abilities and acoustic encounters, with a narrative loosely divided into three parts: "journey," "arrival," and "Green light." Toward the end of the piece, a conversation between inscribed visitor Veit and *Green light* participant Murtaza Azimi emerges. Veit asks Murtaza what the *Green light* means to him. Murtaza answers that when he saw the *Green light* for the first time it triggered memories of diamonds. He continues to tell the story of his journey from Afghanistan to Austria with a stop in Iran for several months, where he worked under rough conditions in a diamond mine to keep himself and his younger sister afloat. Now the *Green light* represents a sense of the future for him.

4 Zygmunt Bauman, cited in Étienne Balibar, "Strangers as Enemies: Further Reflections on the Aporias of Transnational Citizenship" (paper presented at the Institute on Globalization and the Human Condition, McMaster University, Hamilton, Ontario, March 16, 2006).

In his workshop titled "Memory and Mobility: On What It Means to Get Up and Go," Shuddhabrata Sengupta equally facilitated engagement with the transformation of memories, connotations, and concepts. Stories, testimonies, and poems on concepts of "future" or "light" were captured in self-made videos. The intimate narratives by Anas Aljajeh, Qasim Tahmasebi, and Tawab Baran stemming from this encounter can be read in this volume and were shared in front of a large crowd of visitors at *15 Acts of Participation* at TBA21–Augarten (an open event featuring various presentations by *Green light* participants and invited guests that contextualized the project). Tawab's poem voices the despair that is the heritage of Afghans: "I fled but now you say I should return," a line reads. The seventeen-year-old tries to make understood what it feels like to have been forced to leave one's home under hardship and not be welcomed in the new place. Sixteen-year-old Qasim reveals that the only memories he has of his childhood are those of fire, blood, and war. After months and years of traveling to Austria, he now has room to imagine a future that is not war but that is, however, very uncertain.

Strangers as Enemies as Neighbors as Co-citizens

Since the inception of *Green light*, when "Refugees are welcome" seemed the sentiment of the majority in European receiving countries and large crowds showed overwhelming solidarity with the arrivals—welcoming them with clapping hands and encouraging words and spending hours at train and bus stations to offer clothing, water and food, translation services, and housing—the public mood has shifted. Today the borders are closed again, and the camps have been moved back to the edges of Europe. Today the welcoming culture is largely regarded as irresponsible, integration as failed, differences as insurmountable.

What the French philosopher Étienne Balibar describes as "rapid transformations of the status of borders" seems to be amplified and epitomized by the right-wing ideologies in Europe and elsewhere. Borders are not understood merely as architectural fences or walls but are of a legal nature, manifested as police actions or taking more sophisticated forms in social and cultural everyday life. Balibar writes: "I see citizenship not as a fixed notion, as a permanently open problem, which has already been subjected historically to mutations, collapses, and redefinition. In recent discussions concerning the new functions of borders and their relationship to Europe's becoming, not exactly a 'sovereign' entity, but rather what we might call a 'space of exception,' it has been a question not only of the fact that 'borders' tend to become really dislocated, if not ubiquitous, but also of another characteristic which has to do with the inversion of the relationship between the 'border' and the 'stranger/foreigner.'" [5]

Imagining the stranger or foreigner as produced and reproduced by multiple, dislocated borders that are not stable, Balibar here evokes an understanding similar to Sandra Noeth's account in this publication, in which she refers to boundaries as moveable, volatile, changed or in relation between selves and others: "Borders are spaces in their own right—they are always in a state of becoming, always unfinished. Permeable and porous, visceral and felt, the border is situated in—it is part of—my body. [...] *The movement of the border is restless, disquieting. Oftentimes it is creeping, gradual, accumulating, delayed, anonymous. Often it is perceived much later, like an echo in the rhythm of life. Like a continuous state of displacement, unfolding slowly.*"

The moments and events of subtle transformations, shifts of perspective and status between self and other triggered and nourished within *Green light* and particularly *Green light—Shared learning* counter restricted views on translation implied in mass education as well as integration measures. They describe vital and conflictual daily practices of communication and understanding, of taking someone else's point of view, that create disturbances in a well-versed system. They confirm that individuals are not being reduced to their place of origin or immigration status but are regarded as co-producers, and maybe co-citizens, in an act of constantly rebuilding processes of kinship and configurations of "we." These are processes of *unlearning*—comprising the realization that internalized, institutionalized, and socialized othering and bordering can be reversed if we recognize our own situations and contributions to subtle structures of domination and are thus able to take another subject's viewpoint.[6] This is where *Green light* and *Green light—Shared learning* are anchored, finding their most meaningful contributions to rethinking integration as a reciprocal participatory process.

5 Balibar, "Strangers as Enemies," 4.

6 Sara Danius, Stefan Jonsson, and Gayatri Chakravorty Spivak, "An Interview with Gayatri Chakravorty Spivak," *Boundary 2* 20, no. 2 (1993): 24.

AHMET ÖĞÜT
The Silent University—*Orientation Module*
A *Green light—Shared learning* workshop

Vienna May 7–8, 2016

Artist Ahmet Öğüt invited the *Green light* participants to join a two-day research initiative on alternative models of learning and teaching in the context of the Silent University. Initiated by Öğüt in 2012, the Silent University is an autonomous, solidarity-based knowledge exchange platform by refugees, asylum seekers, and migrants who have had a professional life and academic training in their home countries but are unable to use their skills in their current environments due to their (legal and other) status. It provides a platform for knowledge transfer, circumventing the bureaucratic legal structures that may limit the possibilities of intellectual exchange.

Through the *Orientation Module*, the participants in *Green light* became active fellows and contributors to the steadily shaping and expanding network of the Silent University. Researching alternative learning facilities and initiatives that can be used as tools to navigate their own future in Austria, and charting potential educational models that could fit it, the participants created a space of agency within the restrictive legal fabric of Europe. This workshop culminated in the creation of Talent Space at Augarten, a series of project-based programs that engages individual based on their talents rather than their status.

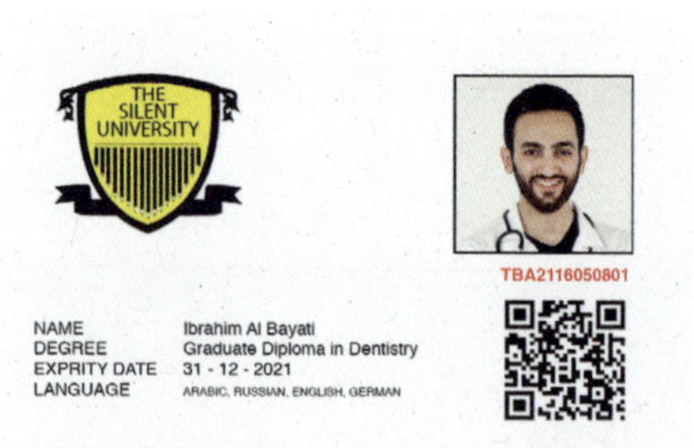

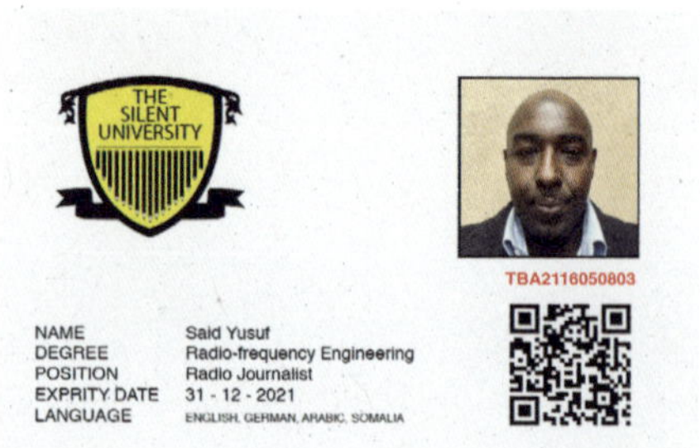

Towards A Transversal Pedagogy
The Silent University Principles and Demands:

1. Everybody has the right to educate.

2. Immediate acknowledgement of academic backgrounds of asylum seekers and refugees.

3. Acting knowledge without language limitations.

4. Acting knowledge without legal limitations.

5. Participatory modes of usership.

6. Artistic pedagogical practices need to be emancipated from commonly used terminologies such as "projects" and "workshops".

7. Pedagogic practices must be based on long-term engagement, commitment and determination.

8. We act in solidarity with other refugee struggles and collectives around the world.

9. Extra-territorial, trans-local knowledge production and conflict urbanism must be priorities.

10. Decentralized, participatory, horizontal and autonomous modality of education, instead of centralized, authoritarian, oppressive, and compulsory education.

11. Acting beyond limitations of border politics.

12. Adhocracy instead of bureaucracy.

13. Action Knowledge can only be produced through assemblage methods.

14. Revolution of decolonising pedagogies.

TAREK ATOUI
***Green light*–Soundtrack**
A *Green light–Shared learning* workshop

In his two-day workshop at TBA21, the Lebanese sound artist, composer, and musician Tarek Atoui gathered a variety of recordings—of instruments, sounds, noises, speech, laughter, the city, and even a musical installation in Vienna's canalization system—with the *Green light* participants and interested visitors, to compose a collectively fabricated acoustic experience.

Exploring the construction of community, spatial compositions, and the diversity of listening abilities, this joint archive elaborates (ex-) changes that take place through acoustic encounters, listening together, and conversations about music and approximates an acoustic narrative in three parts: mobility and travel, arrival, and the activities and resonances of *Green light—An artistic workshop*.

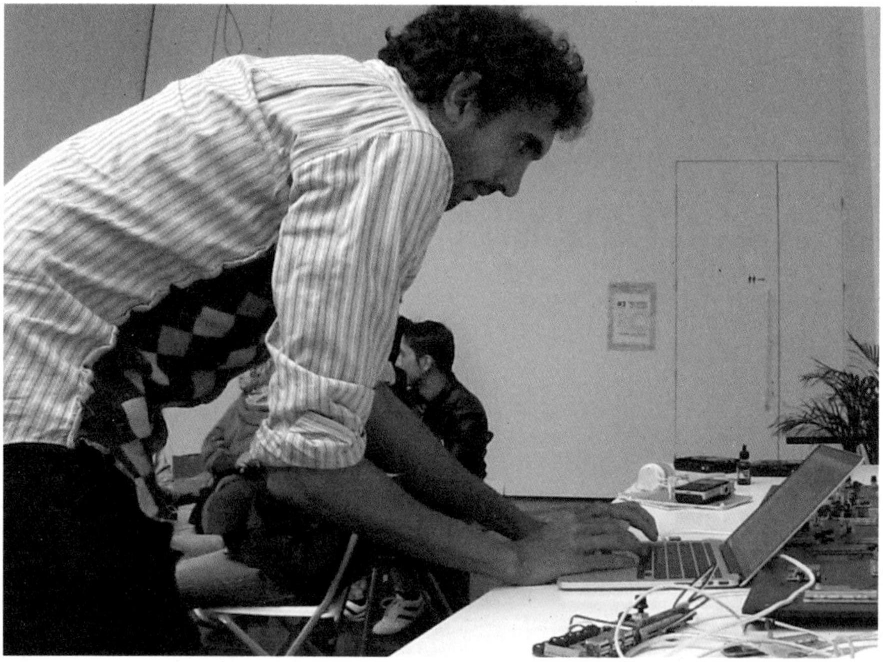

Recordings done by Shamahmood Ahmadi, Ibrahim Al Bayati, Naima Ali, Milad Amiry, Majid Ayubi, Murtaza Azimi, Fatima Chuchari, Ella Felber, Huseyin Haj Hassan, Liya Kasa, Homa Khosrawi, Ibrahim Mawazini, Zia Oryakhel, Hans Schultze, Ewa Sklodowska, Qasim Tahmasebi, Rut Marrow Theodórsdóttir and Vid Jeraj in collaboration with Tarek Atoui.

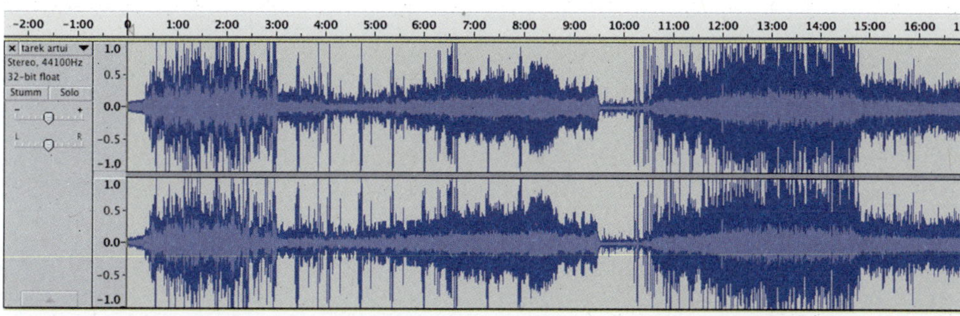

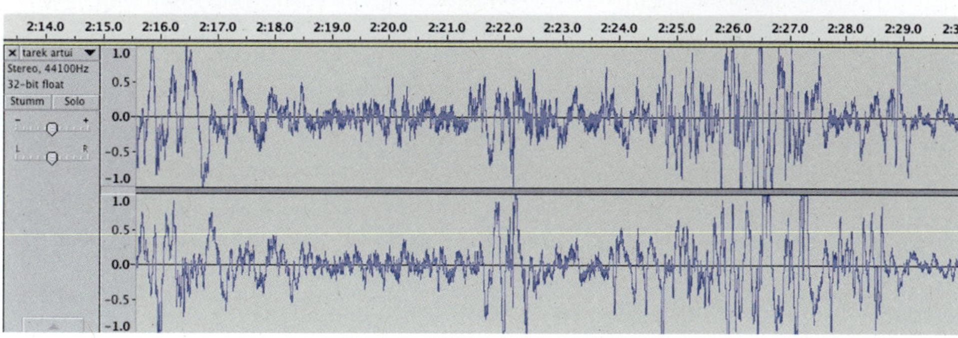

Sounds recorded in the context of freq_out 12 [the last edition] at the Third Man sewer in Vienna. Curated by Carl Michael von Hausswolff and Franz Pomassl. Additional tracks by Robert Aiki Aubrey Lowe & Keith Fullerton Whitman.

DAVID RYCH

Border Act Revisited

A *Green light—Shared learning* workshop

The first interview is a key component of the asylum application process in most European countries, and is without doubt the most important occasion for asylum seekers to explain in detail why they had to leave their country of origin.

On the base of what the authorities are told, they will try to determine whether asylum will be granted or refused. The central question they pose to applicants is whether they experienced persecution or violence, or if they fear it upon return to their home countries, for reasons such as belonging to a specific ethnic group, their gender or sexual orientation, or their political or religious views. During the interview the asylum seeker will be asked to recall details from memory, which are then checked for contradictions, though certain narratives occasionally recur, passed on between migrants, which are said to convince the authorities to grant protection. But what makes a story credible? How does a convincing performance enhance the narrative? How to maintain the integrity of a role? These and similar questions came up during the workshop, in which participants took part in a roleplaying exercise in which they perform as asylum seekers, while at the same time mentally preparing for an interrogation by the authorities at the migration office. Awareness, spontaneity, imagination, and introspection are all elementary aspects of improvisational theater. In a series of intensive sessions with a trained theater pedagogue, the group was familiarized with a number of exercises and techniques preceding a series of stage performances which would directly connect to their personal situation.

Border Act was the title of an art project based on a research on migrant narratives originally carried out in 2015, in which artist David Rych worked with refugees in an identical live setting, which served as a fictitious scenario in which to negotiate reality. The project resulted in an immersive 3D video installation, which would allow the viewer to experience the scene without any restrictions of perspective. *Border Act* is ultimately about point of view, questioning the visual modalities of the documentary format as much as the inherent attempt to establish truth—in parallel with the effort of a jury to determine if a story fulfills all criteria to pass as evidence.

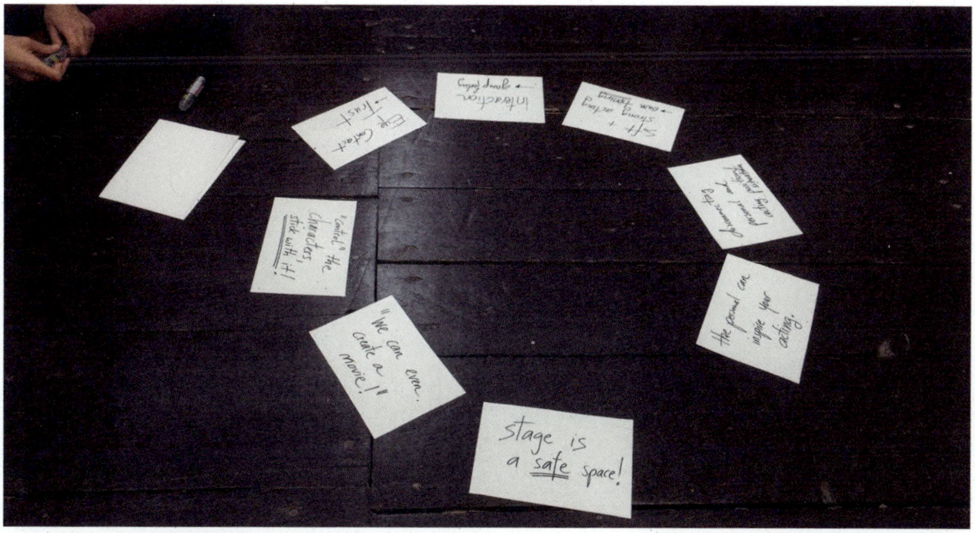
Stage is a safe space!
"We can even create a movie!"
The sound can inspire your acting.
"Control" the characters, stick with it!
Eye Contact
Trust

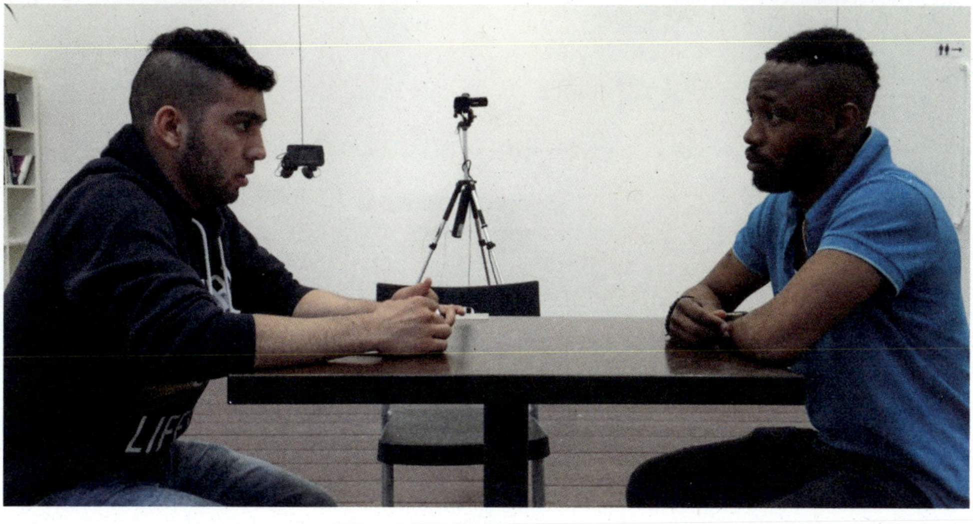

You must have control of your life

Tahajud Alghrabi (48) is from Baghdad, Iraq, where she used to work as a school principal. Following the US invasion in 2004, she migrated between Iraq, Syria, Jordan, and Turkey. In the summer of 2015, along with her husband and their two sons (aged eighteen and twenty), she came to Austria. Today the family lives in a small town near Vienna. Tahajud, her husband, and their older son have all been granted asylum. She is currently working at a school, supporting teachers in the education of children with migration backgrounds.

My name is Tahajud Alghrabi, I am forty-eight years old, I came here to ask for asylum, because—well, everybody knows what happened in my country. I came here looking for safety and to begin a new life.

You are here with your family, right? You grew up in Baghdad but you've also lived in Syria, is that correct?
Yes. I moved from Baghdad to Syria when the war started in 2004. I was going back and forth between Jordan and Baghdad. I needed to earn money and I had a job in Iraq, but at the same time I wanted my children to be somewhere safe. So I was moving between Iraq and Jordan. In 2007 there was so much suffering and we no longer saw any future for us in our country. We travelled to Syria, back when Syria was safe. In 2011, the same things started to happen in Syria, so we moved from Homs to Damascus but life wasn't any better there so I travelled to Jordan. Then there were many legal changes in Jordan so I returned to Iraq for six or seven months. After that I moved to Turkey for over two years.

So you have been on the road for quite a while.
Yeah, and this is the shortest possible version of my life as refugee.

Why did you choose Vienna?
You know, we just searched online for the safest and most social countries.

Do you mean social security?
No, a social country—like within a family. In Vienna, I was very lucky, I found an Austrian family who took care of me and accompanied me to see houses. And I began a new life, here I started over, with a family. So, I lost many things but I lost many things in the camps as well. There are many bad things happening and many difficult situations. Sometimes two families would have to live together in one room. I was lucky that I found this family and that I was able to begin a new life. They pushed me in the right way, really.

How did you get to *Green light*?
I read about it on the Internet.

Really?
Yes, on the Internet they announced that they would do something professional to help the refugees. I was with my Austrian family back then and they told me,

"This is good. Maybe you can be part of it." So I went to the appointment.

The first meeting at TBA21 at Augarten?
The first and the second. I knew the about the appointments from the Internet, so I just wrote down the address and went there.
At the meeting, I also introduced myself to Francesca von Habsburg: "My name is Tahajud," I said, "and I want to join this project. Please, this is important to me. I need this because I want to start anew and I was a school principal before. To me it would mean that I could begin again. I lost many, many years of my life and I am older now. It would mean a lot to me, really. It would be a chance and I need to press forward to begin again. I don't have time to stay at home and wait for somebody to help me. I want to help myself." So I met everybody, and I also met Daniela Zyman and said, "Please, don't forget me. When I come to the project, please let me join." And she said it's okay. And she helped me, she really did. Because on the first day of the project, when the Red Cross were checking names they said I wasn't on the list, and Daniela told them it was okay.

I didn't know how you actually got to the project.
Yeah [laughs], it's actually a funny story. Picture me running around, not knowing the address, and I was late because I didn't have the exact address. And my shoes were falling apart [laughs], and I was like "AHHHH!" And then I told Daniela "Pleeeeease, I know that I'm just dropping in and I am already late. But I must be part of the project!" It really was funny.

Do you remember what your first impression of the project was? When you actually saw what we were going to build, what the rhythms that we wanted to apply and the structures were?
The first thing I thought was that *Green light* means "Go" for your life. I had all these problems and the color and light meant to me that I will begin again. So it's a lovely name for the project. I also expected to communicate with many people and to be able to do something. It was important to me to do things for myself, and being part of this meant that maybe I could find a job in Austria after the project. Because if I wanted to get a job without a certificate, it's difficult. But this will be a kind of certificate, like a CV or a reference letter. It would be an account that I can be on time, that I have a positive character, and that I do a good job. Also, that I like my job and that I respect it. In fact, I respect working, I like doing something. So, when I get a job I try to be my best, because I like it. I can begin again and that will also means that I could find myself again. And I could help the refugees inside the camp, because if I know more about life in this country, I could help other people who don't know as much. I would feel ashamed if I could help somebody and didn't, because all the refugees that came here had suffered a lot. The Europeans—and in particular the Austrian people—really took good care of us. So, I must do something for others as well. Because we speak the same language, we come from the same countries, we share the same stories and cases. So I must, because if I can obtain power I could help, I could do the same things the Austrians are doing to help.

Well, sometimes you can do it even better, because you speak the language and maybe have a better understanding of the people.
Particularly with the question of jobs and

taking care of children, this is important. Because I am a teacher, I can understand what happened to the children. They have lost so much. I've been a refugee since 2000. That means that my children, too, have lost their friends, their country, their home. I have a lot experience with trouble. So I don't want all these people, all of these refugees to have to feel the same things I had to feel. I want to help them—help all of them, if I can. If I do something for myself, it means I can stand up and do something for others. Help myself, then help others. That is my plan. When I was part of the project I was there with people from all kinds of different places. I felt like a mother to them and I have communicated with all of them without language, just through the way we treated each other. I think this is part of the beauty of being human.

You mentioned many times that it was so important to you to be productive, to go out, to do something.
You must have control of your life, so you must do something to control it. When I was part of the project I did something with my hands, I had energy, so I could do something and forget that I was at the camp. It's like a delete button. Because we spent the day there, from noon to 5pm, which is a long time, and we had German classes and the team was really good, they knew they were dealing with people who had suffered a lot and they treated all of us very gently. Sometimes they didn't understand everything because of the language barrier, but you could see in their eyes that they wanted to help. It's important that they wanted to help, and it motivated us. They would always say, "Yeah, you are good, you can start over." And this would help us to really begin again. We learned German with Marianna who was like one of us.

You have gone through many years of travelling and lived at so many different places, and experienced war and fear and loss.
In my country, I had a job, a house, my family, but nothing scares me anymore. So it's ok. I am here in a new country, I don't know the language and it's so difficult. The first days that I was here, I couldn't read a single letter. Couldn't understand one word. It was hard, it feels like being blind. I had so many questions I couldn't easily answer. But I know all you need is contact to other people. With all this contact, people can calm down, and they begin anew and everything changes. Really, people change. Their aggressions wore off and they made plans for the future, and all of them thought this is a project, and it could become a factory. Really, they thought it would become a factory. And that yes, this would be a good way. We found a job, and we found a language. And if there is other work, it's ok—we will learn! But it's important to have a job. For everybody, because it means you are beginning.

You do something, you have a rhythm and you can make plans—suddenly there is time. So while we were building lamps, we ...
... were building ourselves, from the inside.

In *Green light*, there is a close connection between art, art production, exhibition space, and public space and social space and production of communities. Considering your experience with education institutions, how do you see it?
I think what you mean is we mix art with doing something inside ourselves. The social aspect of the project is mixed with the art. And I think it's kind of a

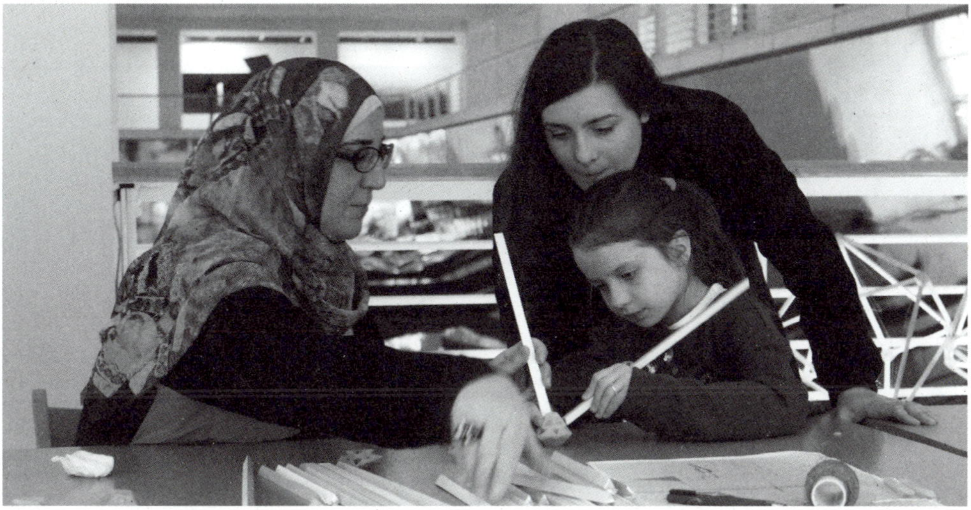

Tahajud Alghrabi at the Green light seminar workshop in Prague

new thing, because we do something similar at school with children. When they have a lot of aggression, I think this kind of art can help: if you have a lot of aggression, you must paint or do something with your hands. It takes out your aggression and it takes the bad ideas from your mind. So this, for me, as a teacher, means that when I build, I can also do something about my feelings. Because we're like a family in this place. And we share this lamp together: one weaves in the threads, one person puts the lamp together—we act like a family. And we have contact with our hands, without talking, because we come from different places. But we respect each other. It means that human beings can do anything without talking.

You say it in very beautiful words. I think that was the best way to put the idea to words: connecting through doing something together. When you look at the *Green light* lamp, what do you see?
I see my first dot to build myself again. This is it for me. This is important. And you know, it's a very small light. So it means we are beginning from the small to become something huge.

And the lamps could also be joined together.
When we arranged them to become a wall, it was amazing, really. To me, it means that all this work, all the nationalities can come together and you can be safe, without argument. Because we are of different nationalities and we made this lamp together and when all these lamps come together, it's like a big globe made by hand.

Like Shuddha Sengupta from Raqs Media Collective said: Here in this room, we have everything we need to build a new world. Whenever people come together you have poetry, you have dreams, you have a carpenter—you have everything within the people to build a new world.

This interview was conducted by Clemens Rettenbacher on December 18, 2016.

The Light That Says Walk

Shuddhabrata Sengupta, Raqs Media Collective

At an intersection in any city, when the light changes to green, you walk. The green light says, "Go," "Come," "Cross over." But the world is full of red lights that say "Stop."

I spent a few days in Vienna, at Thyssen Bornemisza Art Contemporary, last year, thinking about what it means to "Go" and to "Stop," along with a group of young people, refugees fleeing devastation and war, who knew the meaning of the difference between these words better than most. They had gathered to make *Green lights* in a project initiated by the artist Olafur Eliasson. I came to have conversations, and to listen.

Very quickly, we established the boundaries of our languages. My English (and sometimes my Hindustani) began where someone else's Dari and Pashto ended, and sometimes we had to find a little patch of common German, or West African French, or Arabic, to get where we needed to go. Translation, too, was a green light that allowed us to cross over to each other.

Movement was one thing that we knew not to take for granted. The workshop participants had crossed many borders. They knew what it meant to be forced to flee, they knew what it meant to be detained. Arrest meant stillness. Life was on the run. So we needed to slow down. To walk, and to talk to each other while walking. Sometimes we stopped to listen to a song.

There was a boy whose left arm was blown away by a landmine in Syria, but who could hold his stump up and sing like as if his world, and the world in general, was not ending but had just been created.

 When he sang, it was as if the first day was singing in praise of the beginning of time.

There were others who could dance, dribble a football, tell a joke, hold a pose, cook salad, or solder a circuit, as if the world were a playground, a club-house, a never-ending dance party. They have all seen war, many had seen prison. Each had seen death up close. Some, like the smiling, singing Syrian boy, still carried the marks that history had made on their bodies.

We were making *Green lights*. And while we made *Green lights* we talked. I asked them to tell stories about the last cup of tea they had before leaving home. This was based on the memory of a Raqs work (*The Wherehouse*, 2004) where we had collected stories and narratives from refugees in Brussels that were triggered by memories of everyday objects and situations. Like in Brussels, in Vienna we could also read the world in the last cup of tea.

Everyone has a last cup of tea. It tastes different in Libya, Syria, or Afghanistan, but everyone knows what the last cup of tea in your homeland means. It brings with it the bitterness of departure and the sweetness of memory. It is as hot as the anger you take with you, and as comforting as a dream of home. It makes for friendship and solidarity, it brews understanding. And you can read a map of the world in the tea leaves. A map of a broken world that you need to shake to make sense of.

We talked and drank tea. There were tears, confusion, laughter, and the effort to understand the weight of words in different languages. Sometimes we translated silence.

In the end, the workshop resolved to make portraits. Selfies for a selfish world. These were talking portraits. The selfie had to be taken while in conversation with someone else. They were records of dialogue, based on conversation and discovery, and the sharing of an improvised map of the world gleaned from the reading of tea leaves and random sources shared in the circle. The circle of stories began with halting incomprehension, and ended with a sudden flash of understanding. The borders, the border guards, the endless humiliation of the production of papers and narratives, the violence of waiting—all of these can be suspended in a moment of laughter, or in a random act of generous sharing.

When my time came, I had to leave. The lights changed, I crossed back to where I came from. My journeys continued. So did the journeys of everyone else. I hope that none of the people I met in Vienna had to move against their will again.

And this is what we learned, again: freedom is like a little green light in a very dark room, that allows you to see yourself, that allows you to see other people and allows you to see the way to the door.

When I think of my days in Vienna last year, I think of an open door, and a green light, and I know it means both "welcome" and "goodbye."

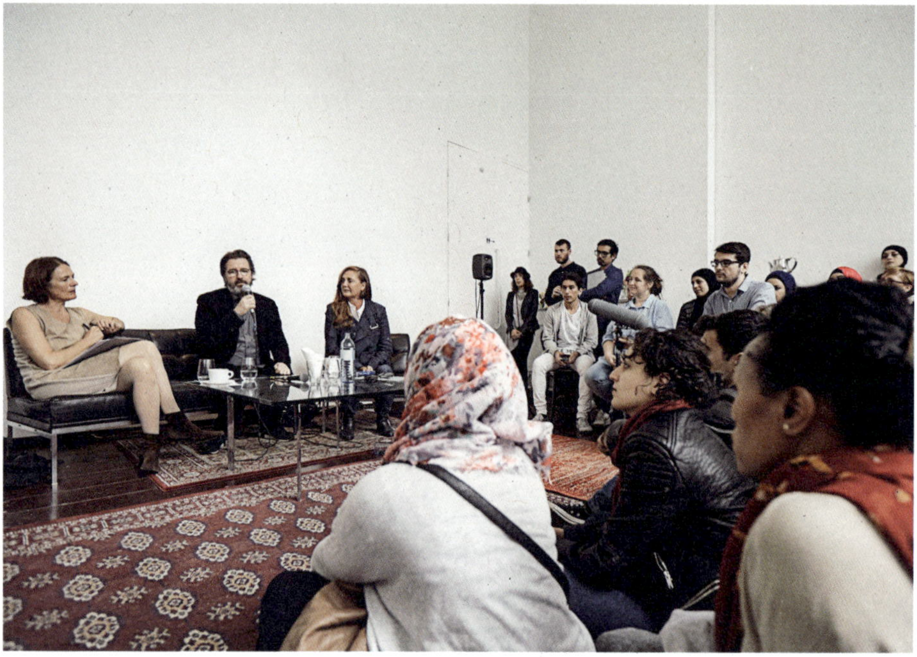

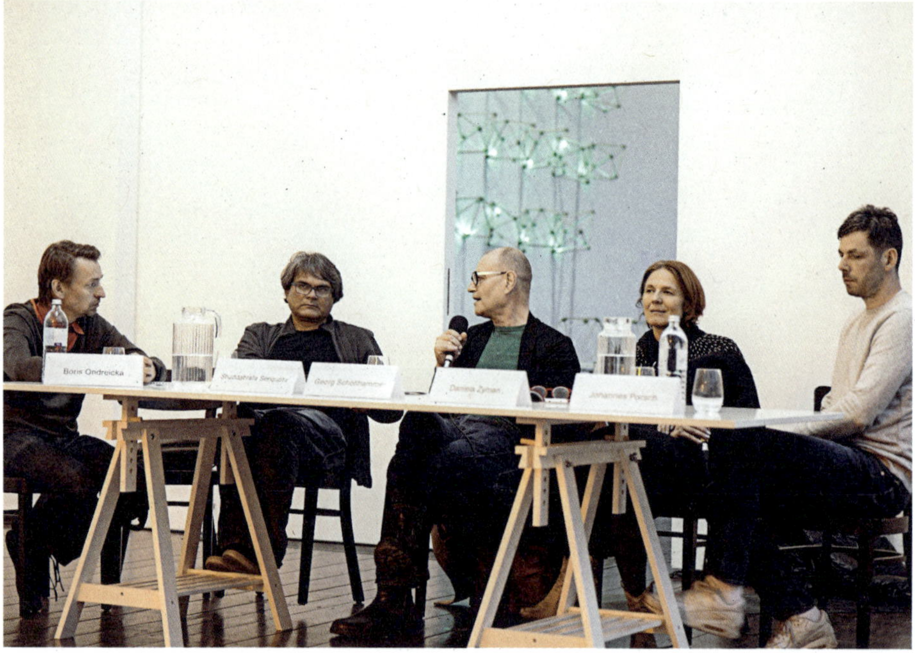
Boris Ondreicka
Georg Schöllhammer
Daniela Zyman
Johannes Porsch

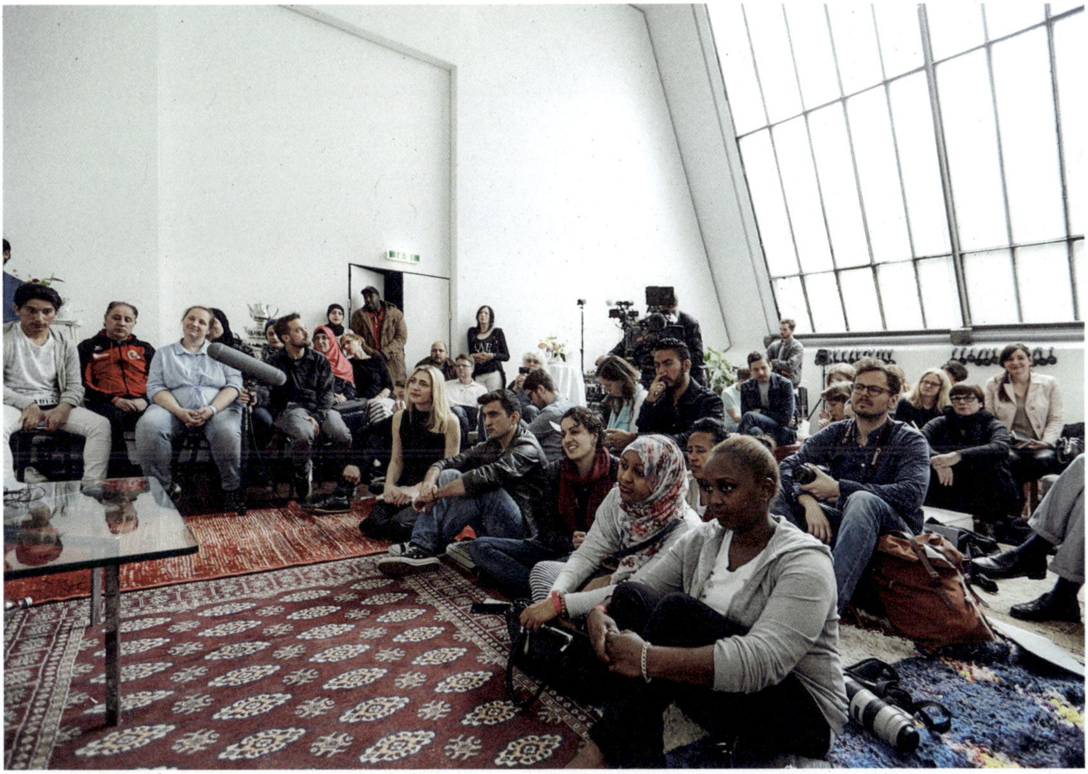

Green light—Shared learning: at TBA21 in Vienna
series of educational events and language school

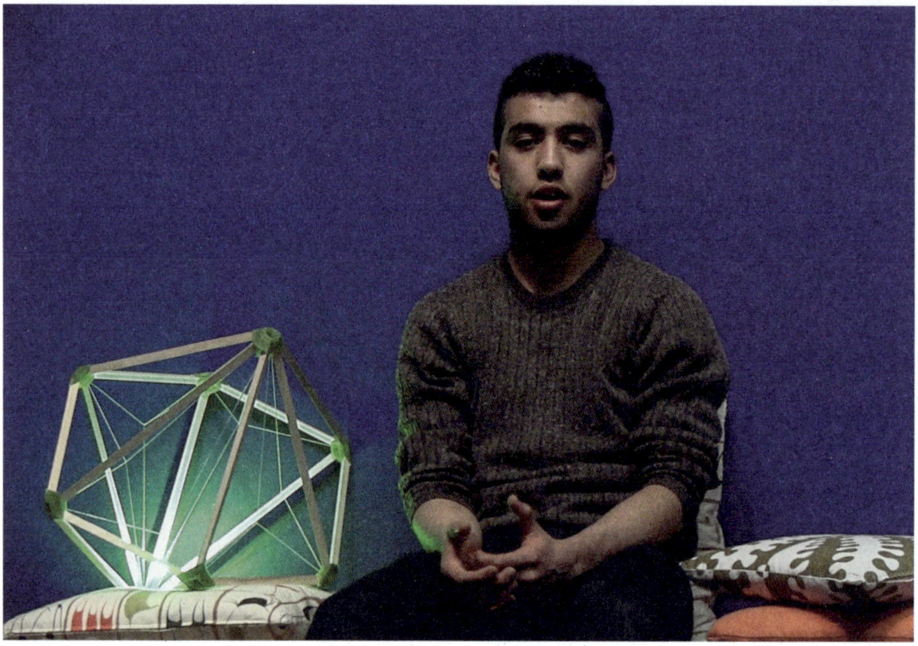

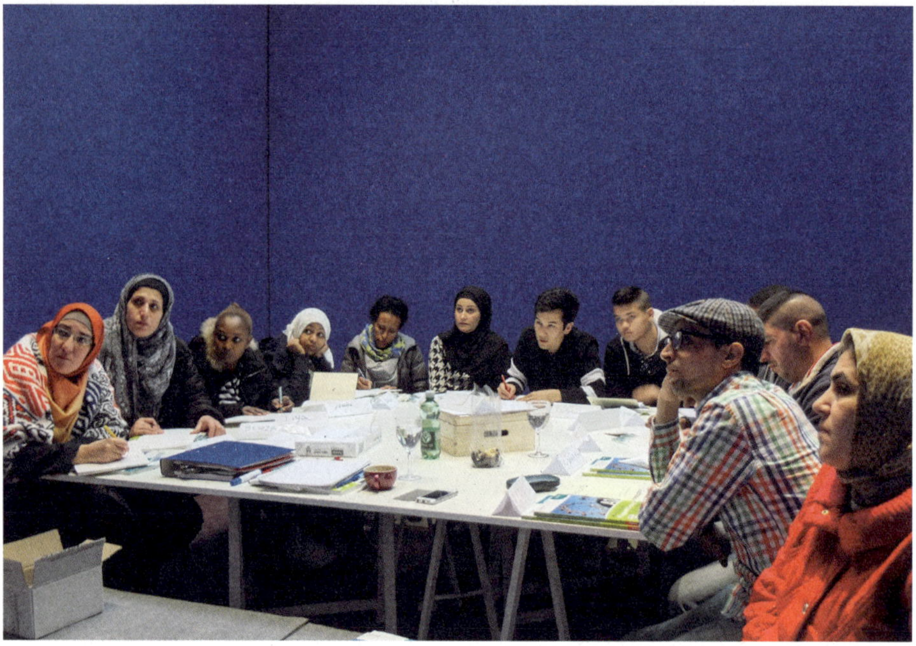

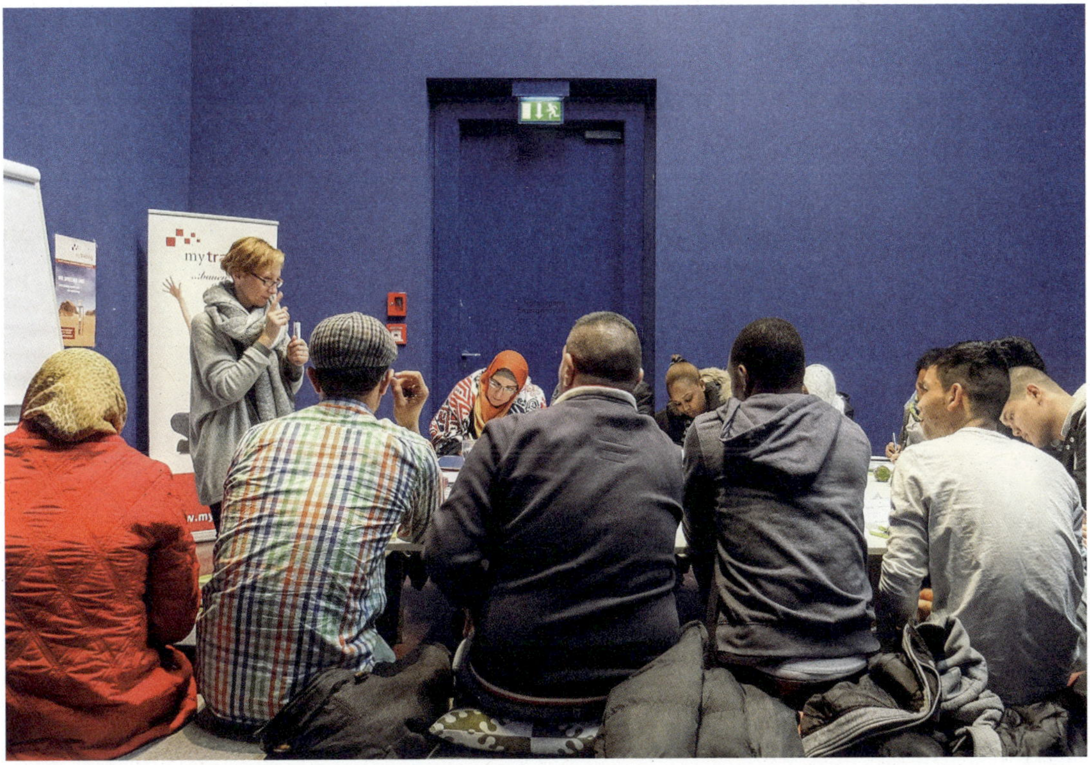

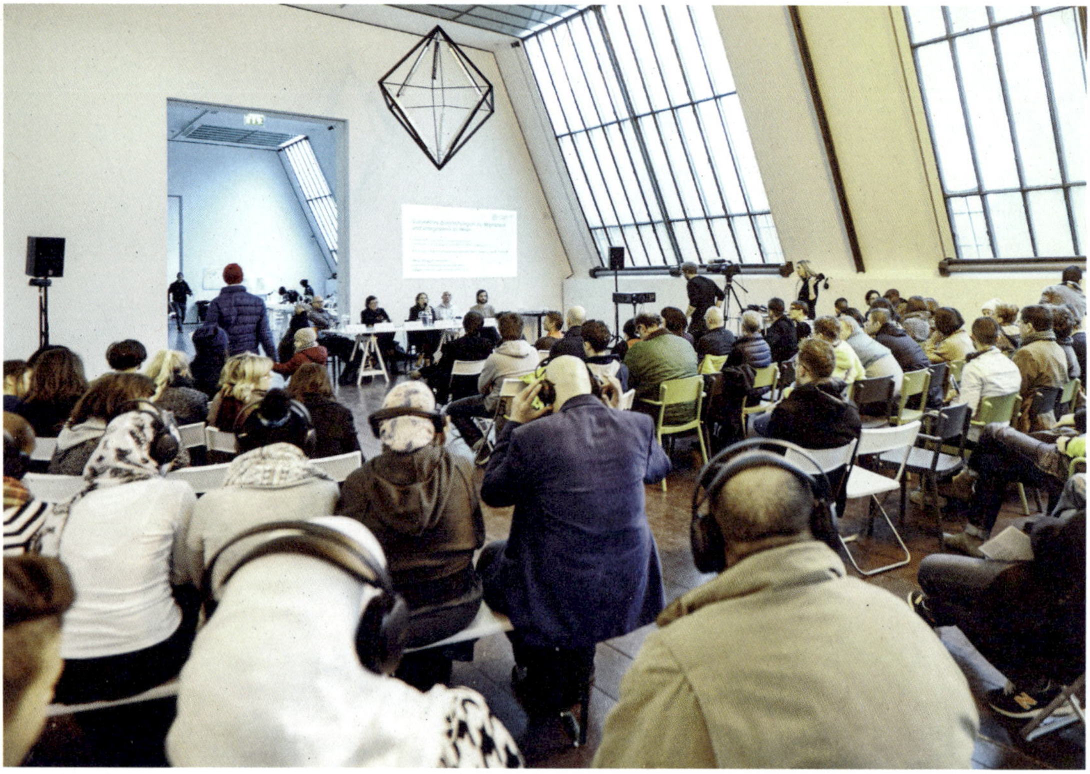

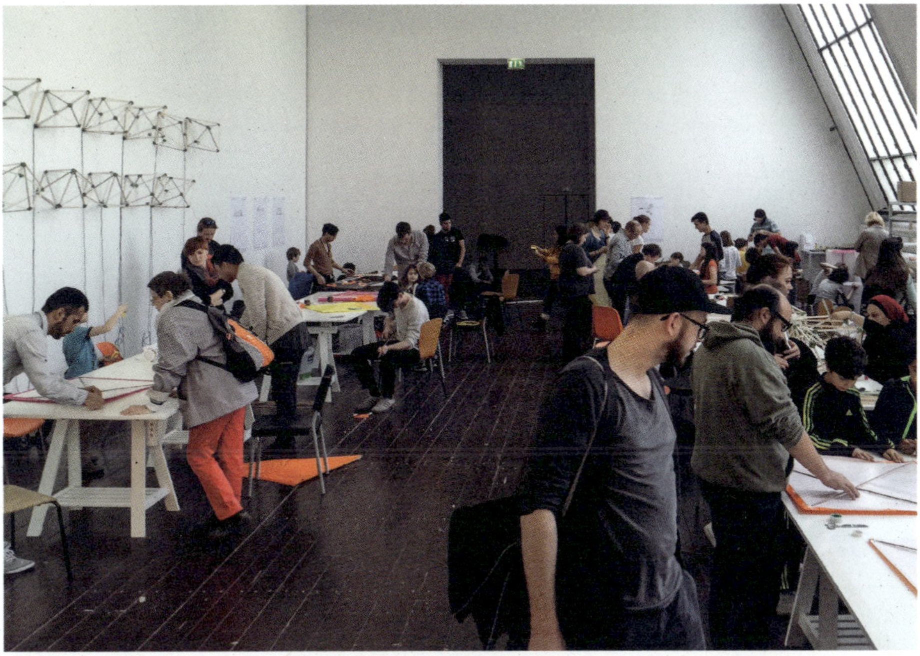

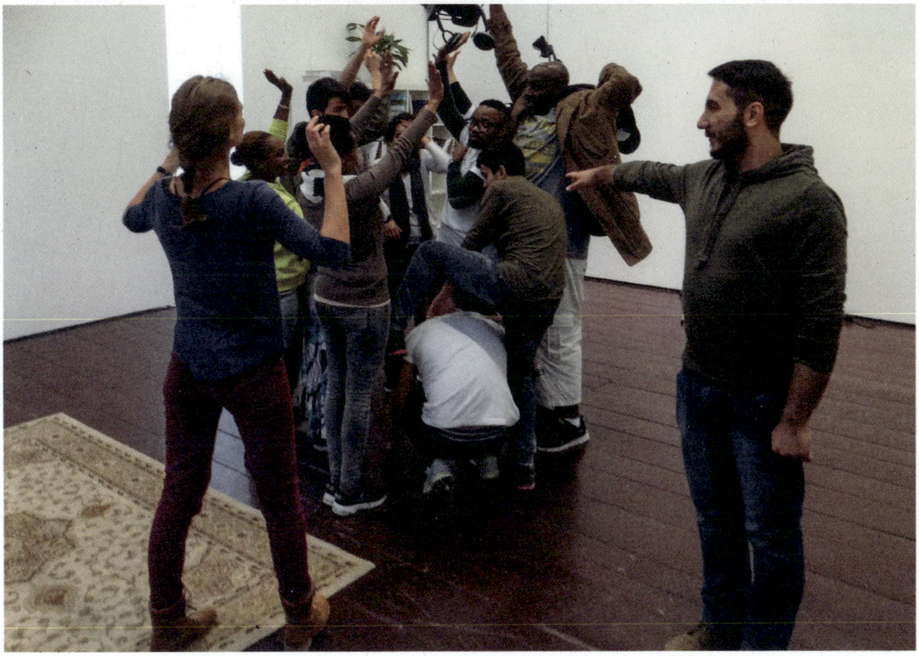

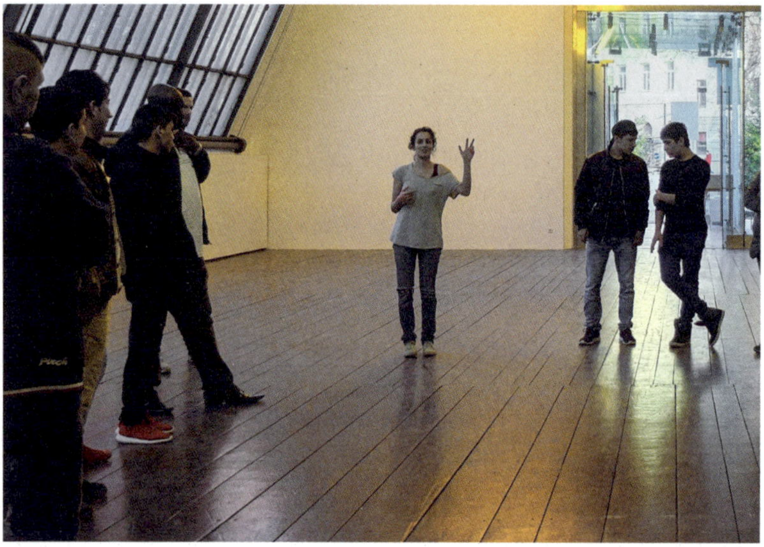

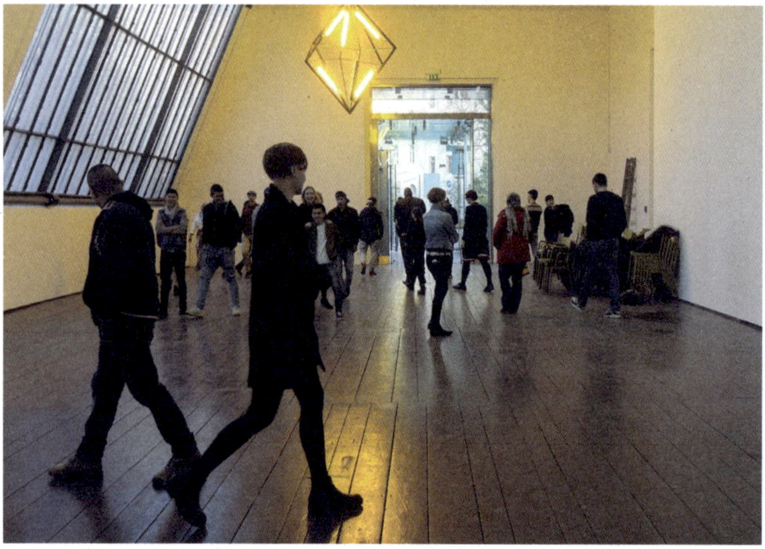

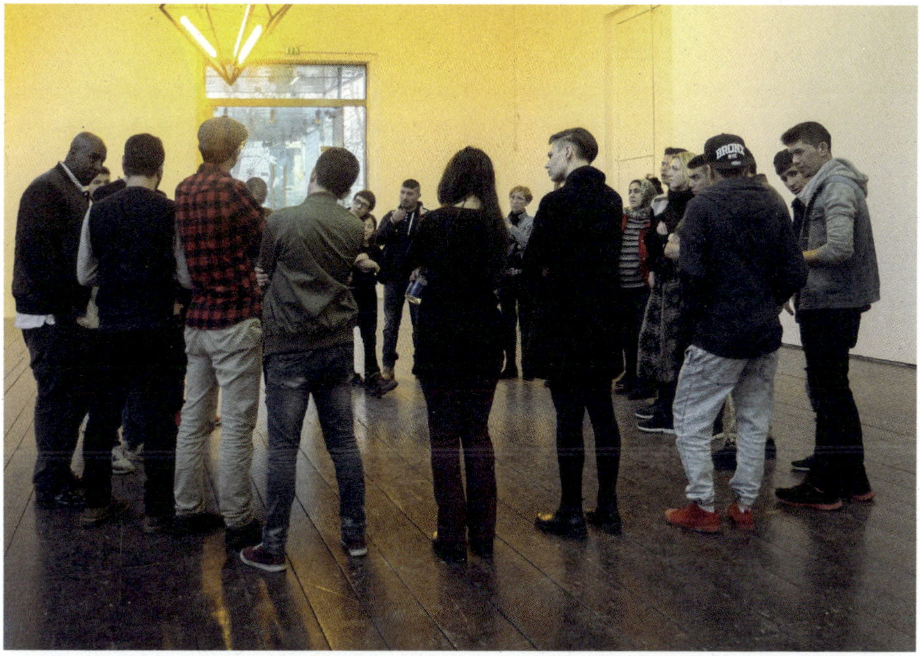

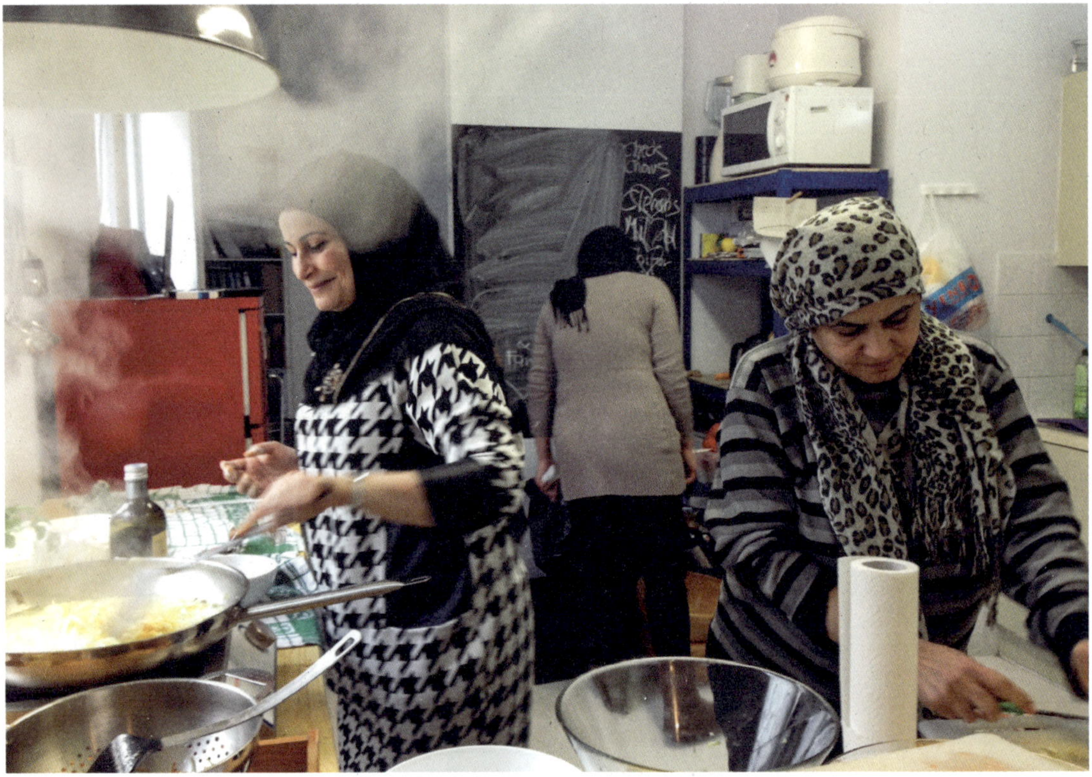

Daily communal cooking at the TBA21–KIOSK, Augarten

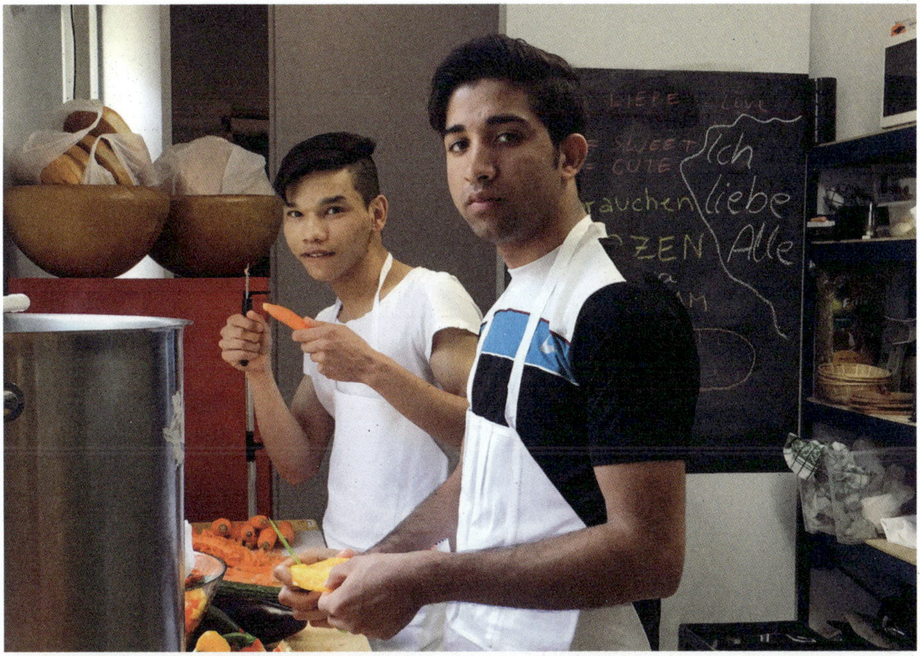
Ich
liebe
Alle

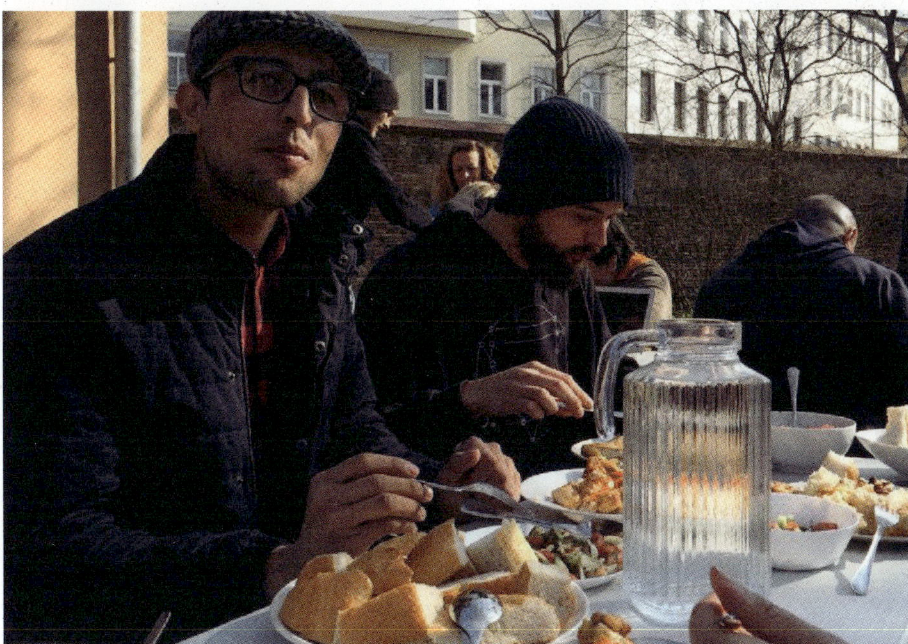

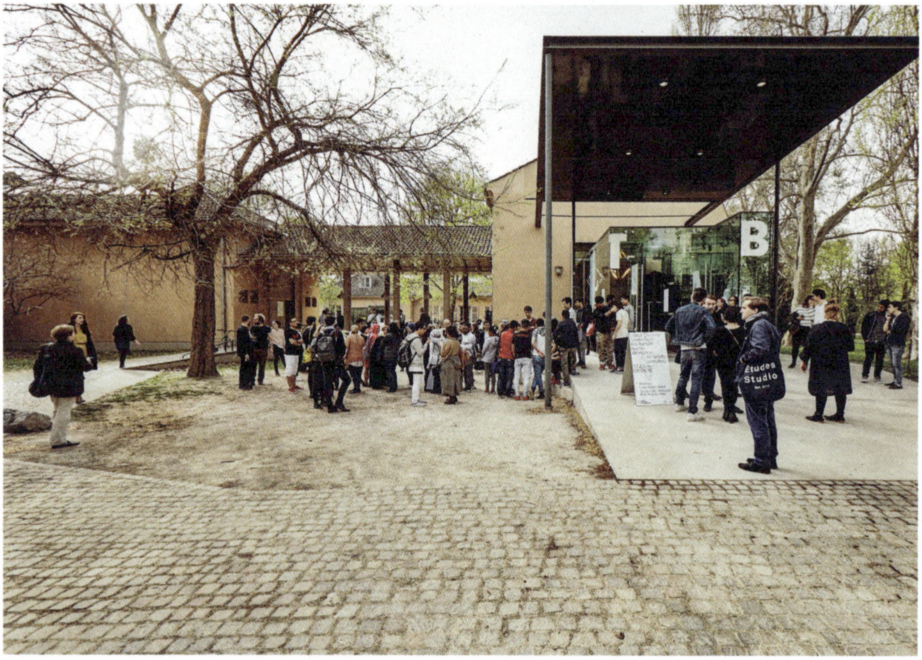
B
Études
Studio

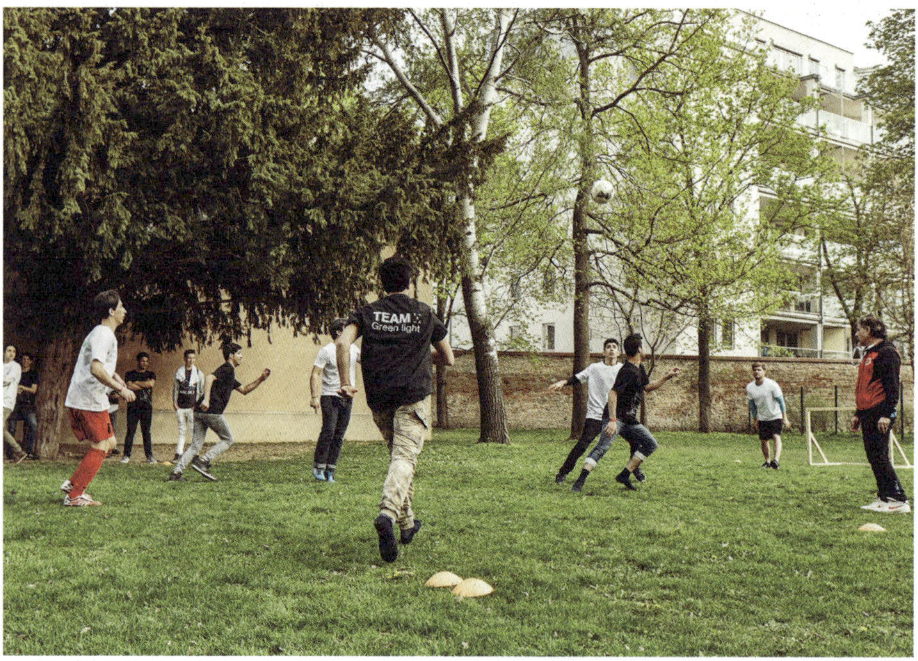
TEAM
Green light

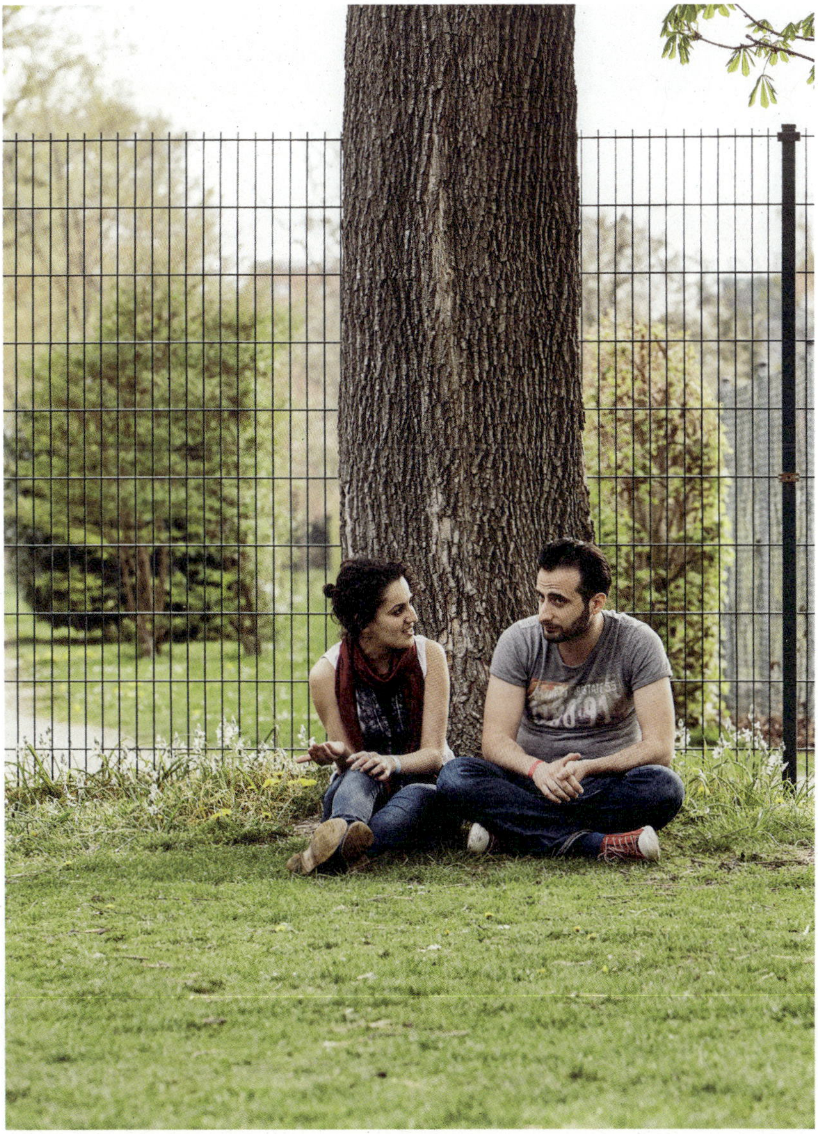

After curricular and recreational activities at Augarten

A place where we could spend our time

Murtaza Azimi (16) is originally from Afghanistan. He arrived in Austria in summer 2015. Today, he is living in the Georg Danzer Haus in Stockerau (Lower Austria), where he is also attending school to obtain a school certificate. He has not been granted asylum yet.

My name is Murtaza, I am 16 years old and I was born in Afghanistan. I went to Iran when I was very young. In Iran, there is no life for Afghans. After one or two years, my dad was deported to Afghanistan. We couldn't get in touch with him and lost contact, though we eventually got in touch with him a few months ago. After my father was deported, we went to Turkey, and there I lost my family, though I found them again later.

Why did you come to Austria?
I didn't realize where I was. I didn't know. I came here, I liked it here, so I stayed. I didn't know exactly what kind of a place this was.

When did you realize where you were?
When I talked to the police.

How did you first hear about *Green light*?
Our guardian Marianne told us that the project would be a chance for all of us who are not going to school yet. A place where we could learn German, and do something like work, a place where we could spend our time.

So did you have any expectations before coming?
No, not really. I was very curious about the project. We knew about German classes, about work, and about school, but I have never heard of a project like that. So I wanted to know at least what it would be about. But first of all, I came for the German classes. They said it would be a native teacher, so I thought I would learn the language faster.

And what was the reason you came regularly?
I've never seen anything like that lamp and anything like that place before and it was the first time in my life that I was doing something like that. Every day was interesting and exciting for me. I never did that kind of handwork before: I sanded, made strings, and sometimes finished a lamp, which was also an art object at the same time, and I did that at a place with lots of different people from all over the world. There were black people, white people, people speaking English and many other different languages. We were all doing something together. I've never seen anything like that before. Really.

What do you remember most?
I realized how quickly my German improved. Before the project I could not compose a sentence. I somehow understood what people were trying to tell me, but I couldn't respond. While working on the project I spoke better and better by the day and I understood more and

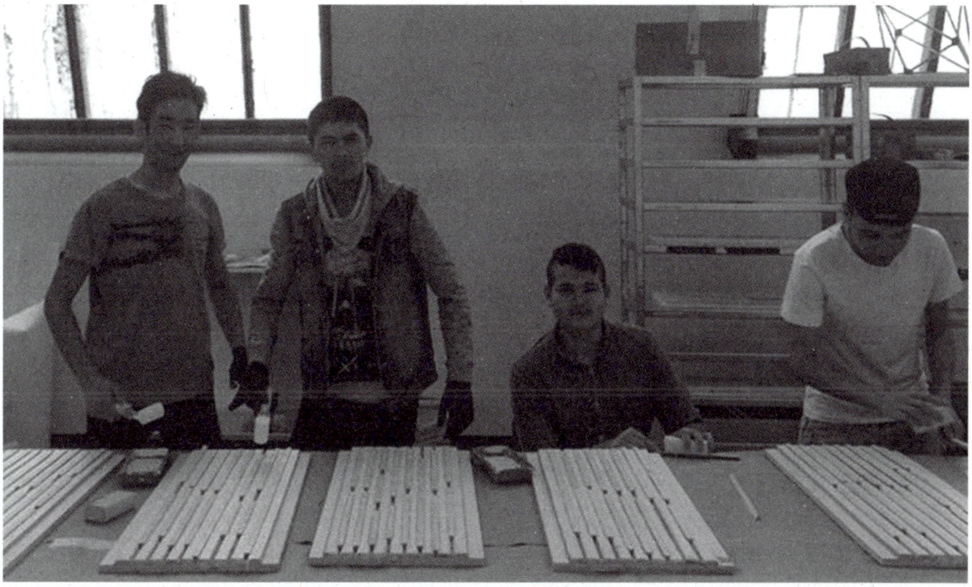

Shamahmood Ahmadi, Murtaza Azimi, Ebrahim Ebrahimi, and Hossein Rezaie painting

more. At the end, it was still a place where everybody spoke German, so I had to learn. And I somehow did, without realizing it.

You learned a language. Did you learn anything else beside it too?
Of course. I learned how to talk to—or at least, lose my discomfort in the presence of—people from other countries. I learned a lot about living together, alongside others. I learned a lot about myself and about good manners and the importance of the way you behave.

***Green light* was an art project primarily. We produced lamps, we ate together, we attended workshops together. What was the "arty" side of it for you?**
To me, it was that all these different people from all those different countries came together and built that lamp. So on the one hand, making the lamp was like making art, or producing art. But it was also the fact that all those different people were taking part in this project and you could never tell what would happen next, so this was also kind of art by itself. I've never seen anything like that lamp before, you know.

What did you like the most about the lamp?
The lamp itself was fascinating to me. A lamp made of wood. That is definitely art.

So, the idea was always to establish a get-together by a common task.
Yes, the project meant structure. Since the project ended, I've been taking language courses and two times a week I play football, and that's it. It's exhausting. Not being able to do anything is exhausting. Not doing anything is exhausting by itself.

This interview was conducted by Anahita Tabrizi on October 17, 2016.

On the Question of Empowerment

Johannes Porsch, Shuddhabrata Sengupta, and Georg Schöllhammer in conversation with Boris Ondreička and Daniela Zyman

DANIELA ZYMAN This is the second panel in the opening program of *Green light—An artistic workshop* at TBA21. This session taps into the ways artistic and institutional practices can—spatially, performatively, and in terms of representation—re-imagine notions of community, co-citizenship, translation, similarity and difference, as well as forms of empowerment in the present context, which is marked by severe forms of transformation, signaling multiple states of "crisis."

I would like to ask the artist and educator Johannes Porsch, who was invited to congregate weekly workshops for ten consecutive weeks in the context of *Green light*. Can you tell us about your intervention, *What Acts Upon (Upon Us) When We Are Acting*, which will involve the *Green light* participants in a very deconstructed platform of acting.

JOHANNES PORSCH I would like to relate my workshops to the discussion on representation. *What Acts Upon (Upon Us) When We Are Acting* can be seen as a critique of representation, looking to theater as a tool through which to think about representation. We (the participants) are not acting within the theater or on a stage, playing characters and roles within the unfolding of a given plot, but we are acting outside and around the theater. Without the guidance of a story we are working with the means at hand, the given situation and circumstances: we are engaging in an action that displaces and expands theatrical action into life and interrupts the familiarity of the everyday.

There are three attitude vis-à-vis the theater; the first would assume that in order to critique representation, we should say, "Let's leave the theater, let's go outside and celebrate togetherness!" This would be Rousseau. The second attitude would be to say, "We stay in the theater, but dismantle it in all its elements." That would be Brecht. The third position could be, for example, "We take the theater with us, but only take from it what we need in given situations." This would be Augusto Boal's Theater of the Oppressed. Of these, I find Brecht most interesting because he dismantles the theater, and understands theater as a system, or as a context of enunciation. As Walter Benjamin said, he loosens the joints of the theater and therefore makes its functional relations flexible. By that flexibility and loosening of what has been fixed in theater, he attains first a critique of theater and second a possibility to act within critique. It is often said that critique does not allow a mode of action, and I think what Brecht does is develop a potentiality of action through a mode of critique.

DANIELA ZYMAN How do you connect your thinking about theater with the project that you have developed here in Augarten?

JOHANNES PORSCH Well, theater is a group production, where a group of people work together. I think this is a very good model to create a community.

DANIELA ZYMAN Georg, what do you think: Does critique allow for a mode of action or does it hinder action? Or put differently: Could you elaborate why you think we are doing what we are doing? As a critical curator and an actor in the cultural field, how do you think we can participate in what Amar Kanwar calls the "scene of crime"? How can we intervene in areas of crisis, uncertainty, and upheaval? I am thinking specifically of Kiev, where you have recently worked, but of course this is a general question. How do you develop tools and an adequate approach to engaging in these scenarios? What urges you to partake in the situation and is there a point in which you think that we should step out and refuse to participate?

GEORG SCHÖLLHAMMER That is quite a heavy question. I'll begin by addressing some topics from the day's previous panel. I think the debate about migration and multiculturalism in Austria has been going on for over 150 years. You could say that it dates back to the Habsburg model, which allowed a certain degree of self-determination to religious groups and social minorities. It brought parts of the Jewish community into the high administration, for example, creating a certain evenness of talking and talking back. So diversity and migration have already played a crucial role in our history. What is happening now is totally different, but I won't go deeper into that.

The second point I want to make about the last panel is that there is an ongoing debate about the institutional and the non-institutional.

What can the institution do? The answer to this question inevitably leads to some kind of modernism. What would the non-institutional be able to do? This is the position of the avant-garde, proposing a kind of self-organization. I recently reread a conversation between Theodor Adorno and Arnold Gehlen from the early 1960s about the possibility of an institution. Adorno claimed, as he had written out in his *Negative Dialectics*, that it was the institutions of modernity that brought us the Holocaust. Gehlen counters with the idea that the institutions of the state, and the institutions that the bourgeois state created and allowed—at least for the middle classes—a certain identificatory moment, which would permit them to be liberal. I would have always been on the Adorno side, but now I am slightly revising that and thinking about the fact that we might have to support institutionality again, to care about our institutions as we see them being corrupted.

If you ask me about art, I don't see a split between art and the other fields, like the social. Culture is a weapon term that is used in a lot of respects in current discourses to separate: culture is bound to mentality, bound to region, to language. It's the 19th-century idea of culture and of nationality that also corrupted the Habsburg Empire. When these debates came up, we suddenly saw separations introduced in the name of liberation and self-determination. Self-determination is thus another very complicated term that we have to talk about. In this context, is art able to really intervene in the social? What does an intervention in the social mean for art? What is the social? Is art part of the social as well? This was what we had to ask ourselves when we—myself and Hedwig Saxenhuber, who is the co-curator of the Kiev Biennial—took on the project. The question was not whether it is wrong to do an art project at a time of war, crisis, and the dispossession of parts of society. This would be the usual job of an art critic of the Left. The question was much more how to create an art project that is against hegemony.

The biennial took place in the Mystetskyi Arsenale, this huge cultural center, which they compare to the Louvre of the East and was the site of President Petro Poroshenko's inauguration. Why did we do it there? It was already a conflicted space, because of an act of censorship that had happened under the director. The artists in Kiev had two positions: the first was, "If we don't occupy the space of the president and voice our claims in that specific space, then we fail to address power and hegemony from the inside. So, let's claim that and see what happens." Our position as curators was in accord: the museum is a house of the people and it is funded by the people, because in the Ukraine the president gets parts of his salary from them. The other fraction claimed, "No, we cannot go into that dirty space where censorship happened!" A lot of people, especially from the Western art world, were asking us how we could possibly organize a biennial at a time of crisis. But that was not true for the young intellectuals and artists, the society and the people we met in Kiev, who said that because they were now victimized and trapped in a space of crisis, a space that can just deal with a mode of crisis and with the otherness of being suppressed by crisis, that a platform is needed that would be civil again—and that is why we did it!

DANIELA ZYMAN Shuddha, any comments on any of that? Maybe you could address the well-versed and never exhausted question of the relationship between the artist and the social, and respectively the role of the institution? And maybe comment on the explosive potential of culture, what Georg calls the "weapon term"?

SHUDDHABRATA SENGUPTA I have always seen the relationship between culture and the social, art, and the political, not in terms of what artists can do in the field of the political, but according to what artists are as citizens. I think that all of us are first of all citizens. Nobody asks a question to a room full of doctors as to what they are doing in relation to politics, though the question could be asked, considering that the practice of medicine is deeply implicated in the construction of social and political realities. Nevertheless, it is a question that inevitably gets asked of us artists. And my initial response to that is that first we have to think about how we respond as citizens, rather than how we respond as artists. I think we all have responsibilities, socially and politically, and living up to those responsibilities should not be the certificate of our artistic practice.

So let me think about the kind of questions that are immediately engaging to me right know. Delhi, where I'm from, is currently going through a political, cultural, and intellectual emergency. There is intense pressure from an extreme right-wing government that is attacking universities and will probably direct its eye to cultural spaces next. There is a concerted effort by militias of the extreme right to use their leverage with the government to actually suppress the normal conditions of thinking in spaces of intellectual production. We tend to think of the production of free thinking and free speech as if it were something special, when in fact it is normal! I refuse to accept the fact that the normal conditions of discussions, debate, and thinking through questions, including the question of self-determination, which is at the heart of the current crisis in Indian universities, is at risk.

Students from universities all over India are increasingly expressing demands around a slogan called Āzādī (आज़ादी), which means freedom. Now, you have a lot of young people in universities suddenly responding to this idea of demanding freedom, sometimes freedom from the Indian state, freedom within the Indian state, there all sorts of discussions and debates around that. As someone who acts within those universities, sometimes in a teaching position, sometimes as an interlocutor to many young friends, my concern as someone who works primarily with the imagination is to expand the definition of what this determination of the self is. Because this is a moment of high theater, where the speeches made on university grounds by students are carried through YouTube videos, competing with the oratory in the parliament. So it is as if there are two cultures of political speech and political representation.

In that situation, perhaps the role of people working with the imagination, like artists, is to ask and constantly make available the process of asking questions about what freedom means, what liberty is. To ask very basic questions, which have to do with the expansion of the imaginative within the political sphere. That is what I can do, that is what my work as an artist trains me to do. So when I return from the studio to the street, not as an artist but as a citizen, I can carry with me certain resources that being an artist produces for me. In much the same way that a mathematician can bring a modus of thinking about relationships of equality, for instance, into society. I think we are all uniquely positioned to bring these conversations to the agora, to the street, to the space of the actual working out of democracy, which is what happens when bodies gather together. And this is what I think is the relationship between the artistic, the cultural, and the political right now in the context of where I am.

DANIELA ZYMAN Thank you! Boris, any questions or comments on your end?

BORIS ONDREIČKA First, I would like to quote Kenneth Burke, who says that life is not like drama, but life is drama! So, how can we divide our primordial bodies from our cultural roles? Following many centuries of what Cicero called cultivation, it's impossible. Cultivation is a term taken from agriculture—which is certainly a violent process. Agriculture makes plants stronger and more resistant, but the process itself is violent. So what we do is conflicted, especially at institutions like TBA21, which in its core function has dual, ambivalent modes. We are a private foundation that works in the public sphere, and permanently confront ourselves with that "agora." What I see as the power of an institution is actually to provide architectural security and hospitality. It is a roof, which protects you from rain. A place where people can gather. That is what Peter Lamborn Wilson, aka Hakim Bey, says. Maybe we don't have to go as far as making huge plans, maybe we can cultivate our abilities of being a magnet for certain nonconformist dialogues, not to allow political correctness to turn into mind control. I think this is somehow feasible in the context of art. So yes, life is not like drama, life is drama! And this process of consideration has to be neuroplastic, it has to be in permanent relation to and critique of other political and economical and cultural notions.

DANIELA ZYMAN I want to circle back to this question of citizenship. The last panel was called "Citizens of Hope." It is actually shocking to recognize how meaningless this word has become in some ways. Shuddha, you say, "My responsibility as citizen"—le citoyen—and there's all this history, this revolutionary potential embedded in this important terminus. And today we are at a moment when it feels that it has become difficult to derive a vision or a modus operandi from it. I wonder whether this is something that you also feel, and in which way citizenship or the citizen as an empowered participant in a political arena can be encouraged to take back the stage.

SHUDDHABRATA SENGUPTA I think it is interesting to mark this moment as a kind of redrawing of a lot of geometrical possibilities. The word citizen sometimes carries a limitation, as if you are a citizen of let's say Vienna, or a citizen of Austria, or a citizen of the European Union, whatever it is. The word citizen, at least in English, is a very recent word, it is not a very old word and it comes, of course, from citoyen. But there is an older word, which may also be interesting for us to think about in the context of migration, which is "denizen," an inhabitant of a specific place. You are a denizen of a city. Denizen is a person with a more or less unqualified right to lead an uninterrupted life. Many communities of wanderers, like Jewish populations in England were conferred rights of denizenship even before the majority of the British population became citizens. In some senses the foreigner, the stranger is the condition for the granting for the rights of those who are not foreign and not strangers. Which is why an index of the health of a polity is always how well does it treat those who are strangers. If it treats them well, so citizens will be reasonably unmolested. All politics in our time is often based on the rights of the citizen and the rights of the Others. We forget that it is the rights of the Other that actually guarantee the rights of the citizen.

Using that as an opportunity to expand our notion of citizenship, what does it mean to be a citizen today? The question of citizenship is always grafted on to a set of oppositional realities. You are a citizen of India, you are a citizen of the potential Republic of Kashmir. So, in Indian universities, when young people say, "Freedom for Kashmir from India," or "Freedom within India for Kashmir," they are often placed as if they are talking on cross purposes, as if freedom from and freedom for, freedom to and freedom within, were mutually exclusive categories. They are mutually exclusive categories as long as we subscribe to the topographic limitations of nation-states. As long as we say that to be citizen of the Republic of India necessarily contradicts the rights of the citizen of a potentially other space. But if we were to say that these are all mutually transacting relationships between different claims to being citizens of the world, within a city, then there's a potential for a different kind of conversation. I have been closely following the political developments of the cantonal constitution of the Canton of Rojava in northern Syria, where Kurdish and other populations have arrived at different forms of social organization and potential transient state-making or non-state making, which are relationships of how people can live together as citizens of different polities, but also co-partners in a space of sharing.

Now those relationships of freedom from, freedom for, and freedom to all constitute different attitudes to the space of being a self and an other for another self. So if we take self-determination to be an imaginative exercise, which doesn't necessarily stop within the overdetermined and ephemeral histories of nation states. The history of central Europe shows us that the histories of nation states are just ephemeral, they come and they go, things change. If we take that as an opportunity to think more imaginatively about how we position ourselves within a moving world, then perhaps we see different possibilities of being citizens of another kind, of being citizens of potentially a different time—not necessarily only citizens of the way the past determines our relationship to political entities, but citizens of an imminent future of the time which is yet to be.

This conversation was held as part of the opening panel on March 12, 2016, at TBA21 in Vienna, which marked the first public intervention embedded in *Green light—An artistic workshop*.

JOHANNES PORSCH
Assembly
A *Green light—Shared learning* workshop

Vienna April and May, 2016

Open Letter

Vienna, April / May 2016

To whom it may concern

"Et qui/aujourd'hui/dira/quoi?"

Sincerely

On the occasion of :
"*Olafur Eliasson. Green Light – Ein künstlerischer Workshop. 15 Akte der Partizipation*", April 7 2016

Contains the following sample:
"*Et qui/ aujourd'hui/dira/quoi?*", from: Jacques Derrida, *Artaud Moma. Ausrufe, Zwischenrufe und Berufungen*, Wien 2002, 13.

Open Letter

Vienna, April / May 2016

To whom it may concern

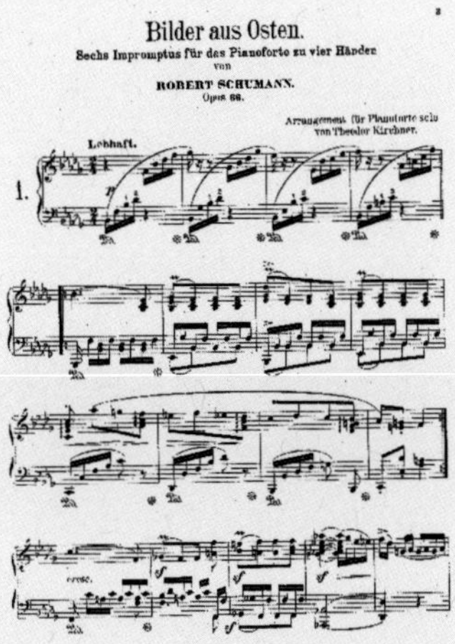

Sincerely

On the occasion of:
"*Olafur Eliasson. Green Light – Ein künstlerischer Workshop. 15 Akte der Partizipation*", April 7 2016

Contains the following sample:
"*Bilder aus Osten*", from: Robert Schumann, *Bilder aus Osten, Op. 66. Sechs Impromptus für das Pianoforte zu vier Händen*, 1848, Edition Peters, Leipzig, N.D., 1.

Exercise No.1
After: "The Stand", Steve Paxton, 1972/1977

Testrun
7 April 2016
3:30 pm
Duration variable

"I think that we are doomed to have to look at what we do.
And we're less [doomed] if we can look at it long enough to be able to [understand] it.

So, stand around."[1]

"[Action] creates a space between the participants which can find its proper location almost anywhere and anytime.

How do we understand this highly, if not infinitely transposable notion of political space?

Space and location are created through plural action. [Action], in its freedom and its power, has the exclusive capacity to create location. [And yet] action is always supported and [...] is invariably bodily, even in its virtual forms.

The material supports of action are not only part of action, but they are also what is being fought about, especially in those cases when the political struggle is about food, employment, mobility and access to institutions.

To rethink the space of appearance in order to understand the power and effect of public demonstrations for our time, we will need to consider [...] the bodily dimension of action,

what the body requires, and what the body can do,

especially when we must think about bodies together in a historical space that undergoes a historical transformation by virtue of their collective action:

What holds them together there, and what are the conditions of persistence and of power in relation to their precarity and exposure?"[2]

1 Steve Paxton, "Why Standing?", URL: www.contactquaterly.com, 4 April 2016
2 Judith Butler, *Notes Toward a Performative Theory of Assembly*, London 2015, 73–74.

Exercise No.2
Reading a Poem

Every Friday 17:00

„ . . . she wanted to find out what *language* says.“[1]

The permutational scheme, which generates eleven lines of six words each is as follows. Choose eleven words.[2]

1	1	2	1	2	3
2	3	4	4	5	6
3	5	6	7	8	9
4	8	9	10	11	1
5	9	10	2	3	4
6	11	1	5	6	7
7	2	3	8	9	10
8	4	5	11	1	2
9	6	7	3	4	5
10	8	9	6	7	8
11	10	11	9	10	11

1, 2 After: Carl André, „Ode“, in: Liz Kotz, *Words to Be Looked At. Language in 1960s Art*, Cambridge London 2007, 151–152.

Migrationalism: Pragmatic Practices between Art, Language, and Bureaucracies

Paul Feigelfeld

As I write this, in the early spring days of 2017, the situation has changed. The so-called Balkan Route, along which so many people fleeing war, persecution, and insufferable living conditions migrated toward Europe, has closed. Hungary is now detaining all remaining and newly arriving refugees in internment camps. Tempelhof airport in Berlin, once the island connecting Berlin with the rest of the world through the Berliner Luftbrücke, still houses hundreds of refugee families, and a container camp is being built on the airfield. Flight and flight, flying and fleeing are not the same.

What are the ways in which we are dealing with this situation? What are the methods that sprung up, old and new, since the summer of 2015, to combine pragmatic approaches to necessities with social collaboration on an individual level as well as a societal one? How do we, and how do different fields or disciplines, change and adapt to ensure aid, create access and establish continuity, integration, sustainable living conditions, and personal relationships for people who have arrived in Europe? The situation is highly complex and requires a variety of diverse alternatives.

But how do we find the right balance between personal engagement on one side and social and political agency on the other; between immediate response to acute and often paradoxical problems—the denial of access to education and work, for example, which makes integration hard to impossible—and the long-lasting transformation of political and bureaucratic structures? And how do we transpose methods from one field to another, from the personal to the institutional to the infrastructural? How does the work of an art institution figure into it? That of an individual artist? Or that of academics? How do we network all these efforts in a sustainable way?

 The refugee situation is clearly not an academic problem, but definitely a problem for academics. How do we make the humanities humanitarian?

The artist Raul Walch created a project called *Azimut*. Together with refugees, Walch flies kites along the peripheries of Europe's refugee camps on the Balkan Route. Thermal lifts and the wind direction correlate with refugee trails and airspace, barbed wire and fences. The patchwork precision of each kite is game and experimentation in one. The kites offer distraction to the refugee children, but also draw attention to the significance of borders. The kites' principle colors, blue, white, grey, and black mean they are camouflaged against the sky. At the same time they adhere to a categorically pragmatic premise: the kites are reflective and thus serve to alert coastguards to the whereabouts of the shipwrecked. The materials used are almost all from the camps and surrounding area: PVC from shipwrecked boats, materials from broken tents, reflectors from discarded life vests.

This multi-faceted approach distinguishes Walch's work. Extensive research and collaboration with refugees and helpers led to the creation of abstract-looking diagrammatic objects reminiscent of the origami-like political situation that gave rise to them. At the same time the contacts, collaborations, and friendships that have formed are not artistic comments from afar, or something manufactured in a studio: they have grown during Walch's journey along these routes, borders and displacement settlements out of necessity and mutual curiosity.

European countries are still deporting, bureaucracies still fail to adapt, and even though Austria did not elect a right-wing president and the Netherlands chose only a right-wing liberal instead of an outright right-wing nutcase, the entire political spectrum has tipped to the Right like a capsizing life boat on the Mediterranean. The fact that remains is that the migration continues. It's not—has never been—a crisis in the sense that it was an event that lasted a short period of time. The flight of people is a state of being, and it might be time to treat it as a historical and epistemological category. It carries with it migrations of ideas, languages, capital, and data. And it navigates and is guided by the infrastructures of data and resources: internet and mobile networks play a central role, as do electrical grids and their differing standards. Power outlets, where refugees can charge their phones, become campfire sites where energy conversion and conversations merge. Access to local SIM cards and the internet is often expensive, maybe even controlled by authorities, who sometimes prohibit smartphones in refugee camps or homes, or even switch off mobile data in nearby towers. This also calls for an infrastructural critique on levels of both governance and business. But it must, and often does, start on a much lower level: personal contact, food, shelter, communication. En route as well as in the limbo people arriving in Europe are often held in for months or years.

The summer of 2015 was a contingency between being and event which resulted in unparalleled civic agency, social change, and the creation of new communities and forms of solidarity. Within weeks of a surge in people migrating across the Mediterranean to Europe and beyond as refugees, citizens in many countries engaged in volunteer work, from immediate and direct aid work along the route, in camps, at train stations, or elsewhere, to more organized projects, initiatives, and NGOs coming to life trying to tackle the problems and deal with the myriad of issues at hand, from something urgent like drowning or dehydration to long and complex problems like immigration law. Many of these activities were coordinated through loose networks on platforms like Facebook and made use of tools like shared Google Docs and spreadsheets to coordinate people, activities, data, resources, and so on. One of these projects is *Refugee Phrasebook*.

Refugee Phrasebook is an open data collection of phrases and translations in open Google Spreadsheets, created and translated by hundreds of volunteers all over the world. It tries to cover all the themes the people engaged with creating it deemed important to help refugees and aid, from general orientation and everyday life to medical concerns and juridical affairs. Within days of its creation in late August 2015, it went viral and grew to hundreds of phrases in dozens of languages. By now, it contains about 1,500 phrases in forty-four languages. The first versions of the phrasebook were printed within days of its inception—incidentally on the office printer at the TBA21 office—and distributed at Wien Westbahnhof railway station and in Berlin, which saw thousands coming at that time. Until now, dozens of different print versions have been created by a variety of people and institutions, and around 150,000 copies have been printed and distributed all over the world, from Lesbos and Idomeni to Norway, and the Google Play Store and iTunes Store. The data is maintained under a Creative Commons 0 License, which means it is entirely in the public domain and can be used, adapted, and incorporated by anyone everywhere. As one of the coordinators of *Refugee Phrasebook*, we know of perhaps most of the projects the data has been used in and most of the print versions made, but the openness of the project guarantees that there is no ownership, central control, or profit to be made. The website is maintained and hosted for free by the Open Knowledge Foundation Deutschland e.V., Leuphana University Lüneburg supported a programming solution to make PDF creation easier, and all donations are used to fund print runs in places where infrastructure is bad and funds are low, like in Idomeni. As a booklet, *Refugee Phrasebook* is a simple and versatile tool for exactly these places with bad to no electricity, phone, or internet connectivity. In worse situations, it has been used as insulation against the cold, and just as it can start a conversation, it can be used to kindle a fire, too. One of the few cases when burning books can help. It was used by Croatian police just as it was used by Syrian refugees and German officials. Incidentally, Raul Walch is active in distributing and using *Refugee Phrasebook*, too.

A central aspect in the creation and most of all the maintenance of projects such as *Refugee Phrasebook* is exactly the kind of infrastructural critique and misappropriation of institutions and adaptation resources I already mentioned. From employing informal and professional skills—like knowing a certain kind of specialist (say, medical) vocabulary—to using office printers, university classes and networks, software, and hardware. Just like *Refugee Phrasebook* itself is a translation tool, peer-to-peer projects like this sparked new forms of translation between different fields. *Green light* is one of them. It was created around the same time, and also functioned as an adapter for other projects, connecting people, ideas, languages, and many fields from design to art and science. All these projects have a few aspects in common: they are both pragmatic and playful, and they combine informal approaches to formal problems with a collaborative effort. They operate on the thresholds of the legal system by offering education where access to the educational system is denied, providing work and creative collaboration and establishing a socio-cultural exchange. And they aim for continuity both in developing themselves further as projects—Walch continues to work in refugee camps and with the materials and discourses created through *Azimuth*, *Refugee Phrasebook* has platformed as a stable resource, and *Green light* is being used and created in a variety of different places around the world—as well as on a personal level. Relationships, friendships, and further collaborations are being formed and help people and ideas.

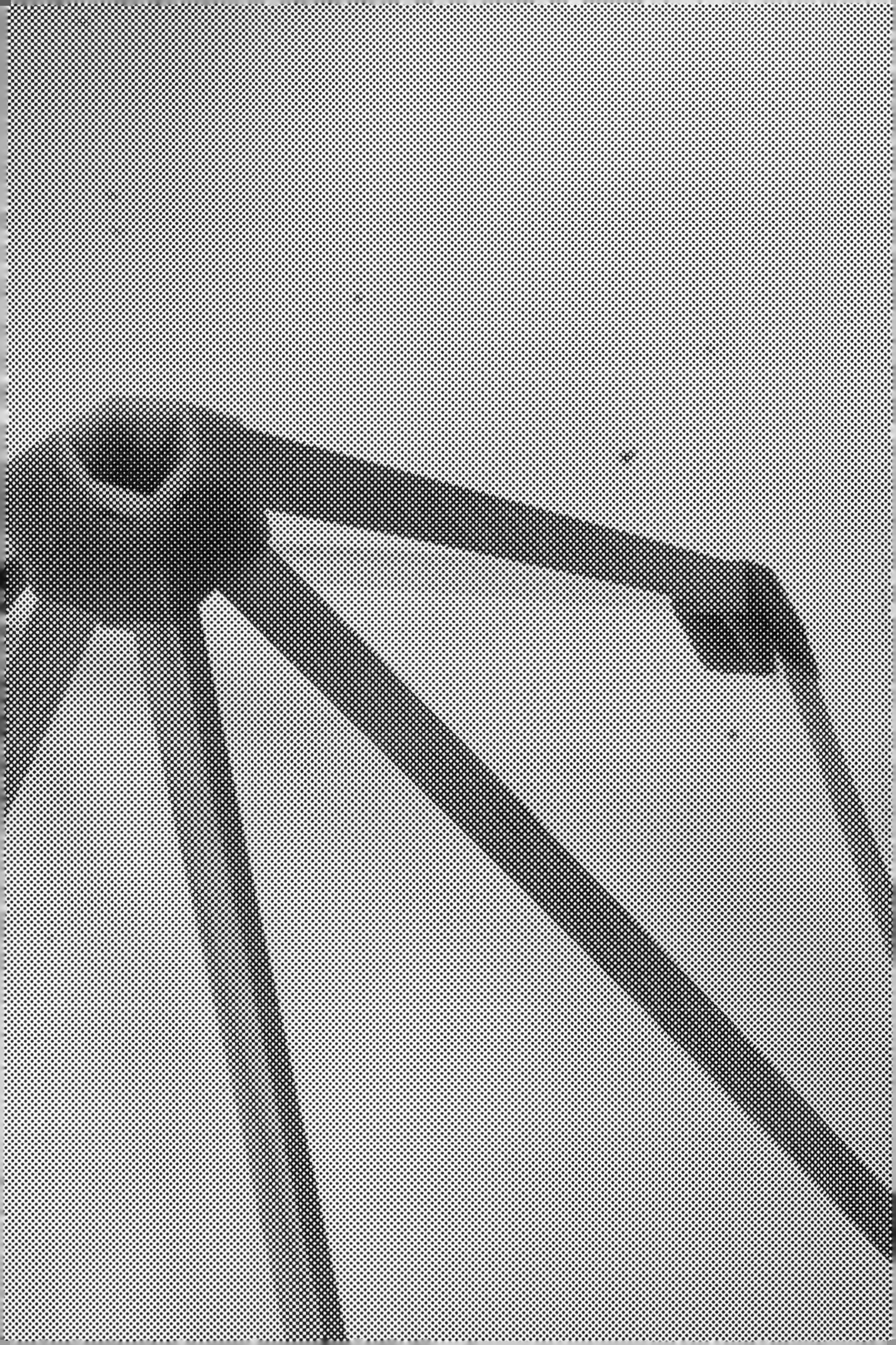

Feeling connected

Kelvin Osazuwa (30) grew up in Nigeria. He left after he was the victim of a hate crime and arrived in Austria in 2015. Kelvin is part of several creative projects in Vienna and would like to become a performance artist. He has not been granted asylum yet.

Kelvin, what are you doing these days?
Actually, nothing. But once a week, for an hour, I have work. I am part of the cleaning workforce at my camp.

But you are also active in your church community?
I also clean there, in the morning, so if we have shared use of the church, I like to keep the house of God clean. Every time I go there, I always believe that whenever something is not ok in my life, when I clean the house of God it will also become clean in my life. I like to attend services, I am also in close contact with the minister and I am a part of the community.

Sounds like an important aspect of your life.
Yeah. And currently, I am also working on an app. It's an app for your phone that deals with documenting difficult situations or violence. When I first arrived here, I encountered so many things that weren't what I expected them to be and that I couldn't read about anywhere. So that was how the idea of the app came to my mind: I thought that it could be useful in dealing with violence, racism, and injustice.

How does the app work?
There is an existing app called Parachute, which allows you to film something you see and upload it live for people to see. They can then decide whether it requires immediate attendance or not. We are trying to get this basic concept more secure, connect it to the police, and make people feel safer by uploading something via our app. In a way, it's about providing safety to the person but it also addresses the community as a whole. It allows us to see many things in our society we can't see at the moment.

So the app is about documenting?
Yeah, things like violence, but not just that. Maybe you are in a critical situation and you know nobody is around to help you. The app connects you with your friends. It allows you to film something and post it immediately. This is why we want to involve the police, NGOs, or other organizations.

Are you working on this alone?
No, I am working with Andrew, who I met through Talent Space. Together we will make sure that this works.

What is Talent Space?
Talent Space is a community we created in context of the *Green light* project. It's a place where you can go and get support for your ideas, sometimes from

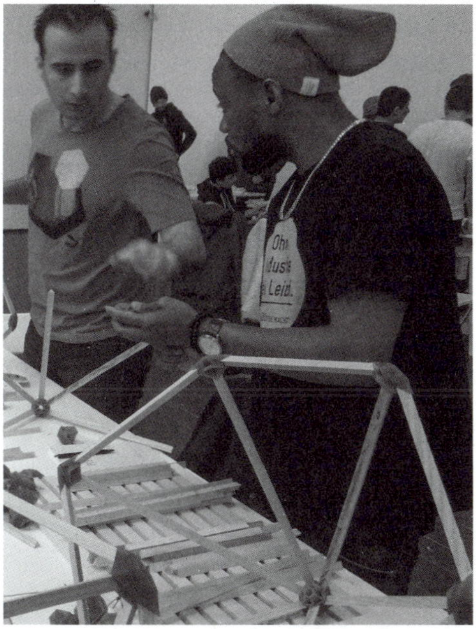

Green light experts Ghifar Al Darkazanly and Kelvin Osazuwa

places you hadn't imagined before. If you have something in mind, it's usually better to work in a team with other the people who also have ideas. And if you have no assets or no clear plan how you can realize your ideas, Talent Space is a place where you can go to figure out something. If you got something in mind, we will try to help you build it up.

It sounds like you are actually quite busy.
I am not. I don't have access to a German course, which is something I would love to do. But the app is on my mind all the time. And there are many other things I would like to do in Austria. I try to pick the language so I would be able to do different things. I try to picture how to get there. I am trying to take steps to get there. But I still don't have asylum and that makes it hard to settle down and sort things out. I want to do comedy, or something in an exhibition context, something that was always dear to me, and make people in Austria smile. But I feel that I want to do this in German—auf Deutsch—which is why I keep trying to learn, why I keep looking for chances to learn. I need chances to speak in a normal environment and I try to talk to people in German whenever I have the opportunity.

You want to be active in producing art?
Yes, I am already part of an African filmmaking crew in Austria—it's rather small, five or six people. Like a little Nollywood in Austria. We are making films. I have a script—or, let's say, more like a proposal—in mind. We will see what happens with it. It's hard to get equipment though, so I am once again searching for partners who have experience. Maybe they can comment on my script and help me with contacts. Show me what to do and how to do it.

A year has now passed since the beginning of the *Green light* project in Vienna: Do you still feel a connection with it?
I never lost it. I still feel the people, they are still around me. Like, I don't see them regularly, but I feel like I never left the project. I don't know, but it's like we are still together and we are still building these lamps. I feel this in my mind, feeling connected. It's a good feeling. Everybody I got to know there has been very helpful. The *Green light* project was something that revived me from where I came from. *Green light* entered my life, when I was new in Austria. It was the place for family. *Green light* was my first family in Austria. I have stayed in that family to this day.

This interview was conducted by Clemens Rettenbacher on April 4, 2017.

I felt that it is life

Homa Khosravi (42) grew up in Iran. She married when she was sixteen and later got divorced. Her daughter and family are still in Iran. Homa holds a PhD in economics and worked as a university professor. She came to Austria in 2016 and is currently attending a German course while she waits for her interview for the asylum process.

I came here from Iran under difficult circumstances. I love living here but I still have a family back in Iran. That's very hard on me. In Iran, I got married when I was sixteen years old because my father forced me to. My father was a very open-minded man, who helped all people, but he was very sensitive about his daughters having contact with other people. I was his oldest child and he thought that I should marry and so I married. But, it wasn't a good marriage, and after some years I divorced. I have a daughter, who is an artist and also teaches. Everything I do in life, I do for her. I started working when I was eighteen years old, I went to work as a teacher, I taught mathematics and physics.

When you were eighteen years old?
Yeah, I like teaching [laughs]. When I was eighteen, I was a student and my father said that he knew I could also work. I wanted to study. Originally, I wanted to study architecture. But my husband didn't want me to, he said I should stay at home. But my father spoke to him and organized for me to go to an all-girls school, and so my husband agreed. I finished my BA in mathematics and physics and then went on to change subjects. I have a PhD in economics that I finished in Armenia. I lived there for five years which was a good experience.

Do you want to talk about your way to Europe, is this is something you want to share?
I don't like talking about the way I came here. But it was really a horrible time for me. I was in Turkey and really, it was a bad situation. It took me only thirty minutes to decide to come here. I traveled by boat with another person. I really don't want to talk about it.

Let's talk about *Green light*: How would you explain the project to somebody who wasn't part of it?
You know, I had many bad experiences in my life. Many times I felt like I wanted to die, really. But this time God sent me something that is good.

What was your first impression when you came there?
I am not the kind of person who goes somewhere the first time and immediately starts to talk to other people. I need to know the person and be certain that I want to be in contact with them. But when I came to the project and saw its aim, saw that it was a good place with good people who are all nice, I changed my mind.

As you know, we tried to create a community in different way, we were convinced that we could become a group by

just working together. Maybe you can tell me how you experienced that?
There were many special things about TBA21. It was especially cool when, sometimes, before or after work TBA21 would organize something interesting for the participants. Supporting people through workshops, but also even more basically through the behavior of the people that worked there. Encouraging us, like though a small celebration, which really is nothing but means a lot for the people who live here. After the *Green light* project I went to work for a tourism project and for a short time at a school. The latter I didn't like.

How did you like the work on the lamp?
I didn't like every part of it, especially not the threading. Ugh, that was annoying. The first thing that interested me when I came there was the 3D printer. I had never seen something like that. I also enjoyed the painting and the sanding. It depended on the day, too. Some days it was hard to focus and I didn't like the work, and others I would enjoy every part of the process. But all together, because I felt calm when I went there, the time at *Green light* was very good for me. When I went there, I was calm.

Is there something that you learned at *Green light* aside from building the lamp?
There were many people with different cultures. People were very patient and helped each other.

And we learned a lot from each other. We were somehow able to go beyond that distinction between "us" and "them"—and all these individuals would come together to be one big group.
In Iran it's difficult. Most of the refugees in Iran are from Afghanistan and the truth is—and this story goes back for a long time—the Iranians treat the Afghans quite badly. I know it's not good. I don't want to judge. Back when I was a child I was afraid of the Afghan people. It's the same thing here: one person from a refugee background does something bad and you immediately have a bad image of all of them. I never would have thought that I would be a refugee myself one day. And that I would feel unable to contact other people because I was a refugee. At *Green light* the contact was very good. I felt that it is life and even if you have a bad time at the camp you can get out of the camp and have a good time, you meet nice people and have good contacts. I felt the life here in TBA21.

This interview was conducted by Clemens Rettenbacher on April 6, 2017.

Apricots under
Green light
Atıf Akın

Our age with its modern warfare, imperialism, and quasi-theological ambitions of totalitarian rulers—is indeed the age of the refugee, the displaced person, mass immigration.—Edward Said[1]

Apricots from Damascus[2] is a publication and exhibition project concerning art in a state of mobility and exile. The expression "Apricots from Damascus" is part of a Turkish idiom which means, "it does not get better than this" (*Bundan iyisi, Şam'da kayısı*, which literally translates as "better than this, apricots from Damascus"). The word for apricot in a number of Romance languages is *damasco*, which indicates that the sweet fruit was associated with Damascus, Syria, for a long time. The apricot was known in Armenia during ancient times, and is said to have been cultivated there. Its scientific name, *Prunus armeniaca* (Armenian plum) points to this provenance. In *Apricots from Damascus*, the apricot—its origins and history—represents a series of connected and multi-layered issues at the forefront of contemporary public discourse, specifically, mobility and language in and from the Levant, as well as the region's complex relationship with the West. *Apricots from Damascus* engages publishing as an artistic practice in an effort to collate interdisciplinary knowledge acquired by communities held together by cultural commons, thus creating new forms and new narratives. The project involved commissioning artists—selected for their experience with mobility or exile—to produce zines, which were published in three languages: Arabic, Turkish, and English.

1 Edward Said, *Reflections on Exile*, 1984

2 *Apricots from Damascus* is a part of apexart's exhibitions and public programs in New York, organized by Atıf Akın and Dilek Winchester and presented by SALT in İstanbul.

My work for the project, *Apricots from the Damascus Room*, is the sixth issue in the series of zines, and one of a handful of commissions featuring an installation. *Apricots from the Damascus Room* is based on the history, architectural layout, and curatorial narrative of the Metropolitan Museum of Art in New York. It extracts and creates its own geopolitical narrative, referencing art, mobility, exile, representation, restoration, orientalism, philanthropy, and architecture. The work's narrative follows the routes of the refugees fleeing from Syria through Turkey, Greece, and finally to the "West," all within the confines of the museum: the installation brings together a series of visual elements beginning with images from gallery 461 at the Met, which includes a residential winter reception chamber typical of the late Ottoman period in Damascus, Syria, followed by the by Koç Family Galleries, galleries 459 and 460, which display carpets, textiles and Arts of the Ottoman Court between the 14th and 20th centuries, and so on. Research began inside the Metropolitan Museum, and the work reveals itself through three types of codes: architectural, computerized, and genetic. As in Olafur Eliasson's *Green light*, procedural thinking and code give rise to modularity, thus creating a cumulative effect, a new formation.

The key to *Apricots from the Damascus Room*'s architectural code is the plan of the Met, published in seven different languages, including Arabic. On the far end of this architectural trajectory, a portion of the genetic code of the *Prunus armeniaca* is displayed. This code represents a particular part of the gene sequence that relates to the immune system of the apricot, which allows it to survive under conditions of environmental stress. Adjacent to this is a series of photographs showing wall tiles and patterns displayed in the Damascus Room and Koç Galleries. Some of the sections of the wall tiles are missing, and a computer-generated code has been used to fill those in.

The wall tiles present a powerful symbol for the movement and migration of forms: unfolding from an invisible source, their patterns are aniconic in character. They arise from the fold, with a line replacing the point as the smallest unit of the form. The use of local five-fold symmetry in Islamic tiles began in the 11th century; examples from this era demonstrate how a period pattern can be transformed into a locally aperiodic Penrose tiling pattern, which most efficiently solves the difficult problem of mathematical aperiodic tiling. Remarkably, these tiles match with crystal diffraction patterns that exhibit five-fold symmetry. This history of forms dovetails with the work of Icelandic architect Einar Thorsteinn, who conducted extensive research about five-fold symmetry, which informed the geometry of *Green light*.

The historical transference of knowledge of modular geometrical patterns is discussed in Laura U. Marks's book, *Enfoldment and Infinity* in a chapter titled "Haptic Transfer and the Travels of the Abstract Line."[3] Marks delves into the journey of Islamic aesthetics westward from medieval times on, suggesting that this journey ultimately informs modernist abstraction and embodiment. She reaches the conclusion that several of the most important modern paradigms, such as pixels, algorithms, morphs, virtual reality, and artificial intelligence were developed originally during the golden age of the Orient, subsequently *migrating* west.

If, indeed, mobility—of ideas, people, flora and fauna, artworks—has a recognized east-to-west trajectory, can we rethink the crisis narrative of this movement ("refugee crisis"), thus enabling new thinking to emerge? My intention here is not to normalize the catastrophes caused by colonialism, global warming, and religious and ethnic conflicts, but rather, to find a common visual and historical language to study and understand the notion and consequences of mobility.

Here, I refer to Janet Roitman's book *Anti-Crisis*, in which Roitman questions how the invocation of crisis in contemporary accounts of economic upheavals and other world events, enables entrenchment, raising certain questions while closing off others.[4] From this, I consider the framing of the recent migrant influx into Europe as something other than a "crisis," in an effort to question a narrative that justifies the delegation of power and action to authorities such as state and international governmental organizations, rather than those very people experiencing their own conditions of migration.

With its emphasis on hands-on participation, *Green light* provides a meaningful context to explore the cultural interactions and consequences of migration. The color green, which is a strong visual elements of the project, calls to mind the concept of alienation. Broadly speaking, green color on skin brings up negative connotations. The image of "little green men" has historically been associated with extraterrestrials and aliens; the Wicked Witch of the East in

3 Laura Marks, *Enfoldment and Infinity: An Islamic Genealogy of New Media Art* (Cambridge, MA: The MIT Press, 2010).

4 Janet Roitman, *Anti-Crisis* (Durham, NC: Duke University Press, 2013).

The Wizard of Oz has a green face; when someone seems sick, they are said to look "green"; in science fiction films, unknown substances like slime are often green.

Eliasson, referring to the modularity of the *Green lights*, says, "You could build a whole city out of these." Built by migrants and others invited to participate in *Green light*, this newly-built city could look like the Emerald City, the dazzling dream city in *The Wizard of Oz*. The modularity of the *Green light* structure transforms the connotation of the *Green light* from alien to "us."

In post-colonial times, the West has largely been built by immigrants and refugees, who provide a labor force, and bring with them ideas, culture, and new perspectives. In his *Reflections on Exile*, Edward Said notes:

> Modern Western culture is in large part the work of exiles, émigrés, refugees. In the United States, academic, intellectual, and aesthetic thought is what it is today because of refugees from fascism, communism, and other regimes given to the oppression and expulsion of dissidents.[5]

Said expresses particular interest in the creative character of exile, noting that much of life in exile is taken up with compensating for the disorienting loss of "home," driving the creation of a new world. He further relates his observation about the condition of exile to occupations that require a minimal investment in physical objects, but, rather, place a great premium on mobility and skill, suggesting that exile is implicitly tied up with movement. He observes, "It is not surprising that so many exiles seem to be novelists, chess players, political activists and intellectuals."

A crisis narrative subjects these events and phenomena to a narrow and limited understanding, and excludes art and art practice. In his book, *Dark Ecology*, Timothy Morton writes, "Art is thought from the future. Thought we cannot explicitly think at present. Thought we may not think or speak at all."[6] Art is not about the time of crisis itself.

5 Edward Said, *Reflections on Exile and Other Essays* (Cambridge, MA: Harvard University Press, 2000).

6 Timothy Morton, *Dark Ecology: For a Logic of Future Coexistence* (New York: Columbia University Press, 2016).

Art is about a time when crisis has not yet happened, or has already been resolved.

A version of this text was presented during *15 Acts of Particiation* at TBA21 in Vienna on April 7, 2016.

We ended up with something useful

Ibrahim Al Bayati (25) is from Diyala, Iraq. He graduated from a medical university in Ukraine and then returned to Iraq to work as a dentist until ISIS attacked his hometown. After completing the *Green light* workshop in Vienna and in accord with the Dublin Regulation, he was deported to Zagreb, Croatia, where he first registered as an asylum seeker in the EU and where his application for asylum is currently being processed.

Ok, my name is Ibrahim Al Bayati. I am from Iraq, from the province of Diyala. In November 2015, I decided to move from Iraq to Austria because the situation in Iraq was not so good since ISIS reached my city. So I planned to run away and reach Austria. I chose Vienna because I knew some people there. And it's a safe city.

How did you know about Austria or Vienna?
I didn't know anything about Vienna and I also didn't know the exact location of Austria. I knew that there was a country called Austria and a city called Vienna, but when I decided to leave Iraq, I was searching for the best city to live, where I could have a really good life and I came up with Vienna. It's such a nice city. Like, to live and have a good life in. And at the same time I discovered I have relatives, like distant relatives, who were also here.

You also lived in Russia for a while?
Yeah, I lived in Russia and in Ukraine, where I studied at a medical university.

Where?
In Ukraine, I spent my last year there. After that, I went back to Iraq to work. But I was shocked at the beginning because the situation was not really stable and it was getting worse and worse by the day until ISIS entered the city and it got so bad you couldn't even go to the hospital to work. I was attacked by ISIS, which was the main reason why I left the country.

How did you learn about *Green light*?
It happened by coincidence [laughs]. Somebody said, "Come to work." At the camp where I was, there were about a thousand people. Every day we would talk to each other and one day, while I was working as an interpreter for the Red Cross, Fatima from our project, came up to me and asked: "Do you want to work with *Green light*? Because I am going there every day and it's a nice project."

What attracted you to the project?
The first thing I was attracted to was just to work here, to be away from the camp [laughs]. Better to have something to do, to work and learn German. Better than sitting around with nothing to do in my room. And the second thing was that the people here are nice. Also the German course with Marianna, it was

amazing and I didn't feel it was too complicated, it was fun and I felt like I was studying at the same time and learning. Also, there was good food [laughing]. I spent my time here well. Also there was the free travel ticket. When I got the ticket I travelled all over Vienna as if I were flying: such freedom! [laughs]. There were so many good things here.

What do you think about the idea that working together in a workshop can connect people, that art can create special places?
For me, *Green light* as a project is something interesting, because for the first time in my life I saw how you can create something like a lamp. Before that, I have never seen in real life how things are made, and it also that attracts people and visitors.

So also the production aspect of the project, you mean?
Yeah, the process and the instruments we used. And also the stuff that was offered to us, the plans and the catalogues showing us how these things are made. To me all of this was new. I am a dentist, so I was not interested in art and I was really blind to these things. I don't know about the people who are used to working with art, but when I walked in to the space, I found it interesting—and that gives you so much energy. Because when you finish your job, you have something tangible in your hands and it is beautiful. So this was the good feeling I got from the *Green light*.

Did you get to meet many new people?
I didn't actually have friends during the project. Only you were my friends—the team that worked with us. But, I mean, the visitors were interested in who we were and how we built these things. So they were not there to be friends with us—which is good, because I don't have time to talk with them every day. But I explained to them how we came here and what we did and all these things.

And what do you think about the *Green light* lamp?
The lamps, I don't exactly know how they will be used. Like, I don't know the correct place for these lamps. Maybe at a restaurant, above the tables where you sit. The light coming from it is romantic. For me, this would be the correct placing. But at home I don't know exactly where to put it. Maybe near the plants, you can put it on the floor and light the green plants at night. That's nice. I don't know where to put it because I have never seen something like it before, it's a new concept to me. The light is not too strong but not weak. It's in the middle. So I don't know.

When you think about the project, what do you think were the strong and weak points in it?
A strong aspect of the project was the fact that we ended up with something useful. It wasn't done for nothing. We did a lot of things which will keep us strong. A weakness of this project was that not everything was very organized and many things got mixed up. Maybe it's the fact that it was a big team connecting about ten people, and everyone has a different idea and everyone is responsible for something else. It's good that everyone had something to do, but it didn't feel like the staff were acting together. I didn't feel all of you had one vision. Every person had a different idea about the project and it mixed up my thinking. I didn't know how to react to all of you.

Looking back on the project now, with your experience and everything you now know, if you were to meet a future *Green light* participant, what would you advise them?
I would tell them, "You should have a big heart!" [laughs]. It's not easy to understand the situation in the beginning. At first, you will feel stressed because you won't know what to do, because it's all new—I mean, it's a struggle to fix the lamp, maybe something is wrong, maybe it's not good enough, maybe the people you work with will say that it's good but deep down inside they don't feel happy about it either, they're just trying to make you feel good and happy. So I would advise people who want to work with *Green light* to be strong and to be open and have a big heart to take everything in.

This interview was conducted by Clemens Rettenbacher on October 29, 2016.

A new kind of education

Marianna Amon was the German language instructor during the *Green light* workshop.

How did you perceive your role as teacher in the context of the *Green light* project?
I embarked on this project with a clear mandate, and knew after three weeks that I would not make any progress with the previous experience I had. I had to find a new, completely autonomous approach to avoid failure, or just to carry on at all.

Where do you see the importance of art in this context, because at the end of day, *Green light* was an artistic workshop? The German course also took place in this setting, in the TBA21 exhibition rooms.
Our work was a joint creative process, with impulses coming from several angles. The idea of going into the class with a fixed concept was something I had to let go of very quickly. I would go into class with a rough idea and let things take shape as I taught—and that's art for me. The flip charts we described, the messages that were sent, the situations we constructed, everything arose from the moment itself. I ditched fixed goals rather quickly, thereby allowing us more and more space.

Do you consider the project a success?
It was a real success for me. Initially, I felt like a complete loser, which forced me to devise new strategies for this process. Which means that I developed and acquired a completely new understanding of my job. It was also a success for me because I met wonderful new people who will continue to influence my life in the future, and because my outlook on

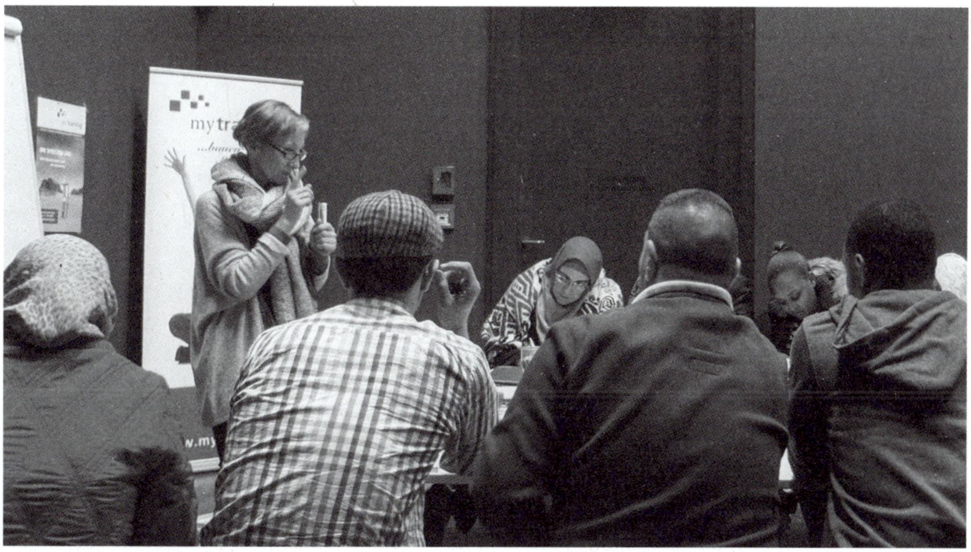

Green light—Shared learning German class

art has been altered. For me, it was a new approach to the idea of art. But I haven't yet completely absorbed everything.

You came into the project as an experienced language trainer and now say that the experience you had did not provide you with the right tools for coping with the situation. That's very interesting and important for future language teachers, too. What are the qualities needed for this kind of project, and how does the teaching differ from a classic language school teaching situation? What have you learned from this?
I faced the challenge of having as many as thirty people from eight different nationalities and four different language levels in one group. That means linking thirty people with thirty different expectations, prior knowledge of the language, levels of education, and opportunities for learning. While teaching I learned that not all the nationalities had friendly relations with each other, which meant it was important to proceed with particular empathy, as well as adjustments. We often learned outdoors, where it was impossible to have listening activities, so instead of which conversations with passers-by. Those students with strong learning skills were assigned to support those with weaker learning capacity. This fostered a sense of togetherness and mutual understanding. I had to set up the classes in such a way that the participants of a course, with my guidance, had to achieve a lot themselves. A project of this kind suits a teacher with extensive experience as a language teacher, who can flexibly adapt to different situations, not only bringing their social education skills to bear, but also an interest in art. I was fortunate to work on this project. It allowed me to broaden my knowledge and skills, which informs my teaching to this day.

This interview was conducted by Anahita Tabrizi on April 2, 2017.

Tawab Baran A poem

Despair is now the heritage of the Afghans!
I have fled, but you say, come back!
I have walked through paths where I risked my life.
My heart was shattered like glass.
I have fled from war and violence,
To find peace and freedom.
But you say, nevertheless, return!
If I were not forced to flee, I would never
have left my home country.
We hope for days of justice,
Which clearly reveals the hardships facing Afghans.
But you say, nevertheless, return!
I have fled and risked my youth, my life.
I secretly shed tears until it was no longer possible.
So please do not say go, but remain man!
So behave fair and show humanity and
do not send me back into hellfire.
But you say go anyway?

Tawab Baran (19) is from Kabul, Afghanistan. He speaks Dari, Paschtu, Urdu, English, and German. He arrived in Austria in July 2015 and initially stayed at the Georg Danzer Haus, then moved to Vienna when he turned eighteen. Tawab writes poetry and produces videos to express his experience of war and fleeing. He has been granted asylum in Austria, and is currently finishing school. This poem was written during Shuddhabrata Sengupta's *Green light—Shared learning* workshop.

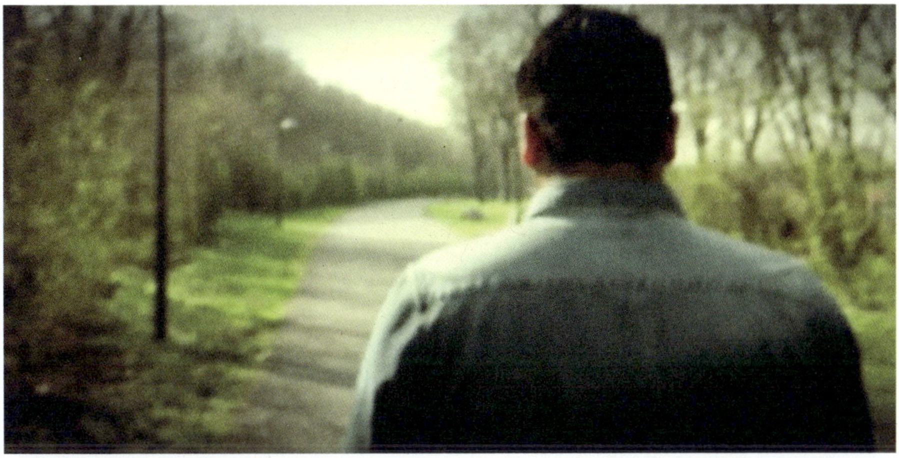
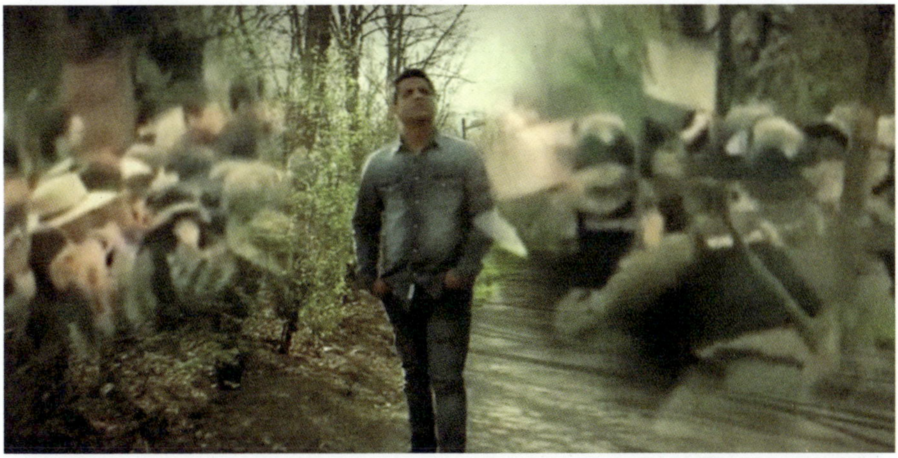
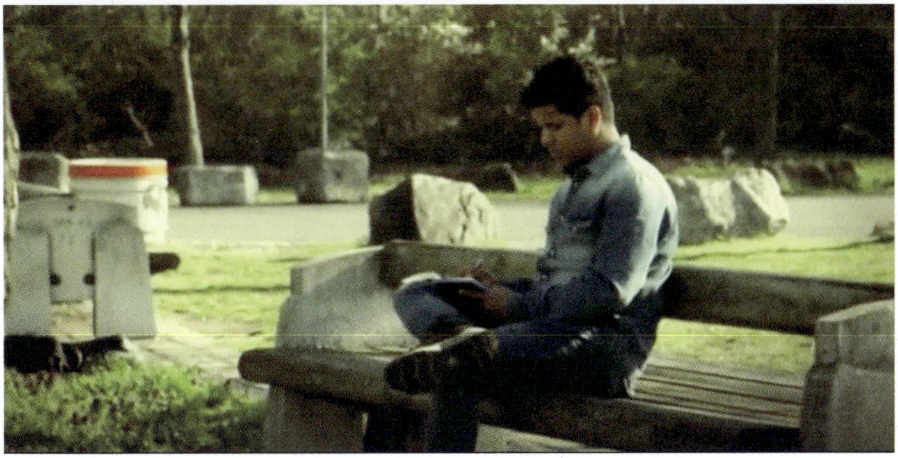

Freedom is a mystic human value
It's a basic need for every human
For every individual
Whatever his nationality, culture, race, color
Or even his religious affiliation

Freedom is also getting rid of all restrictions
and obstacles that stand in front of a human, enabling him to be a protective and effective human
Enabling him to further invest his energies and creativity in any area of life
Enabling him to express his opinion
Enabling him to prove his presence
And enabling him to add his mark
in any aspect of life

Freedom is also getting rid of illiteracy
and a concentration of knowledge
Illiteracy is one of the reasons for repression
One of the ways to prevent freedom
The nations that have been devoted to knowledge
Fought against illiteracy and published knowledge in the community and among all its members
These nations have been enlightened by freedom
Lived luxuriously in freedom

So let’s go get rid of our barriers
Let’s get rid of our limitations
Let’s rise above our knowledge
Let’s move away from our illiteracy
Because as we are humans
Freedom befits us

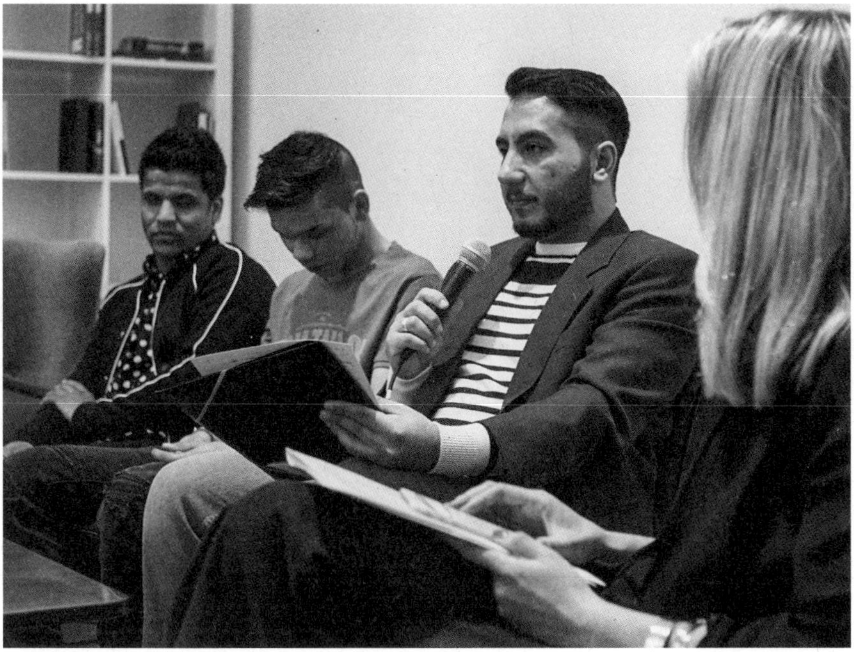

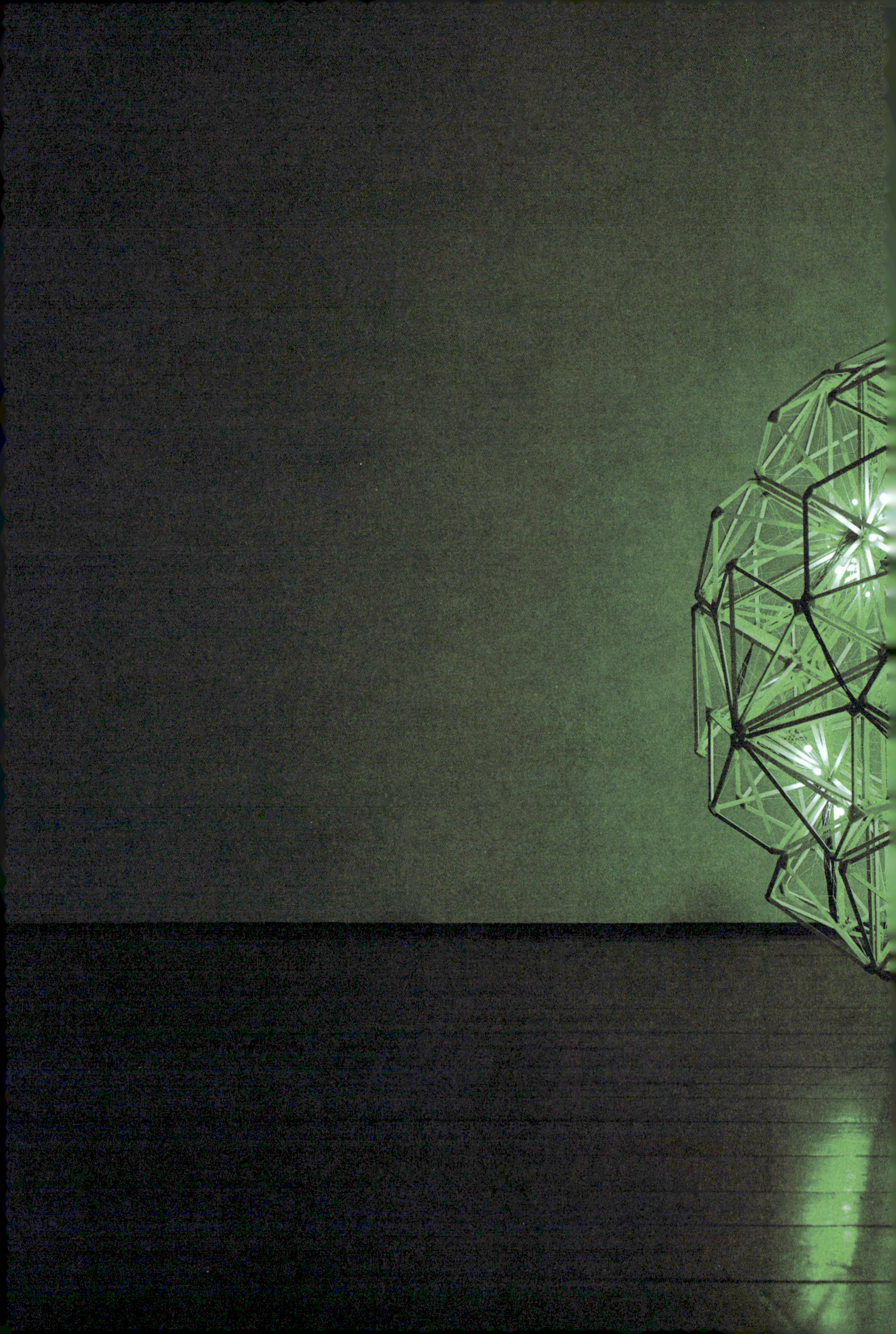

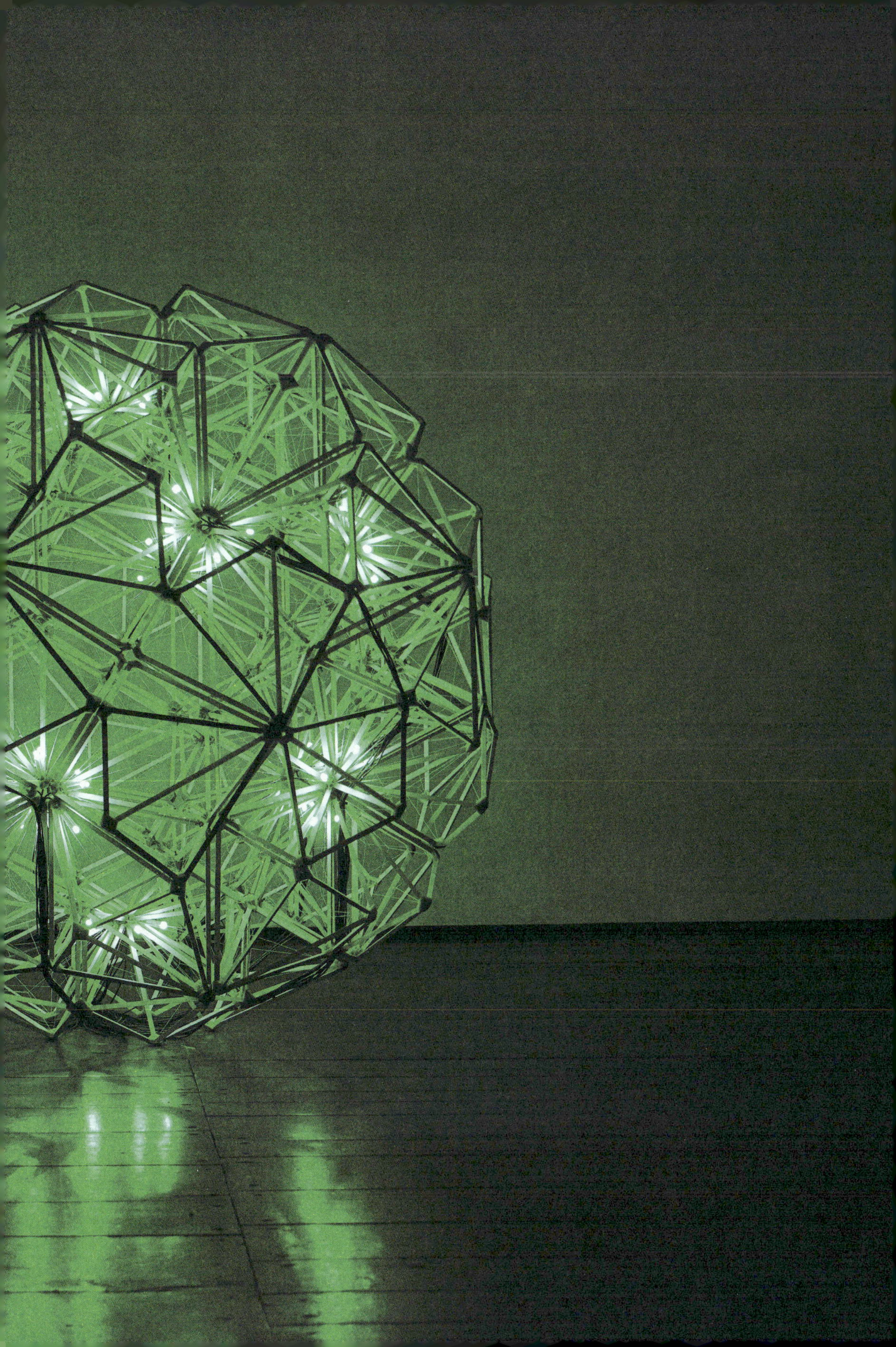

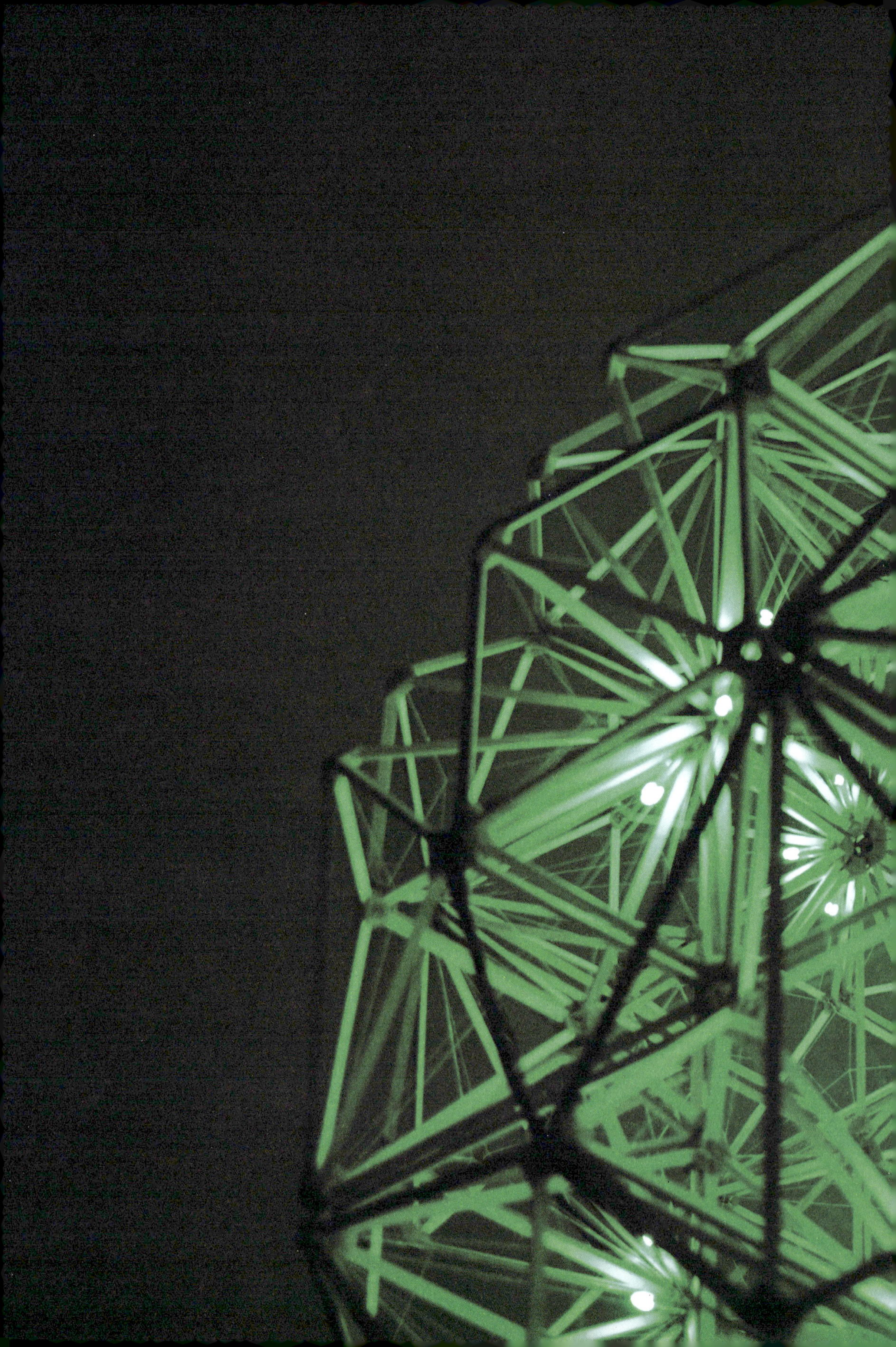

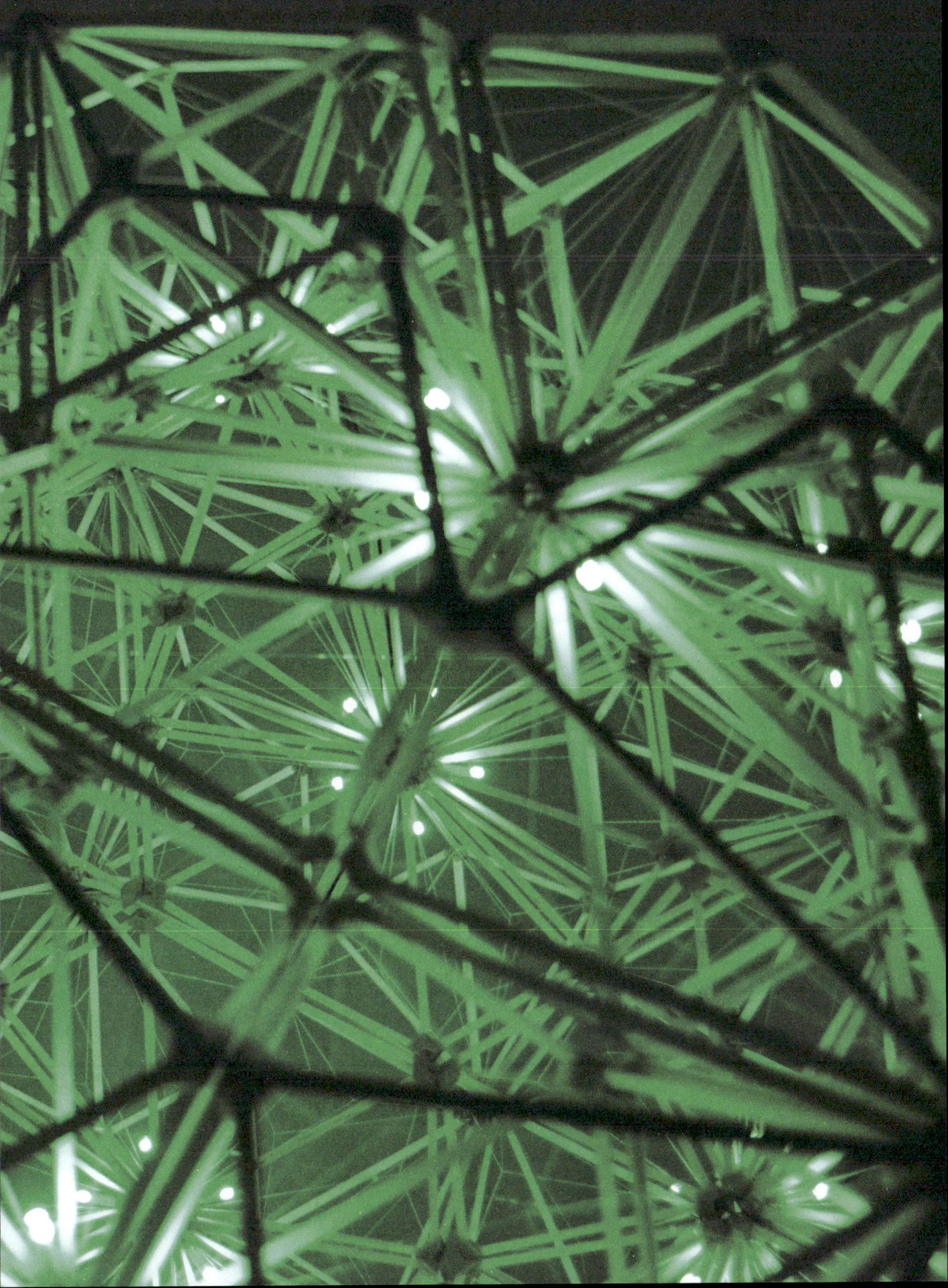

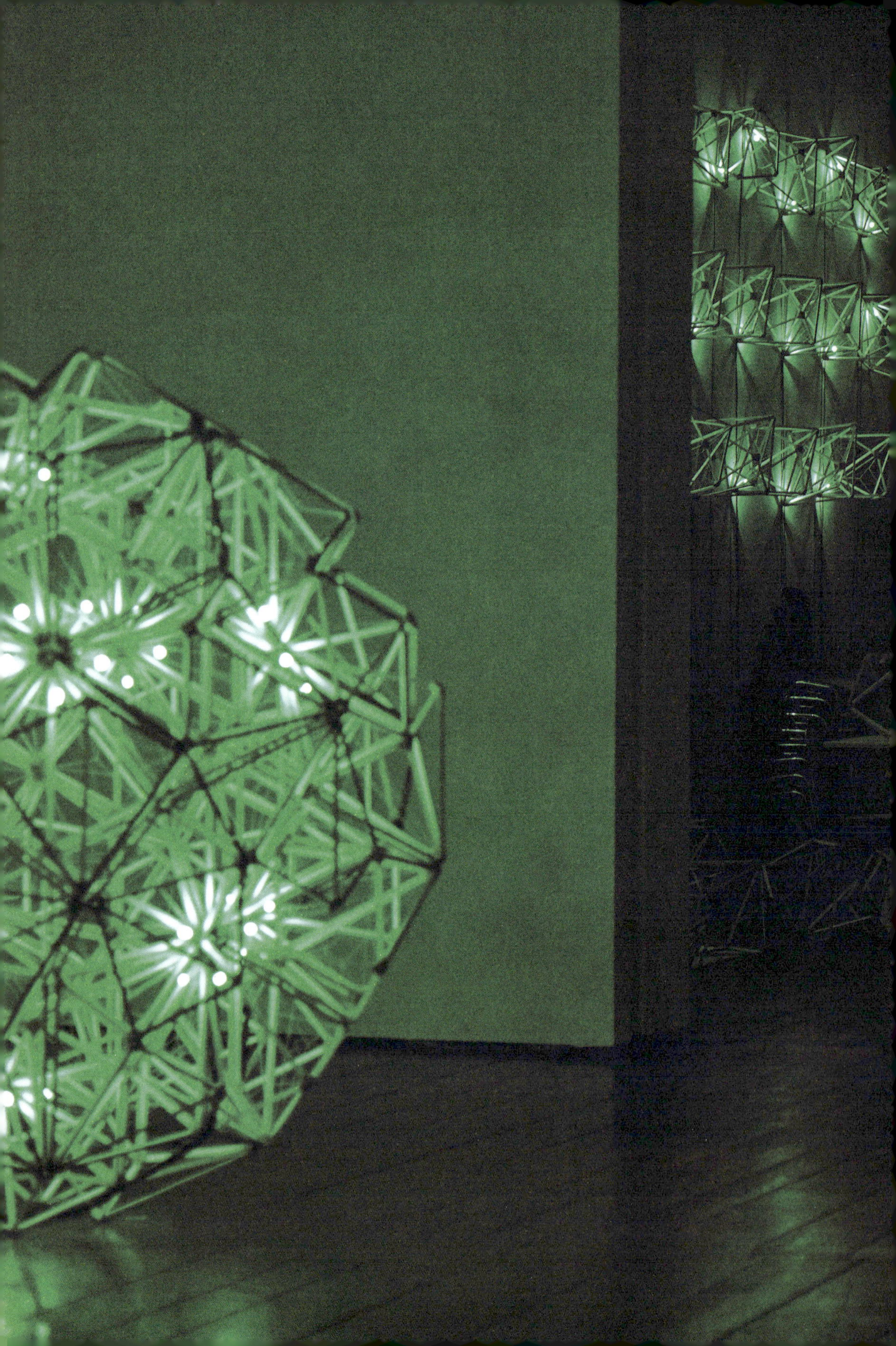

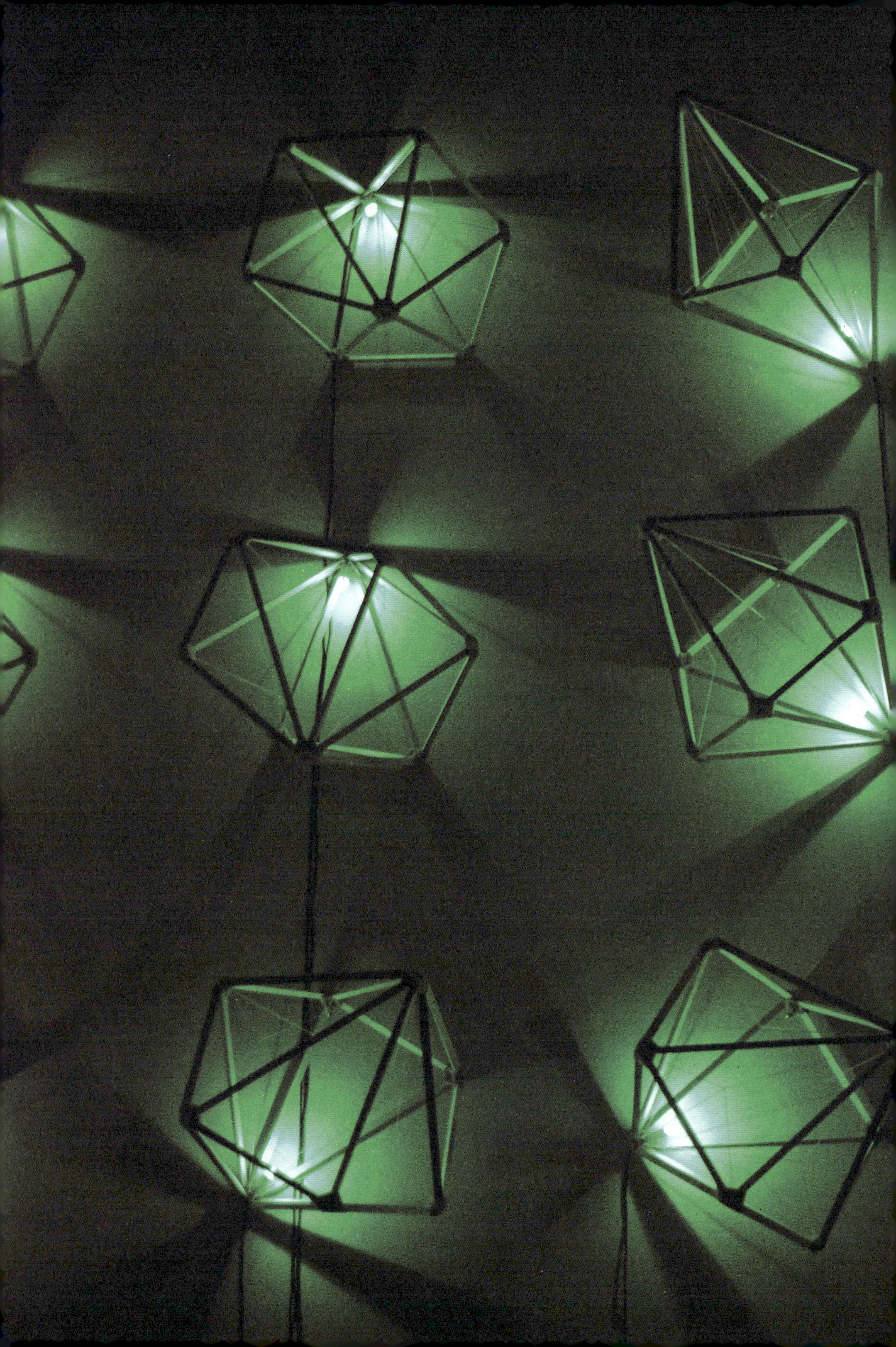

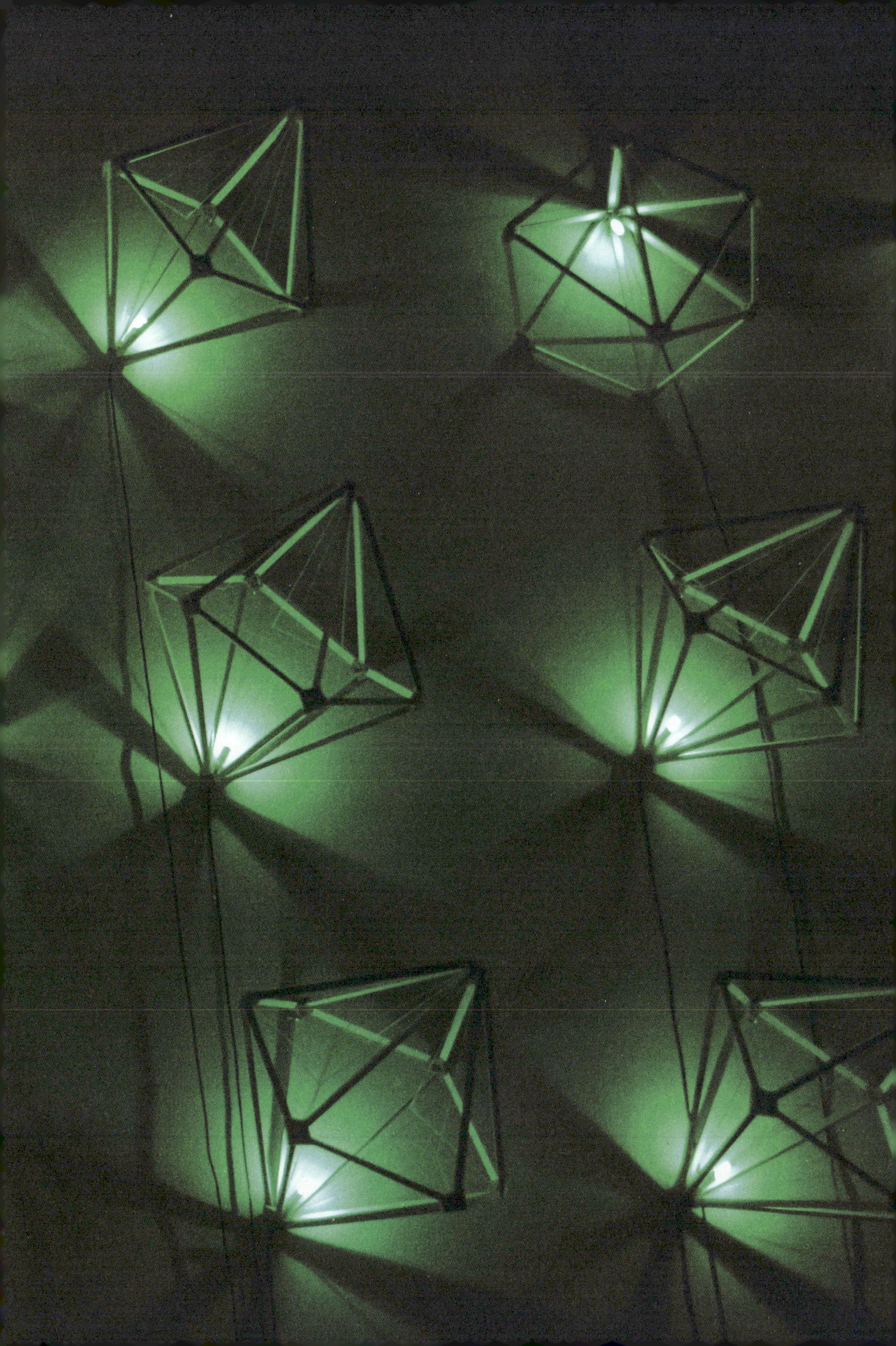

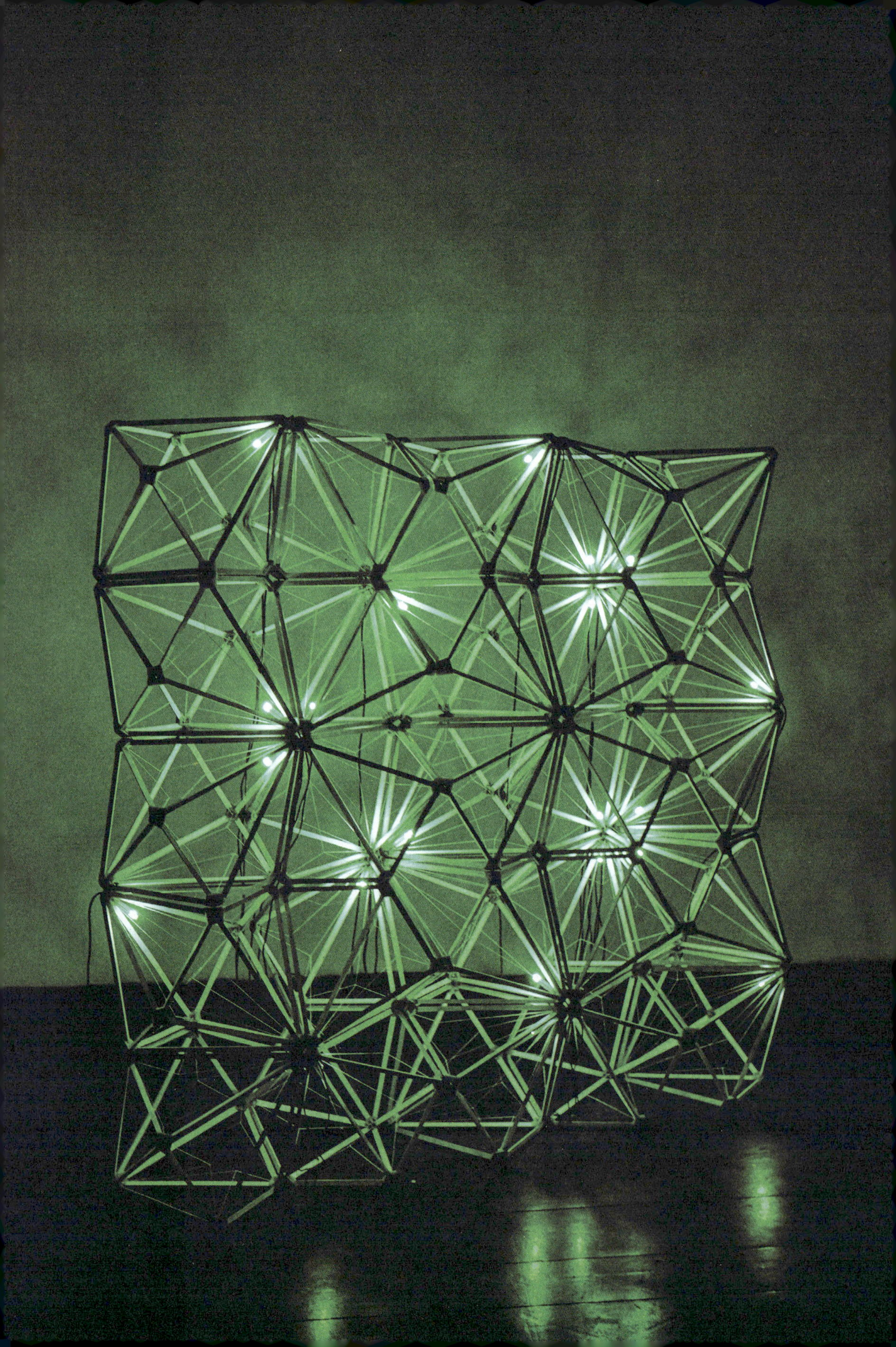

Configurations of *Green light* clusters at TBA21–Augarten, Vienna, and at Studio Olafur Eliasson, Berlin

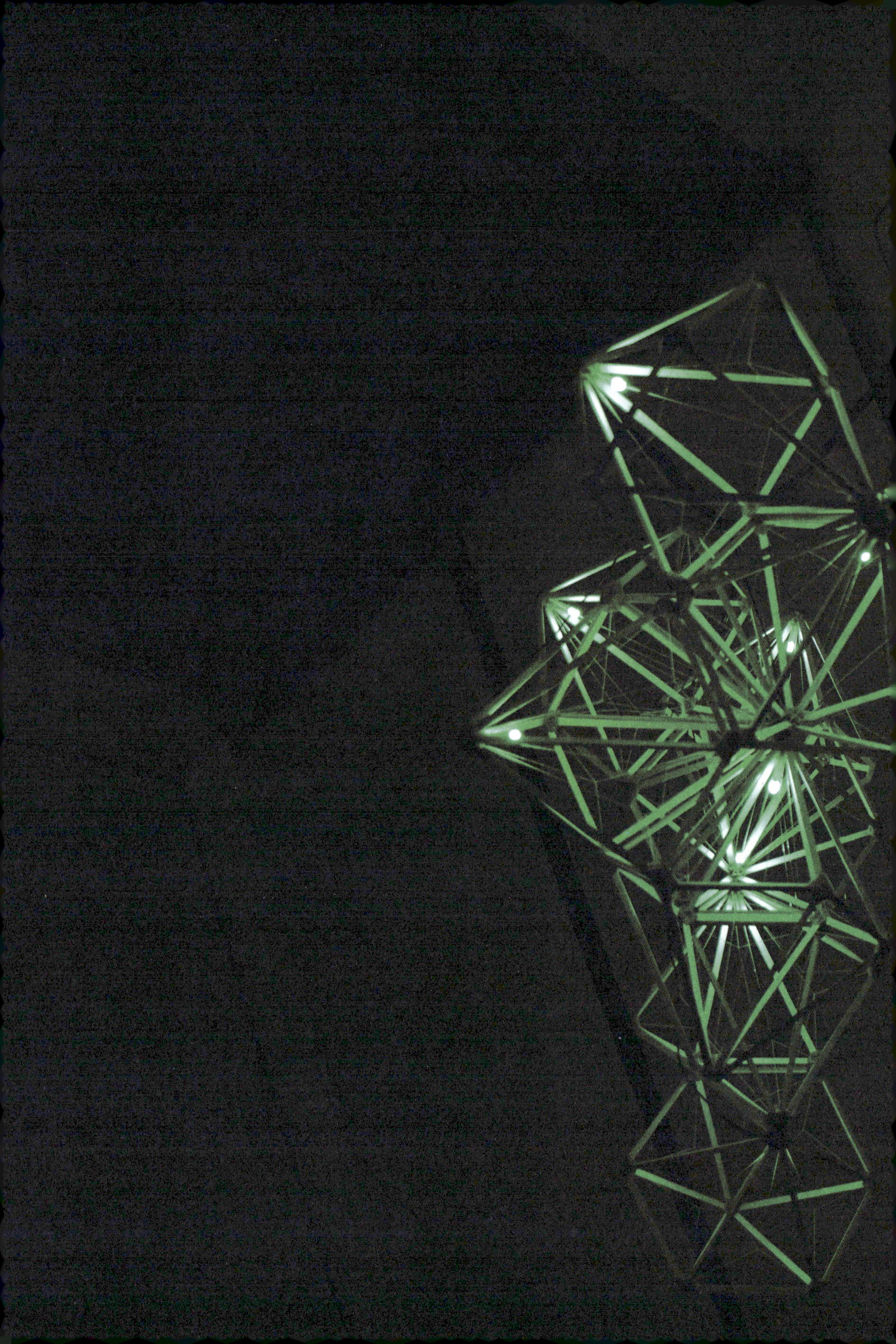

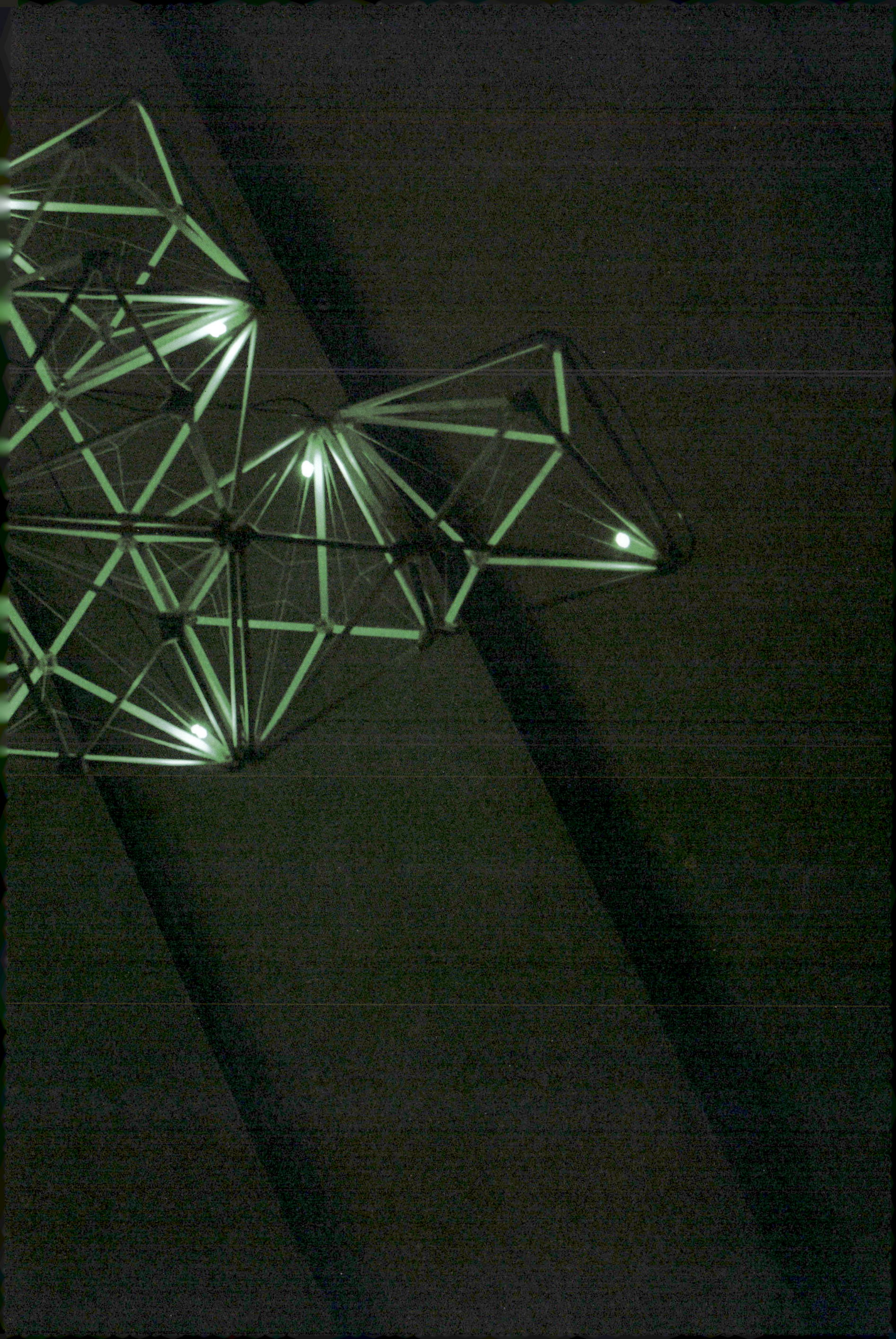

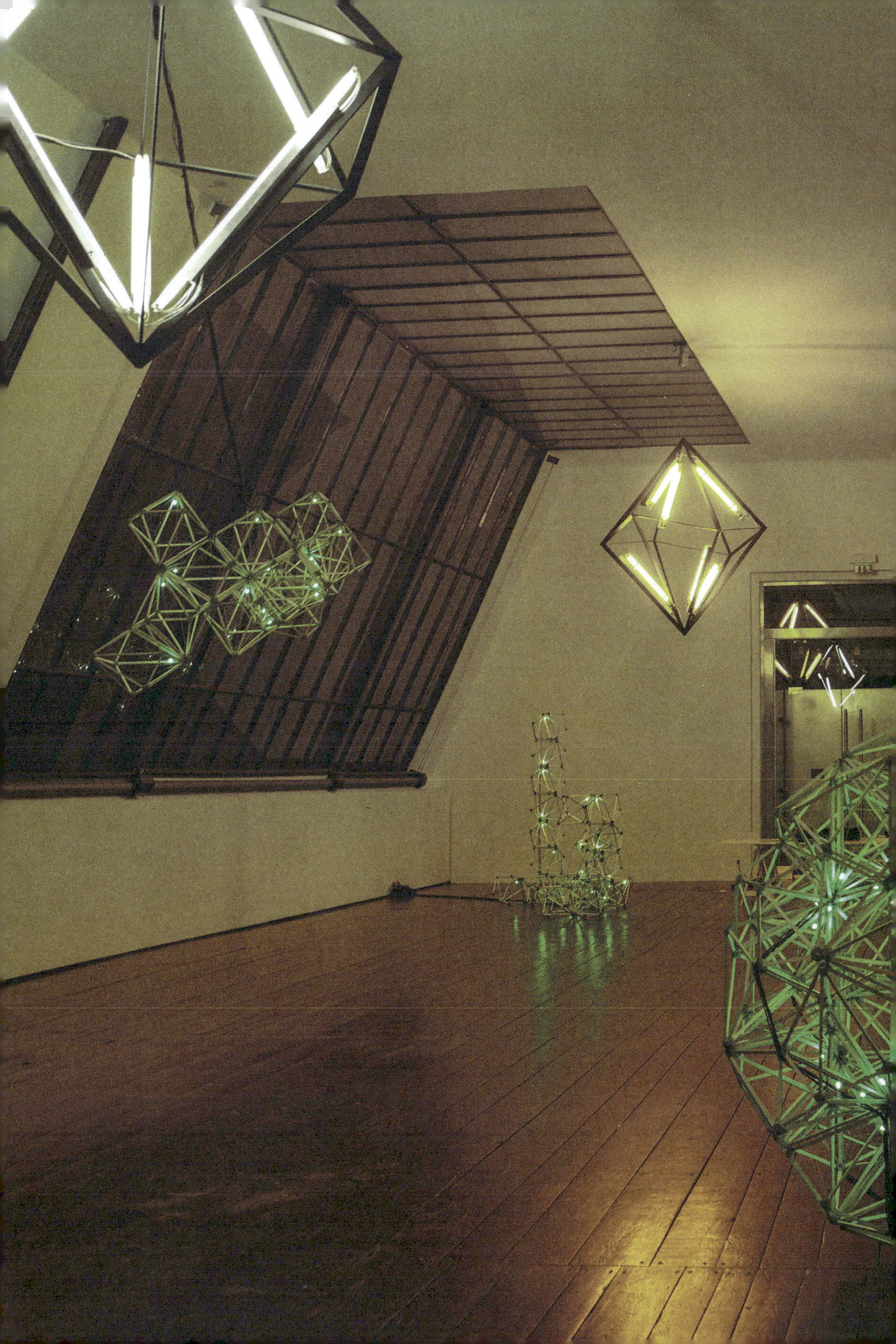

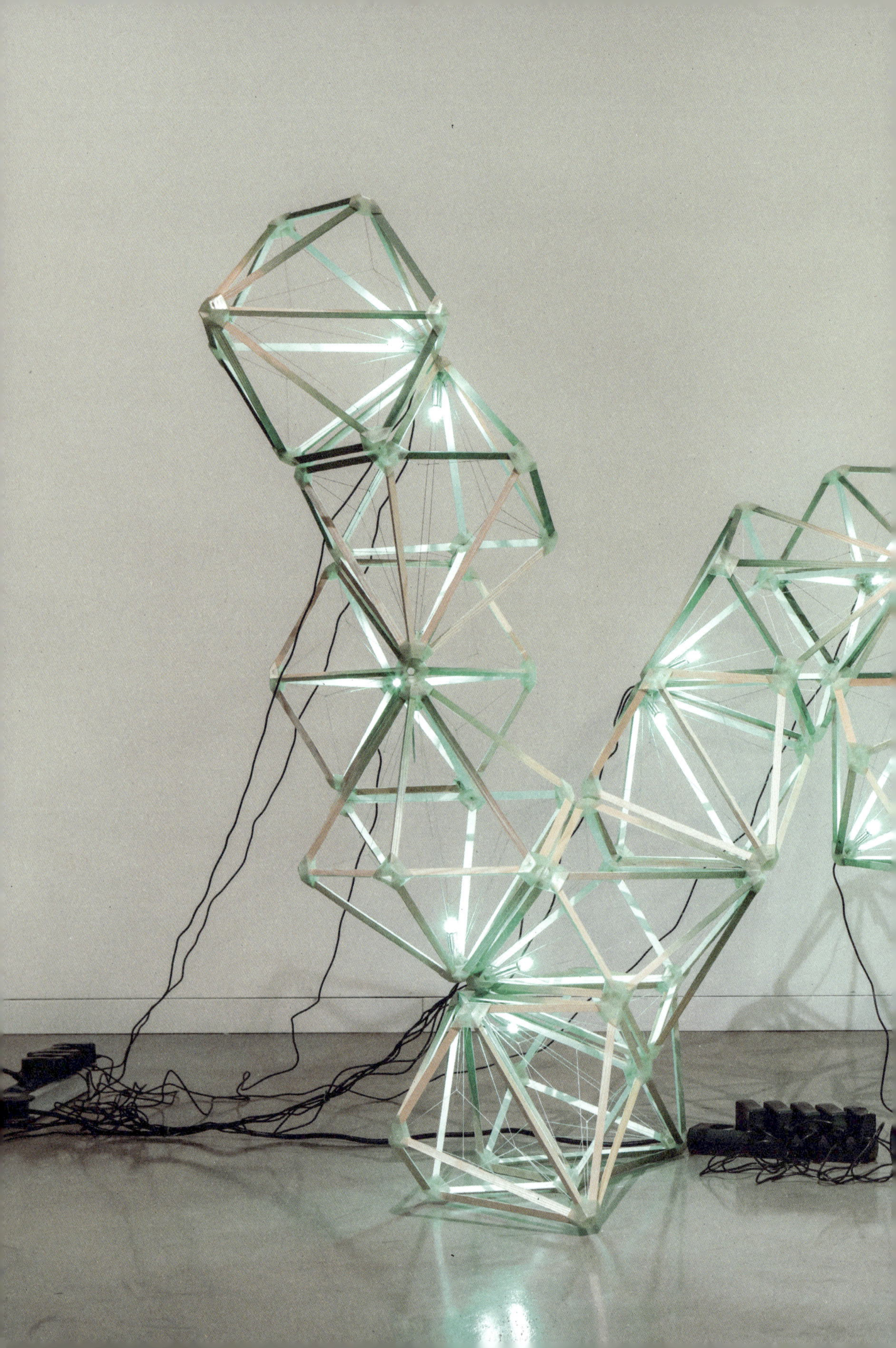

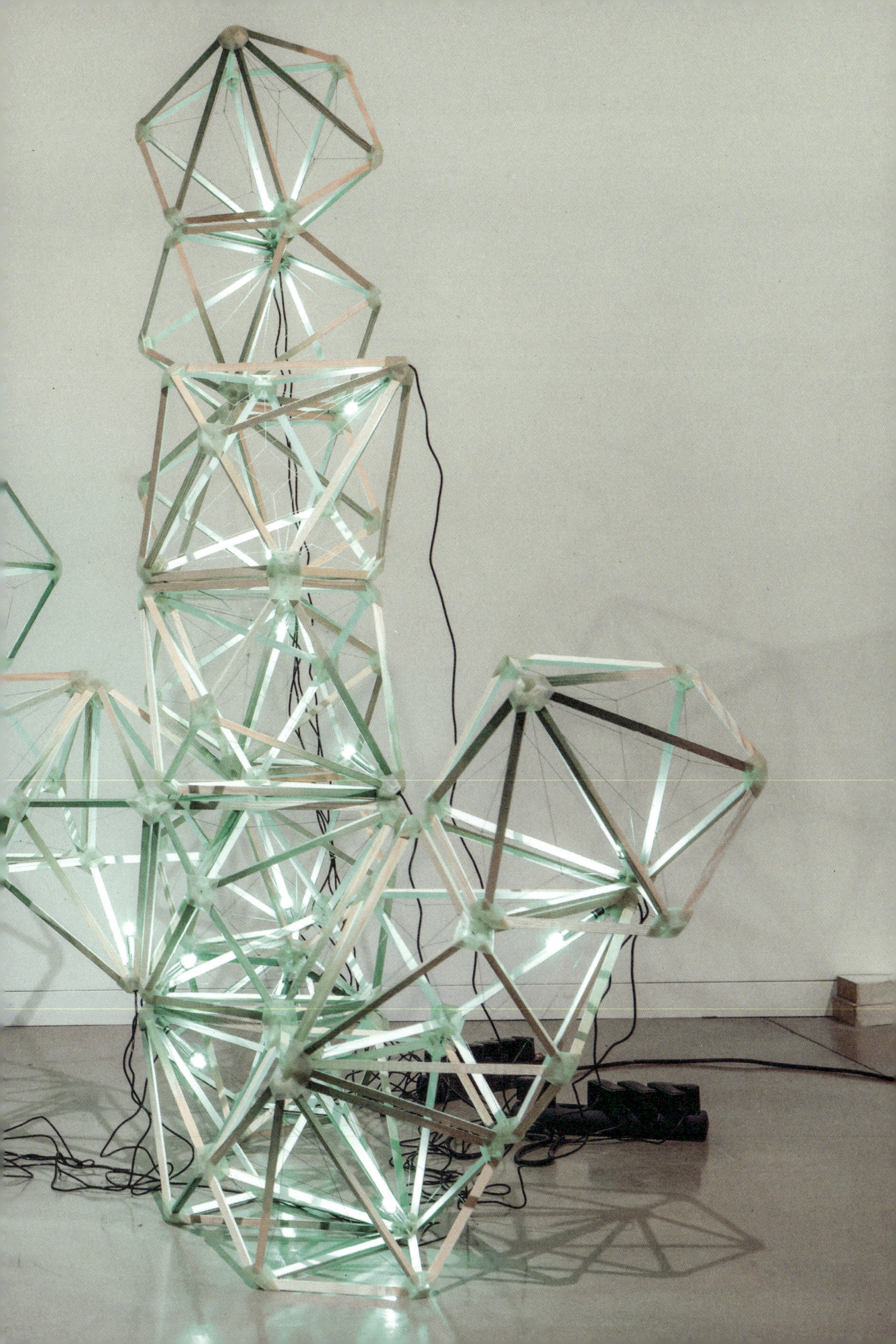

A Creative Laboratory

Alison Weaver

Moody Center for the Arts   Rice University

On January 27, 2017, President Donald Trump signed an executive order suspending entrance to the United States for citizens of seven Muslim-majority countries—Iran, Iraq, Libya, Somalia, Sudan, Syria, and Yemen—for 90 days, and prohibiting all refugees from entering the country for 120 days. The stated rationale was that the order was meant to protect the United States from foreign terrorists, although no data to support the implication that refugees from these countries are dangerous was provided. That same day, the Moody Center for the Arts at Rice University in Houston, Texas, planned a welcome reception for a group of recently arrived refugees to inaugurate Olafur Eliasson's *Green light—An artistic workshop*. By inviting individuals from Afghanistan, Cuba, Iran, Iraq, and Syria to participate together with volunteers, students, and visitors in a project of shared learning, the *Green light* workshop provided a platform for conversation around the issues, anxieties, and outcomes of global migration and its consequences for both refugees and the communities that receive them. In light of radical policy changes in the United States and shifting perceptions around the world, what role could art play in fostering dialogue between individuals from diverse cultural and political contexts? Could creativity inspire actions that affect social and political change? At the Moody, the *Green light* project functioned as a laboratory designed to explore these and other questions prompted by the ramifications of global migration.

On the first day of the *Green light* workshop Hayfaa Al Gburi, a refugee from Iraq, walked into the Moody not knowing what to expect. "I didn't understand anything," she said. Several weeks later, on the occasion of a visit from Olafur Eliasson, she declared, "For me, this is the perfect project! I love this work and this place. I learn everything here. I learn the language and meet wonderful people. When we build the lamps, we work together, people from all countries. We work together, we talk together, we understand." What had transpired in those intervening weeks to transform Ms. Al Gburi's perception of the experience?

After an initial period of training, a rhythm emerged whereby participants worked together on various aspects of lamp assembly, then broke for lunch, conversing in diverse languages and sharing their experiences through gestures and volunteer translators. Music played an important role, with the sounds of different cultures serving as a backdrop for the interplay of languages spoken, and one participant, Mohammad Sheikh Horo, an accomplished saz musician, even shared his talent through an impromptu concert one day over lunch. Through the daily sharing of food and music, and creative hands-on construction, bridges were built across cultures, from as far away as the Middle East to as close to home as the local Houston neighborhood.

Fundamental to the success of the workshop was the participation of volunteers, students, and community partners from across the city. From the overall management of the project to English-language classes, seminars on cultural themes, and assistance with building the lamps, the *Green light* workshop brought together an entire community. Project Manager Sarah Jane Boardman explained her motivations for volunteering: "I am relatively new to Houston and was looking for a way to engage in the local community. After hearing about *Green light,* it seemed like a fantastic opportunity to gain awareness about the resettlement process and to help others assimilate in Houston. The members of *Green light* have given me a real sense of community and of family. Learning about everyone's different journeys to get to where they are, specifically their resilience, tenacity and kind heartedness, has been a humbling experience. It has strengthened my belief in the goodness of people."

The number of volunteers who dedicated themselves to the workshop is impressive: community members drove participants to and from the Moody each day, trained volunteers taught English as a second language, students assisted with construction of the *Green lights*, and experts offered a wide range of creative programs such as a DJ workshop tracing the history of local music; a slide show on the rules of baseball, followed by a pick-up game on the lawn and tickets for families to attend a game in the University stadium; a primer on the organization of the US Government; a photography workshop; and a documentary film on the refugee crisis in Greece.

In addition to individual contributors, community organizations were vital to the project's success. Free Wheels Houston, a local nonprofit that donates used bicycles to refugees, worked with the group to refurbish bikes and distribute them to families. Plant It Forward, a group that employs refugees to create sustainable urban farms, hosted the participants for a day of training in agricultural work. The Moody's primary partner, Interfaith Ministries of Greater Houston, the largest refugee resettlement organization in Houston, supported the project through its connections to the community of refugees and the volunteers who support them. It is through this wide network of mutual support that the *Green light* workshop modeled, on a small scale, how broader social integration can occur. It illustrated not only the ways in which current residents can help recent arrivals, but also how the skills and assets that refugees bring can enrich a community.

The Moody's location in Houston is significant, since Houston has accepted more refugees on an annual basis than any other city in Texas and ranks among the top three cities nationally. Houston's growing economy and rich diversity make it an excellent choice for refugee resettlement, and a welcoming home for people from all over the world. Last year, Interfaith Ministries resettled 680 refugees from fifteen countries: Afghanistan, Bhutan, Myanmar, Burundi, Congo, Cuba, El Salvador, Eritrea, Ethiopia, Honduras, Iran, Iraq, Somalia, Sudan, and Syria. This mix of cultures has diversified the city over the past several decades and continues to contribute to its rich cultural landscape. The *Green light* workshop is a central part of the inauguration of the Moody Center for the Arts, a new building on the campus of Rice University dedicated to trans-disciplinary collaboration through the arts. It signals the idea that creative approaches to seemingly complex issues can provide rewarding pathways and assist us in mapping positive solutions for the future. Following the Houston workshop, our hope is that *Green light* will continue to be a beacon for communities around the world.

The Light

Ian Cion

Artists interested in engaging in civic action have many paths to choose from these days, not the least of which is the continued plight of the dislocated, the disenfranchised, the refugee, the asylum seeker.

It is easy to find a cause to be outraged and motivated by in a world in which at almost every single turn comes more bad news. What's more difficult is to channel creative energy toward making positive impacts in the daily lives of those we encounter.

It is not enough, perhaps, to criticize the heartless and ill-fated actions of those who are driven by fear and isolationism. It is not enough to feel aligned with the forces for good by opinion alone. Opinion does not bring you to a moral high ground. We must enter into the fray of action, we must endeavor to uplift, support, and transform the lives of those in need in their hour of need.

Perhaps this moment is the heart of the crucible in which we are becoming more interconnected, more responsible, more caring, and more alive. We can't just simply say "now more than ever," we can't just say "it is what it is." Transformative actions need not be rooted in institutions, nor lauded, nor even acknowledged. They can happen in the subtle undercurrent of our daily lives, in the way we invite people in, in how we open our door to the world.

Every day the Blackhawks, the Tomahawks, and the drones fly over. Every day reminds us that war rages on. There is no evidence to support the idea that war is the pathway to peace. In fact, after thousands of years of trial and error, from the flint arrow to the nuclear weapon, war still has not triumphed. What, then, of peace? What options do we have before us that we have not yet tried? What deep and thoughtful diplomacy? When the government continues to fail its people, when elected officials continue to remain blind to the needs of the global community, when even school children can understand the profound interconnectivity of all life on this planet and yet adults fail to see actionable steps to align their institutions with this fundamental truth, a radical overhaul of the system is required.

Whom can we rely on? Whom can we turn to? There is a moment, the moment that is maturity, in which we know that we must take matters into our own hands. If, for example, we don't believe in walls, if we don't believe in borders, then we must with all our hearts tear down those walls and borders which keep us isolated, which keep us secure at the expense of our very freedom. We are truly one planet, and truly with the great flow of natural currents, in the sea of time, we share one fate. Cynicism is the sure road to destitution, isolationism the direct path to desolation.

One must come to understand that one's knowledge, efforts, and desires, can be used for good or for gain, and though at the outset of one's journey, this choice can seem difficult, the farther along one travels, the clearer the answer becomes. In moments of weakness and vulnerability it is easy to convince people that the root of the problems is the Other. Because vulnerability manifests the two antithetical responses, fear or courage, it is an important state of being to learn from. Because illumination does not come without risk. New worlds will not be discovered by those too comfortable or too entrenched to leave home. Every explorer is a refugee. Because of the singular direction of the river of time, no home—nor any moment—can ever be returned to, therefore when you meet the traveler on the road, their road is your road, and your road theirs.

It is not in the publicized act, in the bill or the law that the goodness of humanity is contained. Though these things can shed light on our ideals, they are meaningless without the very real, true, and essential daily kindness. All grand proclamations are but sand castles, useless and tired tropes that do not define the character of an innovative people.

Now that the flood of need seems never to slow down, we must become more excellent in our response. We must become masters of caring, we must become physicians that can heal in the most remote regions, we must become poets that can reach into the depth of human character and read the truths of nature in the cosmos. We must inoculate ourselves against the skepticism that doubts our ability and the power of our gentleness. It is true that we have reached a turning point, the threshold that once crossed can never be passed over again. We stare out at the vast horizon into the unknown, which is the only certain. Is not in the parliament, it is not in the launch codes. The way forward inevitably requires that we break from negative habits, from half-baked philosophies of pirate kings, the way forward requires tranquility, integrity, and the code of ethics that prioritizes the accumulation of positive action, of good deeds, rather than the accumulation of objects.

If this is the charge of our current ecosystem, what is to become of the artist? What is to become of the maker of objects? Who are they to make their objects for? And what is the purpose of excellence? Is it for the sake of achievement alone? Is it for vanity? For the ego?

Excellence, in the end, must be in service of ideals. Excellence must be achieved so that ideals can become manifest. Excellence must be achieved to make the impossible possible. The pure inalienable pursuit of excellence is ultimately toward the increasing and ever diversifying flourishing of a blooming cosmos. Excellence is not pursued for accolades or glory, but rather for the refinement of function. There is no more essential task than the cultivation of an excellent self. Interestingly, the cultivation of an excellent self requires dedication to the excellence of the lives of others. No excellence can be achieved without commitment to improving reality itself. Reality is like a shell that we have inherited from others, but eventually it grows too small to contain our multitudes, and we must rebuild our home to accommodate.

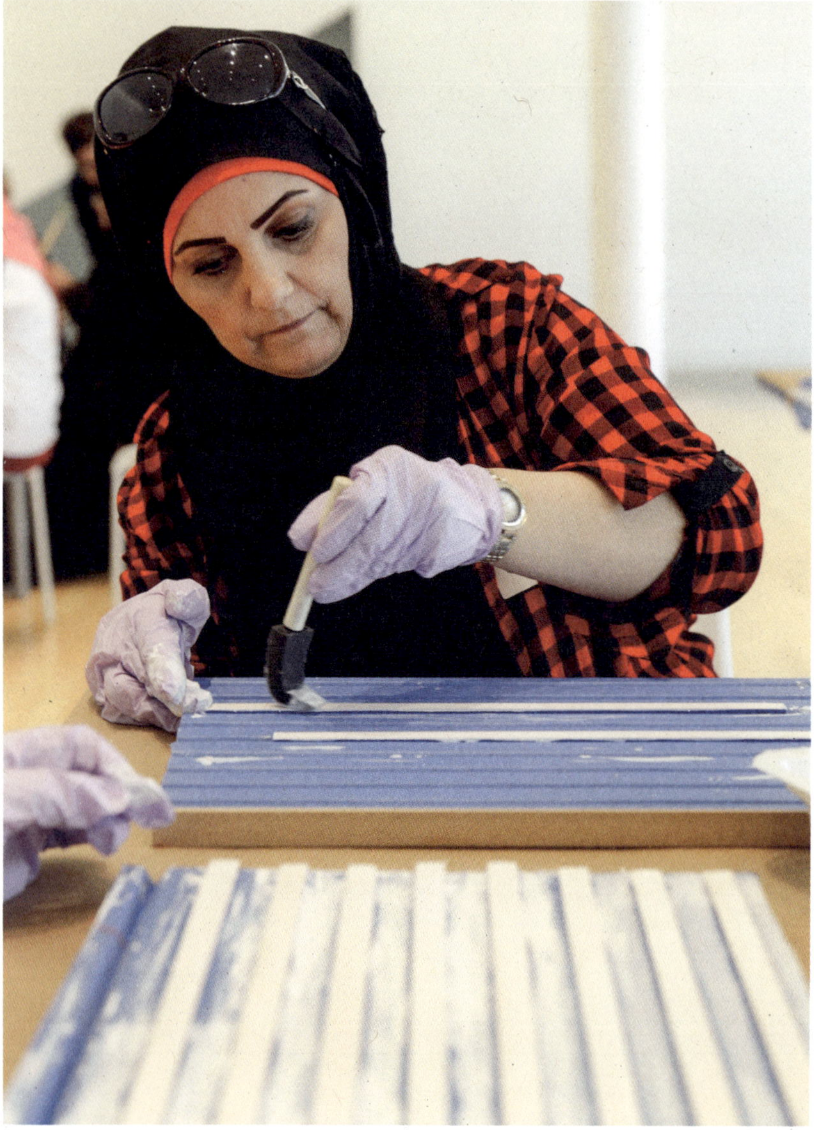

Green light experts in Houston, Texas

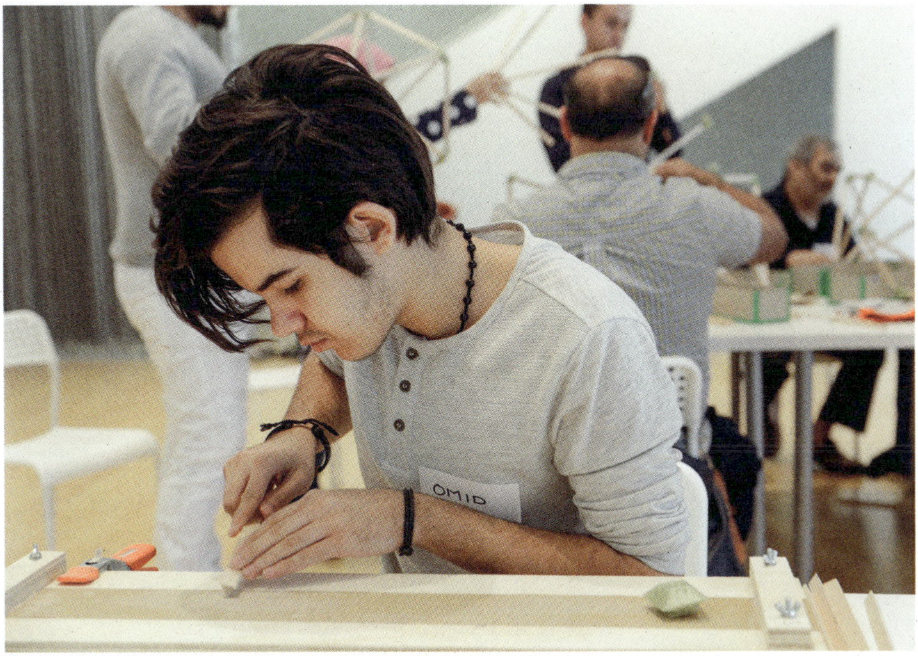
OMID

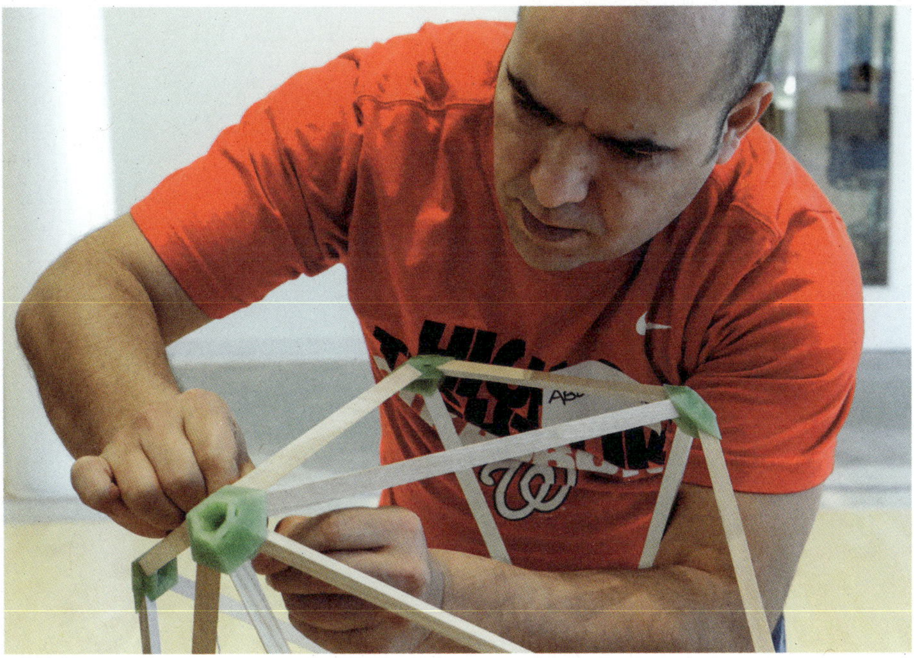

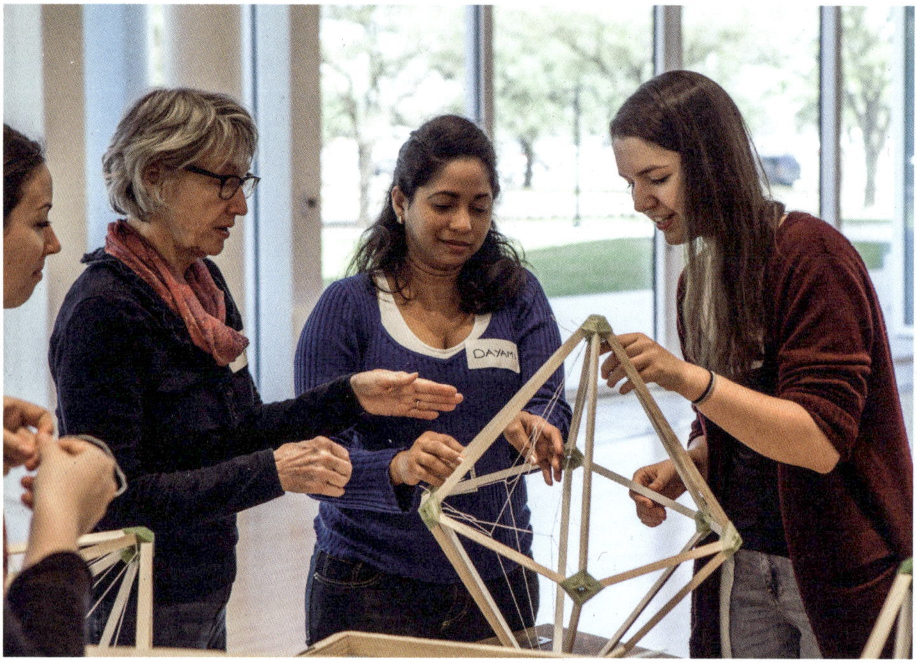

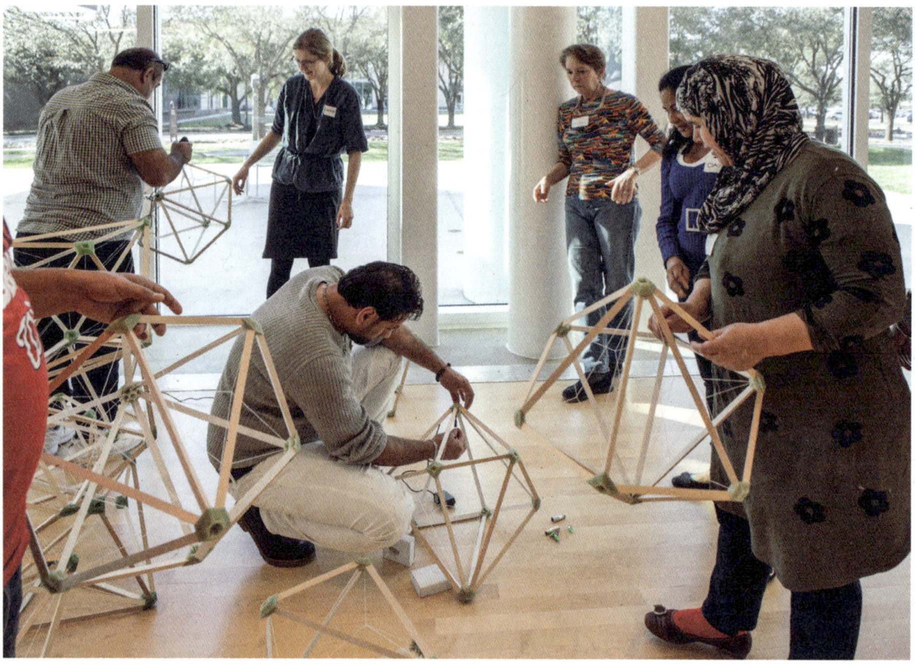

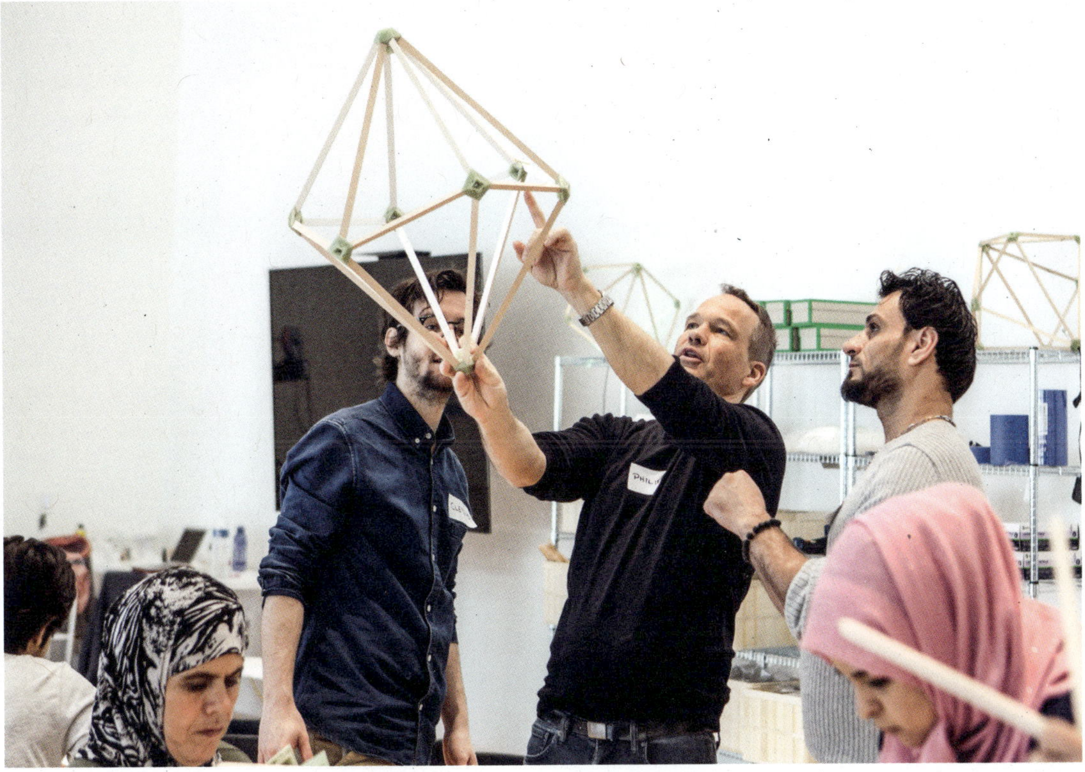

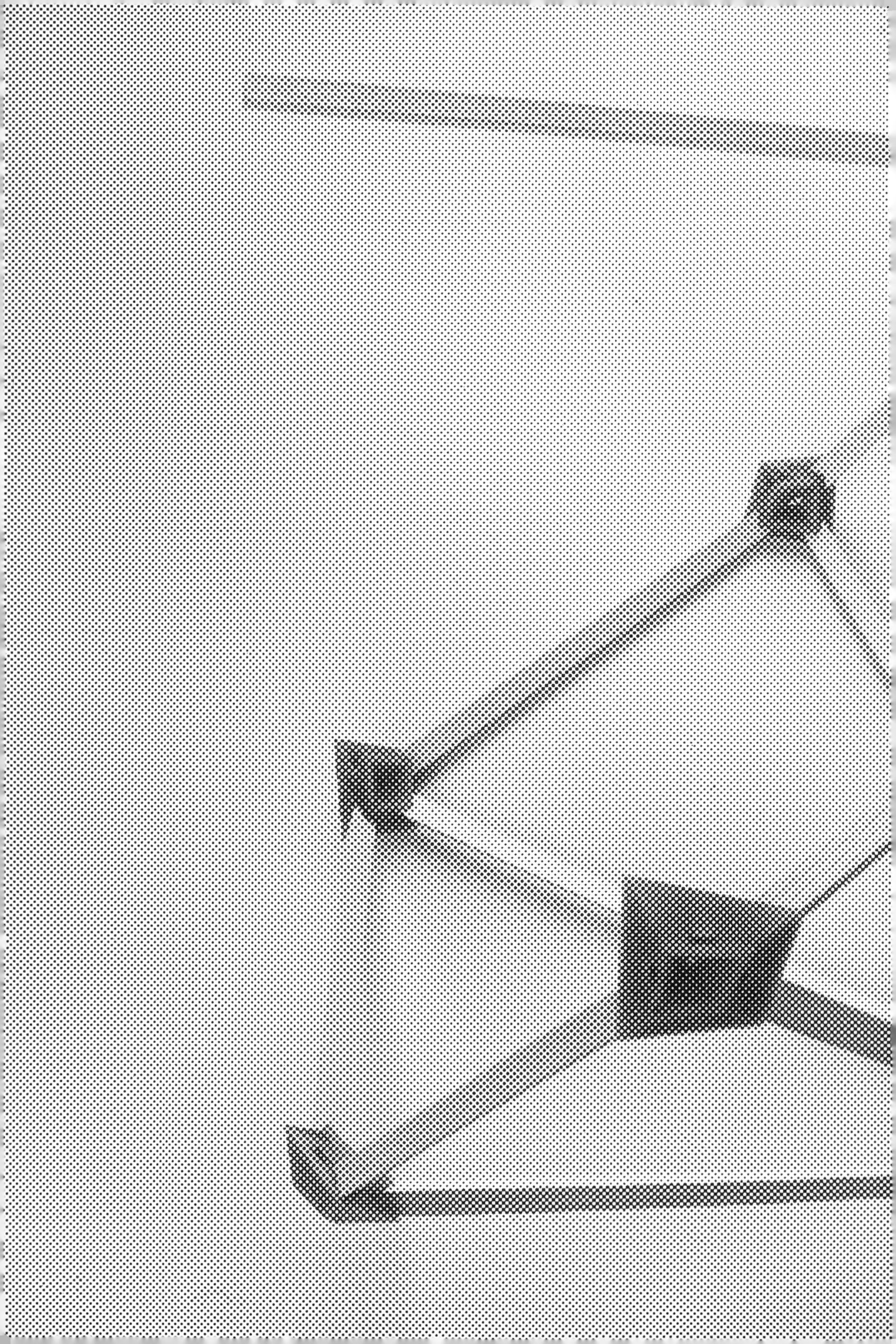

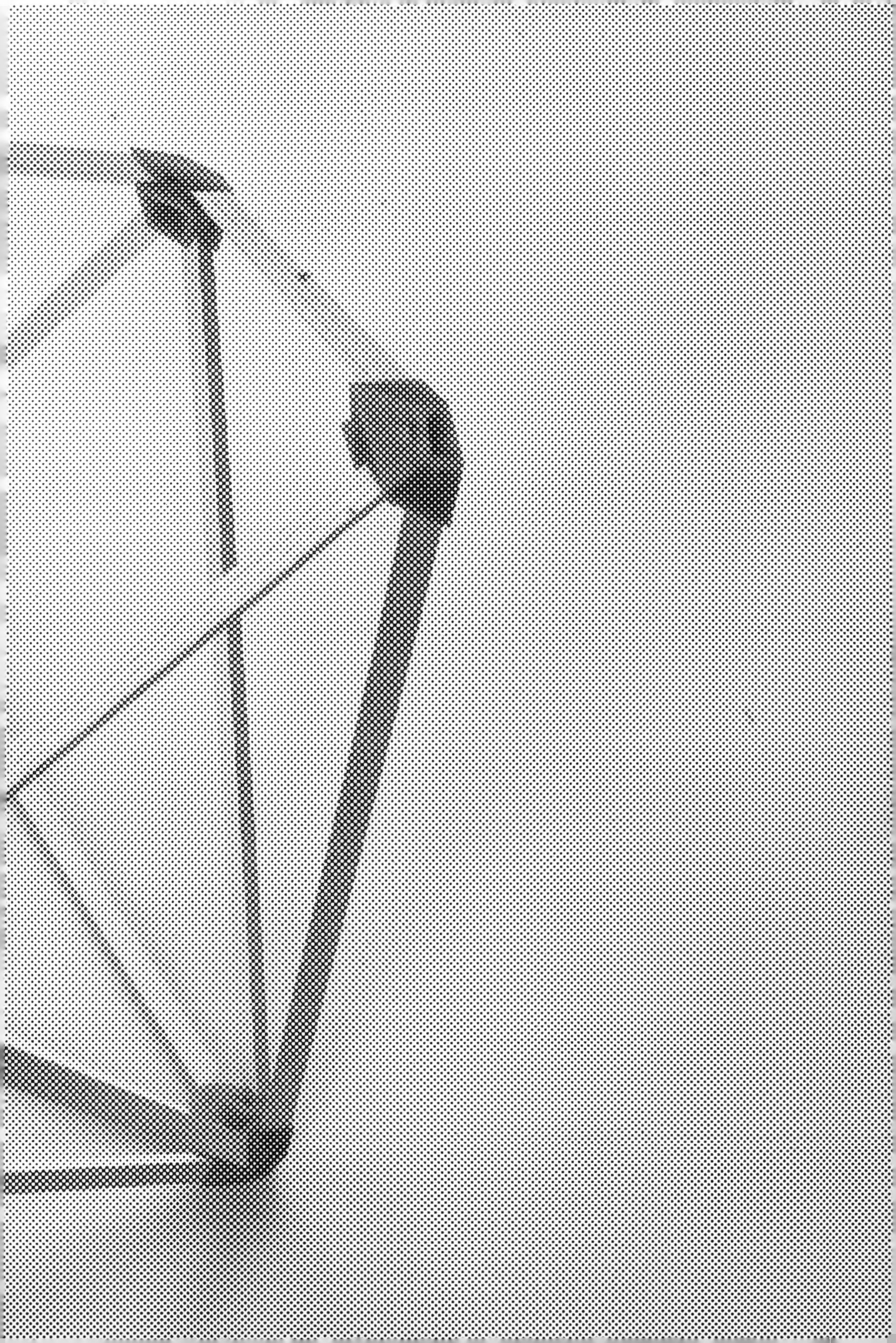

About the artist

The Danish Icelandic artist Olafur Eliasson (born 1967) works in a wide variety of mediums, including installation, painting, sculpture, photography, and film. Awarded with the 2016 Crystal Award for creating inclusive communities, Eliasson ist also known for his environmentalist and socially-engaged projects. Since 1997 his critically acclaimed solo shows have appeared in major museums around the world. Eliasson's projects in public space include *The New York City Waterfalls* in 2008, and *Ice Watch*, shown in Copenhagen in 2014 and Paris in 2015.

Established in 1995, Eliasson's Berlin studio today employs about ninety craftsmen, specialized technicians, architects, archivists, administrators, and cooks. In 2014, Eliasson and architect Sebastian Behmann founded Studio Other Spaces, an office for art and architecture focusing on interdisciplinary and experimental building projects and works in public space. Together with engineer Frederik Ottesen, Eliasson founded the social business Little Sun in 2012. This global project produces and distributes the Little Sun solar lamp for use in off-grid communities and spreads awareness about the need to expand access to sustainable energy to all.

Eliasson's project *Green light—An artistic workshop* was co-produced by Thyssen-Bornemisza Art Contemporary. It debuted in 2016 at TBA21–Augarten, Vienna, before travelling to the Moody Center for the Arts, in Houston, Texas, and the Venice Biennial in 2017.

www.olafureliasson.net
www.studiootherspaces.net
www.littlesun.com
Twitter: @olafureliasson
Instagram: @studioolafureliasson
and @soe_kitchen
Facebook: /studioolafureliasson

Contributor biographies

Atıf Akın is an artist and designer living in New York. His work examines science, nature, mobility, and politics through an (a)historical and contemporary lens. Through a series of activities made up of research, documentation, and design, Akın's work considers transdisciplinary issues through a technoscientific lens. In 2009, he was part of the *Younger Than Jesus* art directory project published by the New Museum and Phaidon. That same year, Akın co-curated the seminal media art exhibition, *Uncharted: User Frames in Media Arts*, and edited an accompanying book. Akın was co-organizer of the zine project and exhibition *Apricots from Damascus*, organized for Apexart and co-produced and hosted by SALT, İstanbul. His long-term, research-driven art project *Mutant Space*, which is focused on nuclear mobility and archaeology was shown at the 2016 Design Biennial, among other venues. Akın teaches at the Mason Gross School of the Arts at Rutgers University.

Tarek Atui is a musician, composer, and sound artist working experimentally with custom-built electronic instruments. He often articulates social realities and histories in his work, while presenting music as a powerful mode of expression and identity. His works are process-based, collaborative projects and include composing sound works, making new types of musical instruments, and large-scale collaborative performances. Atoui has presented his work internationally at the Sharjah Biennial in the United Arab Emirates (2009 and 2013), the New Museum in New York (2010), Mediacity Biennial in Seoul (2010), Haus der Kunst in Munich (2010), Performa 11 in New York (2011), Documenta 13 in Kassel (2012), the Serpentine Gallery in London (2012), the 8th Berlin Biennial (2014), the Fondation Louis Vuitton in Paris (2014 and 2015), and the Tate Modern in London (2016). He was one of the artistic directors of the 2016 Bergen Assembly, a triennial for contemporary art in Norway.

Ian Cion is an artist and writer living in Houston, TX. Cion is currently the Exhibition and Program Manager at the Moody Center for the Arts at Rice University. He joined the Moody from the University of Texas MD Anderson Cancer Center Children's Cancer Hospital where he was the founder and Director of the Arts in Medicine Program. At MD Anderson, Cion implemented a series of large-scale public works in collaboration with patients, families, staff, and community partners. His final work at the hospital was the Space Suit Art Project, a partnership with NASA which resulted in the first art exhibition on board the International Space Station. Cion has taught, lectured, and exhibited internationally for the last twenty years. He earned a Bachelor of Arts, cum laude, from Columbia University.

Angela Dimitrakaki is a writer and Senior Lecturer in Contemporary Art History and Theory at the University of Edinburgh, where she also directs the MSc in Modern and Contemporary Art. Her research focuses on Marxist and feminist critiques of culture and society; art and curating in relation to labor, production, and reproduction; and globalization and biopolitics. Her books include *Gender, ArtWork and the Global Imperative* (2013), *Art and Globalisation: From the Postmodern Sign to the Biopolitical Arena* (2013, in Greek), and *Economy: Art, Production and the Subject in the 21st Century* (2015, with Kirsten Lloyd). In 2016, Dimitrakaki co-edited a special issue on Social Reproduction for the interdisciplinary journal *Historical Materialism* and she is currently co-editing the special issue on Social Reproduction and Art for *Third Text*, forthcoming in September 2017. She is working on two books, *Feminism, Art, Capitalism* and *The Economic Subjects of Contemporary Art*.

Paul Feigelfeld is a media theorist, writer, teacher, and curator, and one of the coordinators of *Refugee Phrasebook*. Until the end of 2016, he was the academic coordinator of the Digital Cultures Research Lab (DCRL) at Leuphana University Lüneburg, Germany. He studied cultural studies and computer science at Humboldt University in Berlin, where he has also been an assistant to Friedrich Kittler and Wolfgang Ernst, and is currently working on his PhD thesis.

Francesca von Habsburg founded Thyssen-Bornemisza Art Contemporary in Vienna in 2002. The foundation represents the fourth generation of the Thyssen family's commitment to the arts and is dedicated primarily to the commissioning and dissemination of ambitious, experimental, and unconventional projects that defy traditional categories. Her passion and interests lie in issues of ecology, specifically the oceans, which she supports particularly within the framework of TBA21 The Current, a research platform seeking to investigate, critique, and propose possible approaches to some of the complex ecological questions of our age. Habsburg has received numerous honors, including the Montblanc de la Culture Arts Patronage Award in 1996, the Merit Award in Gold of the province of Vienna for her cultural engagement in Vienna in 2009, and the Simmons Award for Philanthropic Excellence in 2015.

Timothy Morton is Rita Shea Guffey Chair in English at Rice University. He gave the Wellek Lectures in Theory in 2014 and has collaborated with Björk, Haim Steinbach, and Olafur Eliasson. He is the author of *Dark Ecology: For a Logic of Future Coexistence* (Columbia University Press, 2016), *Nothing: Three Inquiries in Buddhism* (Chicago University Press, 2015), *Hyperobjects: Philosophy and Ecology after the End of the World* (Minnesota University Press, 2013), *Realist Magic: Objects, Ontology, Causality* (Open Humanities, 2013), *The Ecological Thought* (Harvard University Press, 2010), *Ecology without Nature* (Harvard University Press, 2007), eight other books and 160 essays on philosophy, ecology, literature, music, art, architecture, design, and food.

Sandra Noeth has taught in several international institutions such as HZT Berlin, DOCH Stockholm, and MaCh Amsterdam, and was Head of Dramaturgy and Research at Tanzquartier Wien. She has co-authored several publications and edited *Emerging Bodies: On the Performance of Worldmaking* (2011). Her artistic-theoretical projects and teaching posts have focused on the ethics and politics of the body, dramaturgy in dance and performance, and alterity and otherness in the context of non-European dance and body cultures.

Ahmet Öğüt was born in 1981 in Silvan, Diyarbakir in Turkey and lives and works in Amsterdam and Berlin. His work addresses complex topics, such as war, social customs, and political agency, in many cases using humor. The works can materialize through installations, performative or participatory interventions, and actions.

Boris Ondreička is a curator, artist, author, and singer based in Bratislava and Vienna. He has worked as project coordinator at Soros Center for Contemporary Arts, Bratislava; as director of the art initiative tranzit.sk, Bratislava; and, since 2012, as curator at Thyssen-Bornemisza Art Contemporary, Vienna. In 2010 he cofounded the Július Koller Society. Since 1987 he has been lead singer and songwriter for the band Kosa z nosa, Bratislava.

Johannes Porsch is an artist, curator, and author. Recent texts, exhibitions, and publications on the topic of politics of representation and subjectivity include *Unexhibit*, Generali Foundation (2011), *Mobile Springerin Library*, Kunsthaus Bregenz Arena (2012), *Project Proposal #6, Counterproduction*, Generali Foundation (2012), *Unruhe der Form*, Secession, Vienna (2013), *Project Proposal #7, Capital of Desires*, 14th Venice Biennale of Architecture (2014), *Project Proposal #9*, Erste Stiftung, Vienna (2014), *Project Proposal #13, Destination Wien*, Kunsthalle Wien, Vienna (2015), *Project Proposal # 15*, The School of Kyiv, Kiev, Badischer Kunstverein, Karlsruhe, GfzK, Leipzig, Sandleitenhof, Vienna (2015/2016), *Julius Koller. One Man Anti Show*, mumok, Vienna (2016), Tropology, Kunstpavillon, Tiroler Künstlerschaft, Innsbruck (2017).

Clemens Rettenbacher studied political science and philosophy at the University of Vienna, focusing on the history of political ideas, theories of subjectivation and democracy, and gender studies. In his work he discusses the possibilities of transforming existing forms of subjectivation and related strategies of protest, solidarity, and agency. Between 2008 and 2012 he worked as a student assistant at the Institute for Political Science, University of Vienna. Since 2012 he has been working for Thyssen-Bornemisza Art Contemporary as a curatorial assistant, member of the exhibition team, and within the education department. In context of *Green light—An artistic workshop*, he contributed to the development of the *Shared learning* program.

Andreas Roepstorff is Professor, Center of Functionally Integrative Neuroscience and Department of Social Anthropology, Aarhus University / Aarhus University Hospital, Denmark. He edited *Imagining Nature: Practices of Cosmology and Identity*, coedited *Trusting the Subject? Volume 1* and *Trusting the Subject, Volume 2*, coauthored *Concrete spatial language: See what I mean?*, *To musicians, the message is in the meter: Pre-attentive neuronal responses to incongruent rhythm are left-lateralized in musicians*, *Trust or Interaction?*, and *What's at the top in the top-down control of action? Script-sharing and "top-top" control of action in cognitive experiments*, and authored *Cellular Neurosemiotics: Outline of an interpretive framework*, *Mapping Brain Mappers: An Ethnographic Coda*, and *A double dissociation in twentieth century psychology? A commentary on Bernard Baars: The Double Life of BF Skinner*.

David Rych was born 1975 in Innsbruck and lives in Berlin. His artistic practice revolves around notions of identity and reality construction. In the format of documentary film, video installation, and archives, he investigates knowledge production and representation in relation to the relevant political backgrounds. Rych participated in numerous exhibitions and media festivals including the 7th Berlin Biennale, Manifesta 8 (Murcia), Galerie im Taxispalais (Innsbruck), NGBK (Berlin), Centro Culturtal Matucana 100 (Santiago de Chile), O.K Centrum für Gegenwartskunst (Linz), Thyssen-Bornemisza Art Contemporary (Vienna), GfZK, Museum of Contemporary Art (Leipzig), DEAF04 – V2 Dutch Electronic Art Festival (Rotterdam), Transmediale (Berlin), and Secession (Vienna).

Rasha Salti is an independent writer, researcher and curator of art and film. She is also the programmer of La Lucarne for ArtéFrance.

Georg Schöllhammer is an editor, writer, and curator based in Vienna. He is founding editor of *Springerin* and head of tranzit.at. Schöllhammer has worked internationally on cultural projects including Documenta, Manifesta, the biennials of Venice, São Paulo, and Gyumri, as well as The School of Kiev 2015, Sweet Sixties, L'internationale, Former West, and Vienna Fair. He is chairman of The Július Koller Society. From 2004 to 2007 he has been editor-in-chief of Documenta 12 and conceived and directed Documenta 12 magazines. He is an international advisor to the Garage Museum in Moscow.

Shuddhabrata Sengupta is an artist, curator and writer with the Raqs Media Collective, based in New Delhi, India. Raqs Media Collective enjoys playing a plurality of roles, often appearing as artists, occasionally as curators, and sometimes as philosophical agent provocateurs. In 2002 Sengupta co-initiated Sarai, a platform for discursive partnerships between theorists, researchers, practitioners, and artists engaged in reflecting on contemporary urban spaces and cultures in South Asia. Raqs have shown at a variety of exhibitions including Documenta 11 and the Venice, Istanbul, Sao Paulo, Sydney, Taipei, and Shanghai biennials. They were the curators of the 11th Shanghai Biennale (2016). Sengupta was the Keith Haring Fellow in Art & Activism at Bard College, New York (2015–16).

Anahita Tabrizi collaborates with Thyssen-Bornemisza Art Contemporary on the *Green light* project. Tabrizi studied political sciences and international development at the University of Vienna, her Master thesis focused on the European asylum system. She worked as an editor for the students' council magazine *Unique*, and cofounded the alliance "Human Rights Know no Boarders" with several other NGOs.

Alison Weaver is the Suzanne Deal Booth Executive Director of the Moody Center for the Arts at Rice University, which is dedicated to trans-disciplinary collaboration between the arts, sciences and humanities. Weaver is an art historian and former Director of Affiliates for the Solomon R. Guggenheim Museum in New York where she oversaw the museum's programs and operations in Berlin, Bilbao, Venice, and Las Vegas. While at the Guggenheim, she managed the departments of Exhibition Management, Registration, Art Services, and Library and Archives, and together with her curatorial colleagues, implemented a wide range of international traveling exhibitions. In addition to an MBA in non-profit management from the Yale School of Management and experience as a consultant for McKinsey & Company, Weaver has a BA from Princeton University, and advanced degrees in art history from Williams College and the City University of New York. Her academic research focuses on the dialogue between artists in the United States and Europe after 1945.

Franziska Sophie Wildförster was an assistant curator at Thyssen-Bornemisza Art Contemporary from 2014 to 2016, and co-curated (with Daniela Zyman and Boris Ondreicka) the project *Green light—An artistic workshop*. She received her BA in art history and in media and communication at the University of Vienna as well as an MA in visual cultures (2014) and an MFA in curating at Goldsmiths, University of London (2015). She is funding member and co-director of Kunstverein Kevin Space in Vienna. Recent curatorial projects include *Abjects* at Import Projects, Berlin, and a number of exhibitions at at Kevin Space Vienna, including *Kosmo*, *Alexander Baczynski-Jenkins – Sync Crop*, and *Yuri Pattison – Citizens of Nowhere*. She has contributed interviews, reviews, and essays to *Canvas Art Magazine*, Artsy, *i-D Germany*, and Artnews.it.

Nira Yuval-Davis is a Visiting Professor and the Director of the Research Centre on Migration, Refugees and Belonging (CMRB) at the University of East London. She has been the President of the Research Committee 05 (on Racism, Nationalism and Ethnic Relations) of the International Sociological Association, a founding member of Women Against Fundamentalism and the international research network of Women In Militarized Conflict Zones. Yuval-Davis has written extensively on theoretical and empirical aspects of intersected nationalisms, racisms, fundamentalisms, citizenships, identities, belonging/s and gender relations in Britain and Europe, Israel, and other settler societies. Among her written and edited books are *Woman-Nation-State*, 1989, *Racialized Boundaries*, 1992, *Unsettling Settler Societies*, 1995, *Gender and Nation* (1997), *Warning Signs of Fundamentalisms* (2004), *The Politics of Belonging* (2011), *Women Against Fundamentalism* (2014), and the forthcoming *Bordering* (2017).

Daniela Zyman is chief curator at Thyssen-Bornemisza Art Contemporary in Vienna. Between 1995 and 2001 she acted as curator and chief curator at the MAK – Austrian Museum of Applied Arts / Contemporary Art in Vienna and was a founding member of the MAK Center for Art and Architecture at the Schindler House in Los Angeles, which she directed for several years. Between 2000 and 2003 she was artistic director of Künstlerhaus, Vienna, and A9 forum transeuropa at MQ. She has read critical theory at the University of Applied Arts for several years and has edited numerous books and contributed essays to catalogues and international journals.

About Thyssen-Bornemisza Art Contemporary

Founded in 2002 by Francesca von Habsburg in Vienna, Thyssen-Bornemisza Art Contemporary (TBA21) represents the fourth generation of the Thyssen family's commitment to the arts. TBA21's unique collection is the result of its ongoing commitment to commissioning and disseminating multidisciplinary art projects that defy traditional categorization, including large scale installations, sound compositions, endurance performances, and contemporary architecture. Since the foundation believes that art has the capacity to be a transformational force, it explores new modes of presentation that are intended to provoke and inspire change.

Thyssen-Bornemisza Art Contemporary –Office
Köstlergasse 1
1060 Vienna, Austria
+43 1 513 98 56
office@tba21.org

Thyssen-Bornemisza Art Contemporary –Augarten
Scherzergasse 1A
1020 Vienna, Austria
+43 1 513 98 56-24
augarten@tba21.org
www.tba21.org

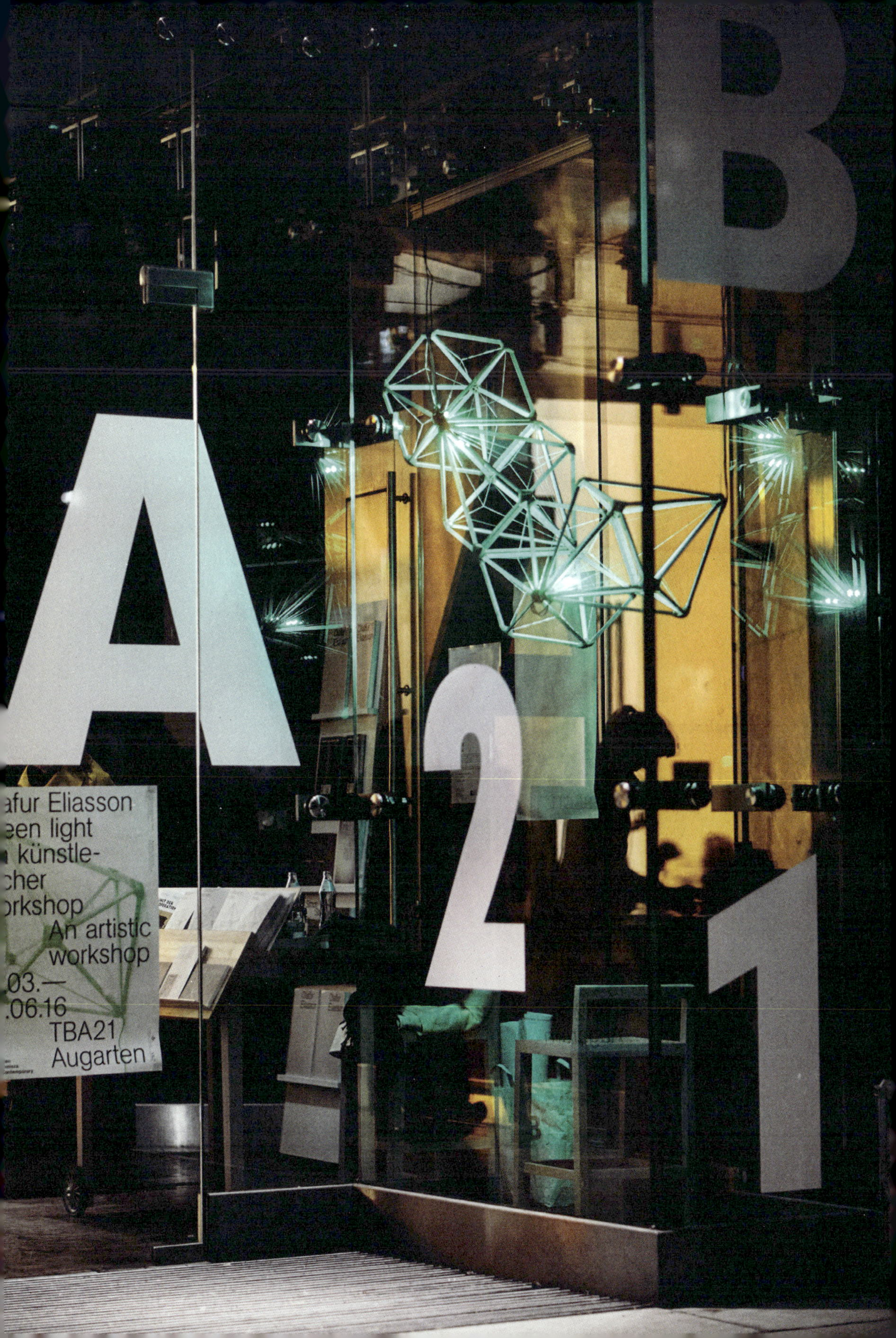
B
A
2
1
afur Eliasson
een light
künstle-
cher
orkshop
An artistic
workshop
.03.—
.06.16
TBA21
Augarten

Olafur Eliasson
Green light—An artistic workshop

Initiated in spring 2016, *Green light* was devised to be further developed in collaboration with institutions and contexts worldwide. To date, it has been realized in Vienna, Houston, and Venice.

Initiated by
Olafur Eliasson
Francesca von Habsburg /
TBA21 Chairwoman

Curators
Caroline Eggel / Studio Olafur Eliasson
Daniela Zyman / TBA21

Project planning and training
Kerstin Palermo / Studio Olafur Eliasson

Installation
Jesper Dyrehauge, Matthias Gerber, Marc Pätzold, Tobias Tavella, Matt Willard, Christian Uchtmann / Studio Olafur Eliasson

Media & Communication
Camilla Kragelund, Martin Enoch, Thilo Frank, David de Larrea Remiro, Kathryn Politis, Geoffrey Garrison, Vajra Spook / Studio Olafur Eliasson

Manufaktur für neue Medien – Istvan Szilagyi & Rocio Burchard; Pickles PR – Rhiannon Pickles

Photography
Sandro E.E. Zanzinger / TBA21
María del Pilar García Ayensa /
Studio Olafur Eliasson

Olafur Eliasson
Green light, 2016

in Vienna:
Wood (European ash), recycled yogurt cups (PLA), used plastic bags, recycled nylon, LED (green)
35 x 35 x 35 cm
Unlimited edition

in Houston:
Wood (American basswood), recycled yogurt cups (PLA), used plastic bags, recycled nylon, LED (green)
35 x 35 x 35 cm
Unlimited edition

in Venice:
Wood (European ash), various types of recycled plastic, LED (green), paint (white, green)
28 x 28 x 28 cm
Unlimited edition

TBA21 would like to thank Olafur Eliasson for a long-standing relationship and his trust. Thanks also go to his entire studio team and all the many many individuals and organizations who have contributed with their generosity and spirit to the *Green light* universe since 2016.

Green light—An artistic workshop at Thyssen-Bornemisza Art Contemporary —Augarten, Vienna March 12—July 29, 2016

Curators
Daniela Zyman, Boris Ondreička, Franziska Sophie Wildförster / TBA21
Caroline Eggel / Studio Olafur Eliasson

Curatorial Assistant
Fanny Hauser

Project planning and training
Kerstin Palermo, Borghildur Indridadottir / Studio Olafur Eliasson

Project Architects
Philipp Krummel, Markus Taxacher

TBA21 Green light Team / Visitor and Exhibition Service
Markus Schlüter, Philipp Bauer, Ziva Drvaric, Christina Gruber, Philipp Kolla, Clemens Rettenbacher, Yusuf Said, Anna Schmoll, Lisa Slawitz, Anahita Tabrizi, David Weidinger

Green light participants
Aliakbar Ahmadi, Shamahmood Ahmadi, Tahajud Alghrabi, Raafat Alhashimy, Naima Ali, Anas Aljajeh, Dunia Aljasararee, Milan Amiri, Mohammad Amiry, Majid Ayubi, Ali Ayzouki, Murtaza Azimi, Tawab Baran, Ibrahim Al Bayati, Fatima Chuchari, Ghifar Al Darkazanly, Beiroza Daud, Ayman Al Dawahra, Ebrahim Ebrahimi, Farhad Farhamand, Husseyin Haj Hassan, Nedwa Hasan, Hussein Hosseini, Liya Kasa, Homa Khosrawi, Ibrahim Mawazini, Fayaz Mir-Amiry, Akbar Muratov, Mayhoub Neesrin, Sahed Niazi, Nesar Ahmad Nourzai, Zia ul Haq Oryakhel, Kelvin Osazuwa, Alarabi Raberi, Emran Ali Rahimi, Hossein Rezaie, Kalaji Samar, Saber Sawari, Issa Shafaei, Qasim Tahmasebi, Milad Wasil

German teacher
Marianna Amon, mytraining.at

Green light—Shared learning
Artistic interventions, seminars, lectures, initiatives with Atıf Akın, Tarek Atoui, Damian Christinger, Displaced, Alexander Ehrmann, Olafur Eliasson, Paul Feigelfeld, HANDS ON, History(ies) of Migration, Mária Hlavajová, Mary Kreutzer & Leila Hadj Abdou, Studio Olafur Eliasson, Rasmus Nielsen, Sandra Noeth, Ben Paine, Johannes Porsch, PROSA, Shuddhabrata Sengupta, Andreas Roepstorff, David Rych, Ahmet Öğüt, Zavoloka

Project partners
Georg Danzer Haus/Verein Fluchtweg, Vienna
Caritas Vienna
Red Cross Vienna

Art Handling
Markus Taxacher, Robert Gruber, Lucas Schmid, Jakob Neulinger

Managing Editor
Eva Ebersberger

Media & Communication
Tereza Horakova, Gérard Rabara, Mariana Rodriguez-Yanez, Katharina Stöhr / TBA21; Ana Berlin Communications

Collection Management
Simone Sentall, Andrea Hofinger, Elizabeth Stevens

Exhibition Photography
Markus Taxacher, Sandro E.E. Zanzinger

Catering
Die AU Café / Restaurant

Administration
Karin Berger, Barbara Hörhan, Azra Demir-Ramovic, Claudia Naue, Paulina Sosna, Florence Wehinger

TBA21—Academy
Markus Reymann, Georg Eder

Green light—An artistic workshop at Moody Center for the Arts at Rice University, Houston, Texas February 24–May 6, 2017

Curators
Alison Weaver / Moody Center for the Arts
Caroline Eggel / Studio Olafur Eliasson

Project planning and training
Kerstin Palermo / Studio Olafur Eliasson

Project partner
Interfaith Ministries for Greater Houston

Green light participants
Hayfaa Al Gburi, Zinab AlAjil, Raghad AlAjil, Hanaa Suwaed, Azad Ismail, Mohammad Sheikh Horo, Najah Al Sholi, Samir Al Khateeb, Elham Hasan, Nawfal Almohy, Dayami Rodriguez-Lopez, Abdulhannan Sheikho, Samira Houshmand, Omid Jahanshahi, Marianela Medina-Cuellar, Fatemah Jahanshahi

Green light—An artistic workshop at

Art | Basel, Basel, Switzerland June 18–19, 2016

International Peace Institute Forum, Salzburg, Austria September 4–6, 2016

National Gallery in Prague, Prague, Czech Republic March 17–19, 2017

Green light—An artistic workshop at 57th International Art Exhibition La Biennale di Venezia May 13–November 26, 2017

Invited by
Christine Macel
in the context of the exhibition *Viva Arte Viva*

Spatial concept and planning
Caroline Eggel, Kerstin Palermo, Brita Jaichner, Kajana Wagner / Studio Olafur Eliasson

Programming and Shared learning
Daniela Zyman / TBA21

Project Manager TBA21 & Studio Olafur Eliasson
Nataša Venturi

TBA21 Curatorial Assistant
Frederike Sperling

TBA21 Curatorial Intern
Beatrice Forchini

Legal Advisor
Marco Franco

Production & Coordination Assistance
Adriana Navarro

TBA21 Communication
Sophie Bayerlein, Elodie Grethen; Daniele Perra, Manufaktur für neue Medien – Istvan Szilagyi & Rocio Burchard; Pickles PR – Rhiannon Pickles

Psychologist
Elisa Danese

Italian Teachers
Laura Schiattone, Rita Fabbri

Coordinators
Mohammed Salhi, Diana Leone

Volunteers
Marta Ruffato, Pietro Consolandi, Giulia Angeloni, Lucia Brergamaschi, Clara Machado Alves, Julian Nativo Matias, Enrica Zaccone, Alessia Prati

With the support of
Prefettura di Venezia
Comune di Venezia
Università IUAV di Venezia
Ordine degli Avvocati di Venezia

Production and material support provided by
Kvadrat, Moroso

Additional support by
Danish Arts Foundation
Paolo Falcone e Olimpia Cavriani, Massimo Redaelli per Fondazione Sambuca
Institut für Auslandsbeziehungen – ifa

Participating non-governmental organizations
Emergency, Georg Danzer Haus, Cooperativa Sociale "Il Villaggio Globale"; Cooperativa Sociale "Giuseppe Olivotti"; Cooperativa Sociale "Il Lievito"; Cooperativa Sociale "Gea"; Cooperativa Sociale "Co.Ge.S Don Lorenzo Milani"; Diocesi Patriarcato di Venezia; Fondazione Groggia; Curia Patriarcale e Fondazione Santa Maria del Porto; Comune di Venezia – Progetto Sprar Fontego: Cooperativa Coges; Comune di Venezia – Progetto Sprar Fontego: Opere Riunite Buon Caritas

Green light participants
Sangare Adama, Naima Adan Mohamed, Seedorf Aigbah, Frank Agbonteam, Miso Ajayi, Marwan Alfrij, Naeel Alfrij, Promise Awose Iyekeretin, Lamin Camara, Enerhu Diamond, Ubaka Dumbiri, Andrew Eboigbe, Marcel Esene, Abdoulie Faye, Yankuba Gassama, Monday Hitila, Denis Igbinedion, Jerry Angel Imariabe Edosomwan, Bakary Jawla, Yousaf Khan Undarh, Shen Limei, Philip Lucky, Asho Mohamed Saaiid, Qadeer Muhammad, Ahmed Muhammed, Akissi Odile N'Guessan, Mahamadou Niakate', Wahidullah Niazi, Akam Noordien Aulla, Iyore Odeh, Dickson Ogwezy, Kelvin Omon, Kelvin Omorogbe Nosakmare, Mo QiuChiang, Lamin Sallah, Azhin Taha, Hawrin Taha, Zubaida Tahiri, Mohammad Usman, Nasrin Hossein Zarandi

Thyssen-Bornemisza Art Contemporary wishes to extend special thanks to its generous sponsor. As one of the leading insurance groups in Central and Eastern Europe, the Vienna Insurance Group and its main share holder Wiener Städtische Versicherungsverein clearly perceive its social responsibilities and have been reliable sponsoring partners for Thyssen-Bornemisza Art Contemporary and other cultural projects for many years. Numerous museums and galleries have insured their collections with Vienna Insurance Group. The main objective for cooperating with cultural institutions is to promote the international exchange in the field of arts and culture.

WIENER STÄDTISCHE VERSICHERUNGSVEREIN
VIG VIENNA INSURANCE GROUP

Olafur Eliasson
Green light—An artistic workshop

Published by Sternberg Press

Green light—An artistic workshop was created by Olafur Eliasson in collaboration with Thyssen-Bornemisza Art Contemporary, with initial iterations in Vienna in 2016 and Houston and Venice in 2017. The project is ongoing.

Editors
Daniela Zyman
Eva Ebersberger

Copyediting
Orit Gat, Karen Jacobson

Translations
Anahita Tabrizi, Andrew Horsfield

Editorial Team Studio Olafur Eliasson
Geoffrey Garrison, Kristina Köper, Biljana Joksimović-Große, Kathryn Politis

Image Credits
Markus Taxacher endpaper, 94–95, 110–11, 148–49, 164–65, 181 (top), 210–11, 230–43, 258–59; Sandro E.E. Zanzinger 16–25, 38, 76, 136–37, 138 (bottom), 139, 140–41, 142, 144–45, 147, 176–77, 180, 186–87, 229, 267; María del Pilar García Ayensa | Studio Olafur Eliasson 52–55, 59, 62–63, 150–53, 244–45; Thilo Frank & David de Larrea Remiro | Studio Olafur Eliasson 56–57, 60–61; Katharina Stöhr 143, 178–79, 182–83, 225; Green light team 113, 123, 146, 184–85, 189, 213; Anudando 138 (top); Ahmet Öğüt 162–63; David Rych 167, 181 (bottom); Frederike Sperling 171, 256–67; Johannes Porsch 198–203; Tawab Baran 227; Anne Houang 254–55.

Graphic Design
Studio Folder

Printing
Rema-Print-Littera Druck-u. VerlagsgmbH, Vienna

ISBN 978-3-95679-333-2

Sternberg Press
Caroline Schneider
Karl-Marx-Allee 78
D-10243 Berlin
www.sternberg-press.com

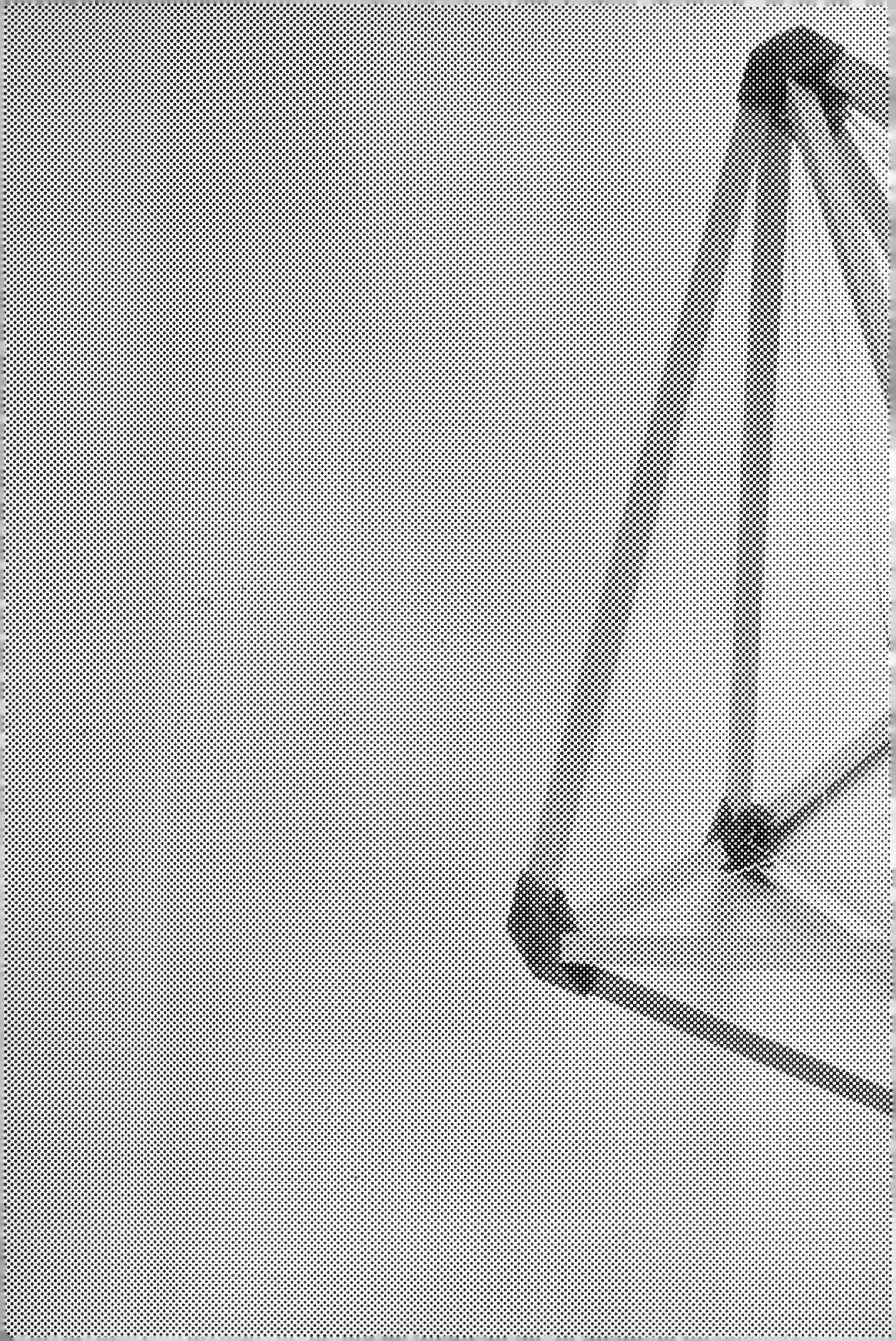